Nordic Consumer Culture

Søren Askegaard • Jacob Östberg
Editors

Nordic Consumer Culture

State, Market and Consumers

palgrave
macmillan

Editors
Søren Askegaard
University of Southern Denmark
Odense, Denmark

Jacob Östberg
Stockholm Business School
Stockholm University
Stockholm, Sweden

ISBN 978-3-030-04932-4 ISBN 978-3-030-04933-1 (eBook)
https://doi.org/10.1007/978-3-030-04933-1

Library of Congress Control Number: 2018968446

This Palgrave Macmillan imprint is published by the registered company Springer Nature Switzerland AG
The registered company address is: Gewerbestrasse 11, 6330 Cham, Switzerland

This book is dedicated
to the memory
of our friend and colleague
Per Østergaard
(1958–2016)
Pioneer of Nordic consumer culture investigations
from Svalbard to the Baltic Sea

Contents

Notes on Contributors

Lars Pynt Andersen is associate professor of Strategic Communication at Aalborg University, Department of Communication and Psychology (Copenhagen campus). His PhD from Copenhagen Business School was on the rhetorical strategies of television advertising. He has published papers on the uses of irony and personification metaphor in advertising, as well as advertising genre and related effects. Research interests include parental consumption, the "tween" consumer, and vicarious consumption as status negotiation. He is currently researching the (re-)construction of the "Nordic" and "Nordic values" in consumer culture and branding strategies.

Eric J. Arnould is Visiting Professor of Marketing at Aalto University School of Business. He has pursued a career in applied social science since 1974. The University of Arizona awarded him a PhD in anthropology in 1982. Aalto awarded him an honorary doctorate in 2016. Arnould's research on consumer culture, cultural marketing strategy, qualitative research methods, services, and development appears in major social science and managerial periodicals and books.

Søren Askegaard is Professor of Consumption Studies at the University of Southern Denmark in Odense. Of northern origin, more precisely from Northern Funen, he is educated in Odense and in Paris (and not least in the general interaction with his colleagues). He considers himself a rooted cosmopolitan. His career has meandered him to and through various positions such as professorships at Lund University in Sweden, Lille University in France, and

Suffolk University in Boston, USA. His publications appear in various journals ranging from the *Flag Bulletin* to the *Journal of Consumer Research*. In terms of research, he is interested in encounters of the local and the global in consumer culture, as well as in humans as imaginary beings and the consequences for phenomena of consumer culture.

Jonathan Bean is Assistant Professor of Architecture, Sustainable Built Environments, and Marketing at the University of Arizona. His research on taste and consumption spans the fields of consumer research, human–computer interaction, architecture, and design. He has received grants from the Social Sciences and Humanities Research Council of Canada, the National Institute for Transportation and Communities, and others. Bean writes the Consuming Tech column for *ACM Interactions* magazine and gave a TEDx talk as part of his immersive study of market transformation in the US building market. His work on IKEA hacking was featured on an episode of the *99% Invisible* podcast.

Stine Bjerregaard is a former PhD student in the Consumer, Culture and Commerce group at the University of Southern Denmark. She now works as a marketing professional—currently with sustainability in the fashion industry. Bjerregaard's research focuses on the early stages of market formation, with special attention to the role of politics and ideology. Theoretically, she works in the intersection between consumer culture theory and market studies, exploring the performativity of ideas and representations. Other research interests include place branding and subtle forms of consumer resistance as it plays out in branded consumption scapes.

James Fitchett is Professor of Marketing and Consumption at the University of Leicester School of Business. He is associate editor for *Marketing Theory*. His research interests include investigations into the politics of consumption, neoliberalism and consumer culture, and theory development in marketing.

Benjamin J. Hartmann is an Associate Professor at the School of Business, Economics and Law at the University of Gothenburg. Originally from Berlin, Hartmann has been a lifetime friend and connoisseur of Nordic consumer culture. His award-winning research generally explores the intersection of consumption, markets, and society, and is published in *Consumption, Markets & Culture*, *Marketing Theory*, *Journal of Consumer Research*, *Psychology & Marketing*, *Journal of Marketing Management*, and *Advances in Consumer Research*.

Maria Hokkinen is a PhD candidate at the Åbo Akademi University in Turku, Finland. Her research interests lie in the field of consumer behavior, with a specific focus on consumer culture theory and consumption in multicultural marketplaces. She is passionate about refugee rights and studies in her doctoral thesis the consumer behavior of refugees in Finland. She works with qualitative methods and is interested in integrating visual materials into interviews.

Dannie Kjeldgaard is Professor in the Consumption, Culture and Commerce group at the University of Southern Denmark and VPP professor at the University of Gothenburg, and is Editor-in-Chief of the journal *Consumption, Markets and Culture.* Kjeldgaard's work analyzes change processes of market-based glocalization, specifically how marketing and consumption as key contemporary cultural practices constitute new sociocultural meaning systems. He is currently working on the historical formation of contemporary gastronomy in a Greenlandic context, the consumption culture of the working poor in France, and cosmopolitanism among less affluent consumers.

Ingeborg Astrid Kleppe is Professor of Marketing at the Norwegian School of Economics. Kleppe has extensive international experience from universities in Canada, the USA, Sweden, and Australia, and has also worked in the World Bank managing poverty surveys in Sub-Saharan Africa. Kleppe has taken her interdisciplinary and international experience into her research. Her current research revolves around marketplace stigma, the new collaborative economy, and visual analysis. She is a producer of award-winning videographies, and her work appears in *Psychology and Marketing, Family and Consumer Sciences Research Journal, European Journal of Marketing, Services Industries Journal,* and *Consumption Markets and Culture.*

Frank Lindberg is Professor of Marketing at Nord University Business School, Norway. He earned his PhD in 2001 at Copenhagen Business School. Since then he has worked as Associate Professor at the University of Nordland and University of Gothenburg, and Vice Dean and Dean at Bodø Graduate School of Business, University of Nordland. Lindberg has been Visiting Scholar at Copenhagen Business School, University of California, Berkeley, and at the University of Southern Denmark. His research covers areas such as the dynamics of markets and consumption, and focuses on tensions and challenges of consumers and communities during the consumption of experiences.

Jeppe Linnet is a social anthropologist with a PhD on hygge, consumer culture, and the Nordic region. His 2011 article on hygge was the first international, peer-reviewed article to analyze the phenomenon in depth. He has been interviewed for numerous articles on hygge in Danish and international media, many of which can be found on his academia.edu page. He is the founder of user and market research agency Linnet Research, and is currently involved in producing four short documentary movies on hygge.

Diane M. Martin is a Professor of Marketing at RMIT University in Melbourne. Her doctoral dissertation, "Women, Work, and Humor: Negotiating Paradoxes of Organizational Life," was honored with the prestigious International Communication Association W. Charles Redding Outstanding Dissertation Award. She served as an Associate Professor at both Aalto University and the University of Portland, and as a Visiting Professor at the University of Gothenburg. She is a Senior Fellow of the American Leadership Forum. Her research employs ethnographic methods in relationships between consumers, communities, and culture. Her scholarship is published in numerous marketing and communication journals and books.

Susanna Molander is an affiliated researcher at the Center for Arts, Business & Culture (ABC) at the Stockholm School of Economics Institute for Research (SIR). Her research focuses on consumer culture, with a particular interest in theories of practice and issues related to parenting, gender, and consumption. She also studies fashion branding from a cultural perspective. With the Nordic context as her primary empirical base, she explores how political projects shape the way consumption is enacted.

Jacob Östberg is Professor of Advertising and PR at Stockholm Business School, Stockholm University. He earned his PhD in 2003 at Lund University, with a thesis that was awarded the Academia Gastronomica Scaniensis research price. Since then he has mainly taught at the Business Schools at Lund and Stockholm universities. Like the Vikings before him, he has traveled near and far, crossing the Baltic Sea to take up a position as Visiting Distinguished Professor of Marketing at Aalto University School of Business in Helsinki, and even following in the footsteps of Halvdan and Árni (who did graffiti in Hagia Sophia around the turn of the first millennium) to Turkey, where he was a visiting scholar at Bìlkent University in Ankara. Östberg's research interests revolve around how meaning is created in the intersection of marketing, popular culture, and consumers' lived lives.

Juulia Pietilä is a recent MSc graduate in International Business and Management at the University of Southern Denmark. Her research interests include sociocultural approaches to marketing and consumer research. Currently, her interests lie with building bridges between sociocultural theory and international marketing practice.

Emma Salminen is a Doctoral Candidate in the Marketing Department at Aalto University School of Business. Her research focuses on nature experienced through consumer culture, changes in social practices, and sustainable consumption from both macro and micro perspectives.

Pamela Schultz Nybacka holds a PhD and MSc in Business Studies and a BSc in Literature from Stockholm University. Her 2011 thesis "Bookonomy" dealt with book reading as a consumption practice, contributing to a rapprochement between the humanities and economies of excess. Schultz Nybacka is a Senior Lecturer at Södertörn University, where she is Head of the BSc in Cultural Management program and of Publishing Studies at the Department of History, Stockholm University. Her research deals with brands and popular literature in consumer culture, critique and new economic criticism, and the organization of libraries and of art.

Jack S. Tillotson is a Lecturer of Marketing at Liverpool Business School, Liverpool John Moores University. He is a Doctoral Candidate at the Marketing Department at Aalto University School of Business in Helsinki. His research investigates various culturally oriented theoretical contexts, including embodiment, myth, identity, and medicalization.

Sofia Ulver earned her PhD in 2008 and is Associate Professor at the School of Economics and Management, Lund University. She defended her PhD thesis on the status and globalization of taste in 2008, and her theoretical domain is critical marketing and consumer culture theory. Her research interest is the intersection between the global market, local society, and consumer culture, how this intersection transforms according to shifts in ideologies, and how the transformations change the way we live, consume, produce, and vote. Her empirical domains have involved ethical and sustainable consumption, political consumption, food consumption, the "home," beauty norms, and market discourses on multiculturalism. She has presented her research at several international academic and public conferences and events. Her work has appeared in *Journal of Consumer Culture*, *European Journal of Marketing*, *Journal of Marketing Management*, *Advances in Consumer Research*, and *Research in Consumer Behavior*, in various book chapters, and in public media.

Henri A. Weijo is Assistant Professor in Marketing at Aalto University School of Business. He is back in Finland after three years in the USA, during which he gained a great deal of appreciation for life in the North. As a result, his ongoing research projects foreground the Nordic context in a more explicit fashion. Weijo focuses his research efforts on ethnographic investigations of consumer collectives, experiential and ludic consumption, nature consumption, friendship, digital consumer culture, value co-creation, and consumer creativity. He does not mind the cold.

List of Figures

List of Tables

1

Introduction: The Institution and the Imaginary in a Nordic Light

Søren Askegaard and Jacob Östberg

As we were finalizing the manuscript for this book, on September 30, 2018, an elderly man died in Odense, Denmark. This man was Kim Larsen, former lead singer of Gasolin'—the unrivaled, biggest rock band in Denmark in the 1970s, with a significant crowd of followers also in Sweden and Norway. After the disbanding of Gasolin', he continued to produce albums (and also one highly successful movie) in genres ranging from the classic rock that was his point of departure to more sing-along kinds of tunes, from solid existential and touching ballads to what many considered "cheesy" and banal songs of dubious quality. His catalogue also contained albums reviving "forgotten" Danish classics from the nineteenth and twentieth centuries. A trained schoolteacher and an avid reader of literary classics, he definitely had a gift for words, although a far

S. Askegaard (✉)
University of Southern Denmark, Odense, Denmark
e-mail: aske@sam.sdu.dk

J. Östberg
Stockholm Business School, Stockholm University, Stockholm, Sweden
e-mail: jacob.ostberg@sbs.su.se

S. Askegaard, J. Östberg (eds.), *Nordic Consumer Culture*,
https://doi.org/10.1007/978-3-030-04933-1_1

cry from the intellectualism of a Tom Waits or a Bob Dylan. If comparison is at all meaningful, the tone of his songwriting had more similarities with the simplicity and the reverence for cultural legacy of a Johnny Cash.

Larsen's death from cancer caused a major media stir as well as thousands of—possibly a million—private mourning and contemplation rituals in many homes, ranging from playing his music all night, or sharing favorite memories of songs (a not uncommon remark was "Larsen's music is the soundtrack to my life"), to showing up with flowers, beers, candles, and little drawings or greetings on spontaneously created sites of commemoration. These sacralized spots—the beers remained largely undrunk by the homeless and the bums of the neighborhoods, although Larsen would presumably have wanted them to serve themselves—were either in the Christianshavn/Christiania neighborhood in Copenhagen (the home turf of Gasolin'), in front of an impromptu graffiti painting of his well-known, sixpence-capped face, or in front of his apartment for the last 25 years of his life in central Odense, conveniently located just next to his favorite beer bar. On the following Friday, an estimated 30,000 people marched in his memory in Copenhagen and 10,000 in Odense.

Even if we as modern consumers are used to the usual over-hyped, mediatized, and more or less commercial exploitation of celebrity and identification that haunts the modern music scene, the depth and scope of the reactions to this passing of a public icon in Danish (and Nordic) musical history surprised many, both avid fans and people simply observing from the sidelines—but nevertheless often touched by the moment themselves. While obviously a large number of people don't like Larsen's work, these voices remained respectfully silent even on social media, where tactfulness is usually not the most widespread feature.

The question is: What is going on? As one journalist reported, he found out about the passing of Mr. Larsen on an airplane on his way to Brussels. And he realized that he could not hold back a tear or two. Considering himself distinctly unsentimental, he began to reflect on the reason for this emotional response. He was not a big fan, had never met the man, had not even been to a concert. And he never found himself looking forward to a new album. He could easily think of better rock poets on the Danish scene. And yet, he knew that he would also never find himself shedding a tear for these other artists.

The media obviously both picked up and nurtured the popular sentiment of loss and grief. The commentaries evoked all kinds of explanatory frameworks. They ranged from the expression of a different (more original) sense of Danishness than the isolationist version promoted by contemporary political populism; the proof of community and sense of belonging in a world of transitory relations, as expressed in a song catalogue that can be used for almost any occasion; the authenticity of a rebel "working-class" hero, complete with deep flaws, conservatism and oddity, and an insistence on supporting the weak and marginalized. This was not just a matter of siding with leftist forces in the political spectrum, since it also included resistance against perceived excess welfare state tyrannies intruding into the personal sphere, such as Larsen's central role in an anti-anti-smoking campaign. To these more concrete examples can be added the power of shared emotions as a carrier of an ephemeral sense of community that in and of itself represents an ideal in the Nordic context.

In short, the legacy of this particular artist may be said to summarize many of the complex and multifaceted elements that constitute the multifaceted and paradoxical formation of Danish and Nordic societies. Social indignation and a tendency to side with the weak co-exist with an expectation that everyone will do their utmost to fulfill the social contract. Celebration of the "popular" co-exists with an appreciation for the value of rebelliousness. Petit-bourgeois, provincial romantic nostalgia for localness co-exists with a sense of responsible inclusion. Fundamental respect for the public institutional set-up that guarantees "good life conditions" and an ensuing trust in government as a positive force simultaneously co-exist with a tacit belief in the positive sides of the Law of Jante, including disrespect for nominal authorities and non-tolerance of bragging bullshit. Emphasis on quality of life and enjoyment pairs with a deep respect for honorable work efforts. A love of the social safety net pairs with a disdain for patronizing coddling. As one journalist pointed out, we all can name both an absolute favorite Larsen anthem (or several) *and* at least one but oftentimes several absolutely loathed tunes. Although the generalization is obviously over-stated, it may be fair to say that the taste for Larsen as a cultural phenomenon (more than for his personality) is orthodox, whereas the taste for his work is distinctly heterodox (Wilk 1997).

Why this fuss about a popular culture figure in a serious book concerning Nordicness and the relations between state and market? Isn't this just nonsensical epiphenomena on top of the historical and institutional forces shaping the "real" character of "the Nordic"? French sociologist Edgar Morin provides us with a response to this criticism when, in his two classics on the cinematographic world (Morin 1956, 2005 [1957]), he underlines the relationship between the products of mass cultural consumption and the fundamental constitution of the human being as living in a world that is simultaneously real and imaginary. The commercial nonsense of mass culture offers pop and plastic, pleasure and repugnance, sense and nonsense. It is not only an object for the study of capitalist exploitation, but also a window to that which is most constitutive of humanity. As Morin writes about the study of mass culture: "Nonsense, no doubt! [but…] Nonsense is *also* what is most profound in man. Behind the star system is not only the 'stupidity' of fanatics, the lack of invention of screen-writers, the commercial chicanery of producers. There is the world's heart and there is love, another kind of nonsense, another profound humanity" (Morin 2005 [1957], p. 87).

What we can learn from this whole story is the importance of the imaginary! Maybe the unspeakable linkage that Larsen seemingly forged with a large part of Danish society was his ability to express the social imaginary which glues together Danish institutional and practical reality. Without really understanding exactly why and how, this artist may have touched on and in a sense "spoken to" central elements of the "Danish imaginary," if we assume and accept that there is such a phenomenon. Consequently, and moving from the Danish to the somewhat larger but not altogether very different Nordic reality, we can ask: What is the Nordic? In order to answer this question, we should of course look at institutional settings, practices, and discourses, but possibly also understand how all these manifestations of a particular social organization might rest on a foundation of the imaginary.

The concept of the imaginary, while marginalized in most social research, is a central concept in much psychoanalytic thinking. Most notably, it represents one of Lacan's three ontological orders, the imaginary order which according to Lacan originates in the mirror stage of infancy. This is a stage in which the infant, through its confrontation with its own image in a mirror or in the mother's (or other significant other's) care, sees itself as an autonomous and complete subject existing in a sort of perfection (for an introduction that also addresses popular culture, see Žižek 1992). Imaginary, something which it is important to retain, does not mean illusory or fictitious in this context, but rather refers to the ability to project and reflect oneself (as well as other phenomena), to create mirrored mental imagery.

We will however use a different approach to the imaginary, which is the one proposed by French-Greek social philosopher Cornelius Castoriadis. His approach to the imaginary is inspired from but also goes beyond the Lacanian concept. Castoriadis transposes the fundamental idea of the imaginary to a social level and in his magnum opus, *The Imaginary Institution of Society* (1975 [1987]), proposes the imaginary as the source for institutionalizing social significations. The imaginary is thereby fundamental both for understanding the individual psyche and for society as a whole (Bouchet 2018).

For Castoriadis, two fundamental questions that are also relevant in terms of thinking "the Nordic" are: What makes societies coherent? And what makes them change historically? In order to answer these questions, he establishes a set of philosophical a priori. First, being is a chaos containing non-regular, disjointed stratifications and partial, temporary organizations. There is no great chain or master system. Second, being is not in time but by the means of time; being *is* time, "being" is always "becoming." And third, time is ontological creation (Castoriadis 1986a, pp. 219 & 222). If these a priori are valid, Castoriadis convincingly argues, the established knowledge and schemes of thinking do not provide satisfactory answers to the instituting power of societies. The instituting process cannot be exhausted by what we usually understand as institutional, rational, functional, material, and symbolic relationships and processes. The instituting power is both implicit and explicit, and, if we do not take the imaginary institution of society into account, the former of the two dimensions fundamentally eludes us.

Castoriadis' radical thesis is therefore to insert an "invisible" factor—the imaginary—into the heart of the institution of the social in order to account for time as ontological creation. He argues for the limits of the functionalist approach to social institutions, but also that the symbolic realm is insufficient for understanding a social institution. "Institutions cannot be reduced to the symbolic but they can exist only in the symbolic" (1987, p. 117), he asserts. Institutions are thus reducible neither to functionalist nor to symbolic entities. There is something at stake behind these levels of reality, he argues. For Castoriadis, this is not to fall into complete idealism or solipsism. Paraphrasing Marx, he says, "Society does constitute its symbolism but not in total freedom" (1987, p. 125). There is obviously what he calls a "natural stratum," the givens of the material and physical world, but there is also history and rationality that co-condition the social institution. He uses the metaphor of a "magma of social significations" to illustrate how the social flows on "something," but this "something" is for Castoriadis of a double nature: it is both of the primary natural stratum, but also of the imaginary.

Essentially, the notion of the imaginary is necessary in order to account for society's instituting process without institutional—functional and/or symbolic—determinism, leaving free space for emergence, the singular event, the ontologically different, Castoriadis' particular ontology of creation *ex nihilo* (Adams 2011). This ability to create *ex nihilo* Castoriadis terms the radical imaginary, and his point is that while it only shows itself in symbolic forms, social history is unthinkable without it. It is, metaphorically speaking, the dark matter of social theory, which we cannot observe, but which must be there in order to make the observations fit. The imaginary, therefore, is a kind of a priori forming of what we can think, say, and do, a frame for possible social valorization, but also something that can change in order to alter the conditions for what we can say, think, and do—without this alteration being reducible to a historical trajectory, the change being already inherent in or given from what was before. Perhaps it is the visual, plastic, and musical arts that most directly channel and reproduce the imaginary (even the art of a Kim Larsen), as the arts are reducible to neither discourse nor symbol. For example, Castoriadis opens his discussion of ontology and the imaginary with the simple question: Why do philosophers never begin their interrogation of a paradigm of being with a reflection on Mozart's Requiem, what it can reveal to us about Being (1986a, p. 222)?

This is Castoriadis' radical thought. He underlines that it is the imaginary institution of significations "which for each society posits what is and what is not, what has worth and what has not, and how, in what way is or is not does or does not have worth that which can actually be or have worth. This is what establishes the conditions and the common orientations of the doable and the representable, and in this holds together, in advance and by construction, so to speak, the indefinite and essentially open multitude of individuals, acts, objects, functions, institutions in the second-order and functionary use of the term, which in each case, concretely constitutes a society" (Castoriadis 1987, pp. 368–369; see also Bouchet 2018).

The imaginary is therefore not the doable or the representable, but their conditions and orientations. It is not the institutions themselves, in their functional and symbolic instantiations, but their framing. The imaginary is the horizon, always a certain direction and a limit beyond which we cannot perceive (yet—since the imaginary as we have seen is malleable). It is according to these principles that we can propose a reflection of central elements of the Nordic imaginary as instituting the particularity of the Nordic, knowing full well that our narrative, our set of elements, represents a leap from the imaginary to the symbolic. It reduces irreducible (and chaotic) Nordicness to a system of elements; it fixates in time what is essentially creation. Alas, we social scientists have only the symbolic instrument of language to express ourselves in and must make do. The following should then be read as a set of symbolic "symptoms" of the Nordic imaginary, symptoms that *are* not but may be able to represent an indication of what "the Nordic" is.

Sketching the Nordic Imaginary

Before we consider the different chapters and their contributions to unpacking Nordic consumer culture in its particular institutional context of state and market, allow us to engage in a set of completely speculative reflections on at least parts of what would constitute the Nordic imaginary and hence the particular set of institutions. It follows from Castoriadis' (1975) discussion of the role of the imaginary for social cohesion (and social change) that one fundamental issue of the imaginary—almost by necessity—is the relationship between individual and society. In order to situate the Nordic imaginary, we could take as a starting point a central axis in the Old Norse cosmology, namely inclusion–exclusion (Hastrup 1992). The axis is not just a separation in terms of space between order and chaos, sociality and wilderness, warmth and cold, light and darkness. It is also a classification of humans. The old Norse word *útlagen*—outlaw—designates someone who has been rejected from the community. An outlaw is not someone who puts himself outside the law through his actions. It is someone who has been put outside the law, meaning outside the social order. Being inside or outside becomes the decisive matter. On the smallest of scales, one can think of this inclusion and exclusion as expressed in situations of hygge underscored by the necessary *hyggebelysning* (Danish for "lights for hygge"). *Hyggebelysning* almost by necessity involves dimmed lights (fires) so as not to illuminate (warm) all the space. Hygge confirms community and its togetherness through the excluded presence of (cold) darkness, of an outside.

Because of this historical cosmology, the notion of community and its borders is foundational to Nordic communities. In addition, Hastrup and Löfgren (1992) argue, a particular type of moral economy specific to the Nordic realm characterizes Nordic local communities: an economy of happiness. From the sagas throughout medieval literature to peasant societies of the nineteenth century, historians and anthropologists can trace this idea that happiness is a finite and pre-defined resource. There is only so much luck given to us as a community, and someone's luck is by necessity someone else's misfortune. We can find here both the origin of envy and the Law of Jante, but, as a mirror image, also the foundation for a deeply rooted egalitarianism. We should not, Castoriadis (1986b) asserts, search for the roots of the value of political egality in Christianity—which would be overlooking more than a thousand years of institutional history (Render unto Caesar…). It is, rather, a highly improbable, imaginary social signification of European societies. Nor were old Nordic societies particularly egalitarian. However, we might assume that once egalitarianism established itself in modern Nordic societies, it was reinforced by this ancient Nordic economy of happiness—just as it may also contribute to the understanding of why Nordic welfare states can be seen as based on "deeply held norms of reciprocity and conditional obligations" (Bowles and Gintis 2000). These authors do not cite Marcel Mauss (1950), but basically this is a Maussian argument about social cohesion and reciprocal exchange.

The egalitarianism of the economy of happiness obviously also engenders a certain skepticism toward elites. Since the representatives of political power usually constitute social elites, this might be seen as an obstacle to the development of a strong state in the Nordic countries. As is widely known, this is not really the case. Hence, the question becomes: What kind of state can be accepted in a context of egalitarianism? The Nordic state model is exactly one which is revered insofar as it does not consider itself and its representatives an elite. The state is there to manage an economy of happiness—to serve the community through redistribution and thereby make sure that those with fortune contribute part of their surplus so that the less fortunate are not excluded from society—not to celebrate itself as "an elite." The first author of this introductory chapter has often entertained his French in-laws with the (for them) unbelievable but true story about the Danish minister who had to resign, due to the fact that she had stayed at a fancy Parisian hotel during an international meeting. It is worthwhile recalling Berggren and Trägårdh's (2015) concept of statist individualism to remind us of the (ideal) mixed role of the state in the Nordic countries. In the modern Nordic imaginary, the state is there to secure individual freedom to pursue a career, lifestyle, interests, and so on within the confines of the community and the law, not to establish itself as a controlling force or an elite to revere. Consequently, a paradoxical love–hate relationship to the state is widespread in the Nordic countries. We of course all (or almost all) love and respect the welfare state and its programs securing the population a maximum of individual freedom, but when the state interferes too much in people's individual lives or when it takes on the character of a self-legitimizing and over-reaching bureaucracy, it is widely condemned. A large majority of Nordic citizens have plenty of personal experiences recounting both of these aspects of welfare state policies.

The particular form of the Nordic welfare state, which permeates almost all social matters but still should not appear as a "state"—that is, a permanent elite that stands outside and above the population—gives rise to a paradox. The Nordic welfare state is a state that is there to make sure that no one gets left out and no one accrues too much power. It is in this respect akin to French anthropologist Pierre Clastres' (1974) idea of Amazonian "societies against the state." There, political power is dispersed so that the chief's prime function is to be a war leader in case of external conflict, but internally to ensure that nobody assumes excessive power within the community. As anthropologists have often observed, the chief is in service to the community, the community is not subservient to the chief. This is obviously a principle characteristic of all democracies, but it is difficult to identify societies where this principle—as an ideal and as a legitimization of governmental institutions—has carried it so close to the principle Clastres found. This is of course not to say that the Nordic populations and the Nordic imaginary do not embrace the modern state and its welfare programs. But, akin to the case with the royal families (which we will discuss a little further on), the state is embraced and supported to the extent that it preserves community and inclusion and does not stand out as something outside the community, as a governing body outside and above the people.

Institutionalizations of the Nordic Imaginary

The belief in welfare, of the specific kind provided by the benevolent state, is perhaps the most central defining characteristic of the modern Nordic countries. As these backward-striving, peasant countries catapulted themselves out of poverty around the turn of the twentieth century or even later, the key element was the largely shared belief in a potent state that would look after the needs of its citizens; needs, as indicated by the dire conditions at the time, that many of the citizens had not previously been able to gratify themselves. The state therefore, in the spirit of an entity with a greater understanding of the needs of its citizens than the citizens themselves, gave itself permission to extort high taxes in order to redistribute wealth in a manner that would benefit the citizens, but perhaps more importantly the state. In this spirit, the aristocracy and the bourgeoisie should abandon—or at least tame and conceal—dubious, degenerate, wasteful habits on one end of the spectrum. So too should the peasants on the other end of the spectrum, and they should all congregate around the middle in celebration of the shared ideals of the newly sprung welfare states, exemplified in taxation, redistribution, and moderation in all aspects of everyday life.

The benevolent welfare state, however, did not rise to this prominent position on its own accord, but was riding the crest of modernity. As has been discussed by countless authors, the overall spirit of modernity was the desire to control and order the world, with the goal of building a grand future for humankind. More specifically, it dealt with controlling nature through scientific technologies, and in the process celebrating rationalism over the emotions, the mind over the body and science over superstition and religion. While the Nordic countries were relatively late to the table, they no doubt dug in with some gusto once they got to enjoy the fruits of modernity.

One example of the enthusiastic welcoming of modern ideas was how quickly and thoroughly religious beliefs were complemented, and in many instances supplemented, by an equally strong belief in modernity. The Nordic countries are still amongst the most secular in the world, which for decades has puzzled international onlookers wondering how we could possibly believe in the state rather than God (Berggren and Trägårdh 2015; Brown 1955). Another particularly prominent example of the strong belief in modernity can be illustrated by the publication of the *acceptera* manifesto, written by a number of architects and other creatives in 1931 (Asplund et al. 1931). The *acceptera* manifesto was produced after the Stockholm Exhibition in 1930, where the Swedish version of functionalism was introduced to the world. One of the key principles of this manifesto was that design should be guided by function rather than superfluous ornamentation. The authors of the manifesto saw the superfluous ornamentation of the past as deceitful. They instead worshiped the ideals of brute functionality. If it works, it is by definition beautiful! Moreover, what the authors found especially offensive was the tendency of factories to mass produce items of poor quality aimed at the lower classes, items whose entire raison d'être was to mimic the aesthetics of the bourgeoisie. These principles subsequently inspired a number of iconic designers including Alvar Aalto, Arne Jacobsen, and Carl Malmsten, designers who still benchmark Nordic design aesthetics.

And still, while celebrating the rationalizing tendency, the citizens of the Nordic countries were clearly never as modern as they would have thought they were (and still do). We should of course not be surprised. Latour (1993) underlines how "we have never been modern" and Castoriadis' (1975) whole point is that functional or rational logic can never exhaust the social institutionalization process. The distinct feature of modern society is, as he points out, that it amongst all known social forms does not allow space for the imaginary to "have a flesh of its own" (op. cit., p. 224). Modernity has chased out the imaginary with rationality, but the imaginary instead emerges exactly through beliefs in analytical objectivism.

Neither Latour nor Castoriadis addresses something that is particular to the Nordic countries. However, in the Nordic context, we might add that one anachronistic aspect of a pre-modern imaginary occupies a central position in the social institution: Denmark, Norway, and Sweden are (still) monarchies. Only Finland and Iceland—for various historical and political reasons that are too complex to delve into here—are organized in the "usual modern" way as republics. Not only are the three aforementioned countries monarchies, but the positions of the royal families are strong and their popularity amongst both old and new citizens is high. This paradoxical position between pre-modernity, modernity, and increasingly late/post/high/liquid (or some other prefix of choice) modernity sets the Nordic countries in a particular position when it comes to various expressions of taste as they play out in Nordic consumer culture.

This is reflected in several of the opening chapters of this book. Weijo (Chap. 2), for example, sketches the rudiments of a Nordic sociology of consumption, and asks whether there might be a way of doing taste that would qualify as distinctly Nordic. In answering this question, he draws on the concept of the Law of Jante (Danish/Norwegian: Janteloven), a concept with Danish-Norwegian origins that is nowadays used across the Nordics, whereby it is essential not to be ostentatious in one's display of distinctions. Weijo's analysis exposes something unique in the cultural tendencies of social conformity and muted displays of distinction. This surface-level equality undergirded by multiple layers of status hierarchies that the consumers of the Nordics constantly navigate in many ways can be characterized by quoting Orwell's *Animal Farm*, wherein the pigs stipulate that "All animals are equal, but some animals are more equal than others…"

The consumers of the Nordics thereby seem to hold the imaginary equality of our countries in such high regard that they appear quite willing to overlook much of the glaring evidence pointing in the opposite direction. Perhaps this strong belief in imaginary equality also goes some way toward explaining the paradoxical acceptance of royalty in some of the Nordic countries. The acceptance of the royal families' particular and anachronistic status is exactly dependent on the fact that they perform in order to deny or at least ironize distinction and privilege. In order to uphold the idea of egalitarianism, Nordics are observant of signs that even the royal families are just like everyone else—mere mortals with flaws and composite personalities—and because of this they do not pose a real threat to equality. If the government is the executive expression of the paradoxical "society against the state" mentioned earlier, the royal families are its symbolic incarnation. Their institutional power is to demonstrate that regardless of political tendencies, *everyone* is included in the community under their reign.

Ulver (Chap. 3) also sketches the contours of a uniquely Nordic mode of consumption, although with an emphasis on Sweden. In doing this, she builds on another fundamental paradox housing "conspicuously strong ideological contradictions absorbed and governed in the state model." More specifically, she builds on the idea of statist individualism, as outlined by Berggren and Trägårdh (2015). In essence, the state has come to play the role of a guarantee of individual autonomy from archaic structures, most prominently the family. The state in the Swedish/Nordic setting thus sets us free to realize ourselves any way we want, which is exactly where the market steps in and capitalizes on our perennial search for belonging. Just like Weijo in Chap. 2, Ulver touches on the intricate dance involved in making distinctions without explicitly appearing to want to make distinctions, which she conceptualizes as "elitarian equality." While both Weijo and Ulver discuss various ways in which consumption and distinction are organized in the Nordic countries and how there is an implicit set of rules that needs to be followed, Martin, Lindberg, and Fitchett (Chap. 4) add another ingredient to the mix by looking at the nexus of inclusion and exclusion through the tensions between temporary visitors and locals. The temporary visitors lack the necessary experiences and competencies to interpret the implicit rules and thereby come to violate the spirit of the Nordic social contract, while not actually violating statutes and rules.

Hokkinen (Chap. 5) also picks up on the theme of inclusion and exclusion, and takes her departure from instances where the implicit rules of how to consume in the Nordics are violated. More specifically, she looks at the relational conflicts that arose between the local Finns and the newly arrived Middle Eastern refugees who came to Finland in the wake of the 2015 refugee crises. What Hokkinen manages to bring to the table are aspects of the welfare state system that become the focal point when those who have supposedly not contributed to the system are enjoying the benefits. In what ways are you allowed to enjoy the benefits of the system and what objects and modes of consumption are legitimate? Next, Molander, Östberg, and Kleppe (Chap. 6) use the case of fatherhood in Sweden to illustrate how consumer culture evolves at the nexus of the (welfare) state, individual consumers' lived lives, and companies' marketing activities. The chapter implicitly draws on the idea of statist individualism brought up in Chap. 3, whereby the Swedish state's feminist agenda has liberated both mothers and fathers from their traditional roles. This freedom, however, should not be confused with some sort of anarchy where anything is allowed. Instead, the freedom is highly regulated by various actors, who both prescribe and capitalize on particular modes of being a progressive father. Salminen (Chap. 7) also discusses this balancing act between supposed freedom and regulations. Using the empirical domain of Nordic sailors, she discusses how consumers' nature experiences are orchestrated through an interplay of Nordic ideologies of nature as well as Nordic governmental apparatuses. Here, the peculiar status of nature is foregrounded with an explication of the Nordic everyman's rights, building on the ideological position that nature should be free to enter and experience equally for everyone, regardless of ownership. But, paradoxically, the Nordic states also set strict governmental rules undergirded by contrasting ideologies that restrict certain nature experiences.

As of late, the Nordic model has definitely won many hearts and inspired politicians all over the world. Recently, notable political figures like Bernie Sanders in the USA and Emmanuel Macron in France have praised the Nordic countries for their success in building societies that are simultaneously economically successful and socially inclusive. Bjerregaard and Kjeldgaard's chapter (Chap. 8) testifies to the seduction and the self-seduction of this discourse of the exemplary society in an analysis of Chinese-Danish cooperation to establish Danish-style eldercare in China. Seen from the perspectives evoked in this introduction, the chapter demonstrates clearly how institutions are rooted in a particular imaginary, and how copying an institutional system without the imaginary that sustained it in the original context is problematic if not impossible. This of course represents a challenge both for politicians who are inspired by the Nordic model but also in a neoliberal age, for the commercial visions of exporting systems that recurrently appear and to some extent legitimize the Nordic public sector. The ambitions to export welfare in Chap. 8 are nicely complemented by Schultz Nybacka's (Chap. 9) analysis of the popularity of Nordic Noir crime novels, and more specifically *Schwedenkrimi*, in Germany, wherein a different set of seductions are laid bare. From a German perspective, the Nordic countries have held a peculiarly elevated position, being idealized both from the perspective of how society is organized and for the lure of vast, untouched nature. The genre of Nordic Noir turns this on its head, hinting at the co-presence of a more sinister undercurrent of corruption and violence underneath the pretty surface. Schultz Nybacka shows how this effect is orchestrated and amplified by translating and packaging the books in particular ways that give them a specific Northern ambiance: snowy, solitary, and sinister. Andersen, Kjeldgaard, Lindberg, and Östberg (Chap. 10) follow this path of how the Nordic is orchestrated by looking at how Nordic brand actors perceive and enact Nordic values. In uncovering the mythological framework that stands as a foundation for Nordic branding strategies, they find various cultural tensions—such as balancing modern Nordic aesthetics with Viking imagery and Norse mythology; egalitarian inclusiveness with fine dining/haute cuisine culture; traditional gendered fashion with post-gendered/LBTQ fashion; and ethnocentrism with multiculturalism—that are used to construct a particular mode of sanitized Nordic mythology. In a similar vein, Pietilä, Tillotson, and Askegaard (Chap. 11) set out to pay "greater sensitivity to place and history" in operationalizing regionally based marketing and consumer research (Chelekis and Figueiredo

2015, p. 321). Through an interpretive inquiry into print advertisements that invoke the idea of Finnishness, they find that mythical portrayals of Finnishness in advertising appeal to, reinforce, and extend a collective sense of national and cultural identity. They also show how advertisements leverage national symbolism and implied domestic product origins to propagate localist, protectionist, and regionalist narratives with moralistic undertones, and how a mythical portrayal of a rustic lifestyle of the past enables Finnish consumers to regain a material connection with a "paradise lost" of traditional Finnishness.

Many of the chapters address various attempts whereby aspects of what is conceived as uniquely Nordic has been taken out of its original context in attempts to add ambiance to various commercial endeavors. This ranges from selling the idea of (supposedly) progressive Swedish masculinity (Chap. 6), Danish-style eldercare (Chap. 8), and *Schwedenkrimi* (Chap. 9), to a wide gamut of other Nordic (Chap. 10) or Finnish (Chap. 11) market offerings. This idea that the Nordic countries hold an appeal that either could—there is money to be made here!—or should—we cannot deny the world this!—be generously made available to the world is a recurrent feature wherein Nordic marketers have become increasingly successful. As seen in the chapters in this volume, there are many different ways in which the Nordic myth markets are tapped for suitable semiotic resources, and they all rest on some idea of translating select elements that would appeal to a broader market. In this regard, we cannot help but refer back to the opening of this chapter, where the passing of Danish artist Kim Larsen was discussed. As described, Kim Larsen really struck a chord with Danish, and Nordic, audiences and came to be seen as someone who continuously, throughout his long career, managed to capture the spirit of the times. At no time was this perhaps more apparent than during the early Gasolin' years and in a touching scene in a much-acclaimed documentary about the band (Østergaard 2006) when they are about to "make it in America"—a fantasy that virtually all Nordic music acts secretly (or not so secretly) nurture—in order to spread, and of course capitalize on, the gospel of Gasolin'. In the documentary we get to see how everyone involved in the band excitedly awaits the opening show in New York City and how no one can foresee a scenario that does not involve success. Gasolin' is speaking the international language of rock 'n' roll, after all! And then…

nothing. They don't even get to fail, because no one, literally no one, shows up. It would be a stretch, of course, to claim that contemporary marketers have learnt a lesson from Gasolin'. Judging from the chapters in this volume, however, it becomes quite clear that those trying to capitalize on the Nordic—be they marketers, brand managers, publishers, bureaucrats, or politicians—have realized that there is nothing inherently appealing about the Nordic. Instead, the Nordic appeal has to be carefully constructed in order for the surrounding world to take an interest.

In the first of the two conversations that end the book, Linnet and Bean (Chap. 12) discuss a uniquely Danish concept that has captured the world's attention in the last couple of years: hygge. A concept largely hijacked by the self-help business in endeavors to "help" consumers worldwide construct their own little zones of hygge, sufficiently sheltered from the harsh realities of the contemporary world, hygge is an example of how a concept deeply rooted in the cultural history of Denmark can be sufficiently emptied of its original meanings to appeal to a broader market. As opposed to Gasolin', the audiences turned up in masses around the world when hygge made its international debut. The two authors are both experts in the field who have approached the concept of hygge from various points of departure and their conversation circles around themes such as the anatomy of hygge, how it is constructed, what myths undergird it, what hygge allows for and what it forecloses, and how hygge has become objectified in order to be turned into something marketable. The concept of hygge also, as already indicated, cuts right to the larger theme of inclusion and exclusion, as the warm and cozy atmosphere that is essential to hygge is predicated on an outside that must be kept, well, outside. And this is exactly where the seemingly innocent concept of hygge connects to world politics, since discussions about what should be defined as outside the perimeters of the Nordic have split the Nordic populations apart in the last couple of years.

The final chapter consists of a conversation between Hartmann and Arnould (Chap. 13), where they discuss the legacy of Per Østergaard, to whom this book is dedicated. Per was instrumental in making us realize the particularities of Nordic consumer culture and how this was not necessarily just a matter of self-congratulating navel-gazing, but could help us understand larger issues of the connections between the state, the market, and the consumers. The chapter takes its departure from some of Per's texts, but quickly meanders into adjacent areas discussing, as Per often did, the intellectual state of the field of marketing and consumer culture theory. While Per's deep knowledge of and engagement with various philosophical perspectives are (unfortunately) not a hallmark of Nordic scholarship, the conversation reveals how essential this type of knowledge is for going beyond the appealing surface-level explanations that we are typically fed with. The closing sentences by Arnould get right to the point: "You know that television series, Broen? It's perfect. It's the perfect metaphor and indeed the bridge is a perfect metaphor for Per's work. It bridges time, space, cultural tradition, and it deals with a situation in which everything is fine and all middle class and then there are two [very disruptive] things that don't quite get together; that are joined by a bridge."

A Nordic Consumer Culture Manifesto?

In one publication appearing only a few years prior to his death, Per Østergaard presented a reflection on the history and legacy of the consumer culture theory research community in terms of a set of "manifestary moments" (Bode and Østergaard 2013). If we retain this trope, this volume is a physical manifestation of countless conversations that have been going on amongst the included authors, as well as several other friends and colleagues, over the years (see, e.g., Østergaard et al. 2014). What started out as casual remarks—many times as reactions to accounts of consumer culture coming from scholars based in the USA, UK, or continental Europe—soon were complemented by more systematic analysis. In the process of trying to pin down what defines Nordic consumer culture, we kept coming back to the idiosyncratic mix of the state, the market, and the consumers, which is reflected in the subtitle of this book. Putting this obsession with trying to pin down the peculiarities of Nordic consumer culture into some perspective, we note that over the years there have indeed been previous more or less official attempts to define a particular Nordic mode of market existence.

We have already mentioned the *acceptera* manifesto (Asplund et al. 1931), whereby influential creatives attempted to guide both producers and consumers toward an enlightened—in the modernist sense—aesthetic ideal. We would like to bring up two more such manifestos here, as they aptly illustrate how questions of authenticity and sincerity keep coming up as Nordics grapple with both technological progression and globalizing tendencies. The first is the notorious *Dogme 95*, the film manifesto written by directors Lars von Trier, Thomas Vinterberg, Kristian Levring, and Søren Kragh Jacobsen in 1995. The manifesto consisted of "The Vow of Chastity" where they set up 10 commandments that should be followed by filmmakers. Examples include only shooting on location, only using handheld cameras, and not using special lighting. Many of the *Dogme 95* films—such as *The Celebration*, *The Idiots*, and *Italian for Beginners*—were celebrated by audiences and critics alike. The second is the *New Nordic Cuisine* manifesto from 2004. This was conceived on the initiative of René Redzepi and Claus Meyer—nowadays mostly famous for having started restaurant *Noma* in Copenhagen—and subsequently signed by chefs from all over Scandinavia. Just like the two previous manifestos discussed here, this one also emphasized a return to something more authentic, adhering to the principles of purity, simplicity, freshness, and an increased use of seasonal foods. The publication of these principles signaled the start of a new culinary trend in Scandinavia that has gained worldwide attention and acclaim.

The point here is not by any means to talk about the market success of these manifestos—even though it is noteworthy—but rather to indicate that the obsession with writing manifestos reflects a particular type of reflexivity on behalf of Nordics: a constant obsession with what we are doing and why, as well as what we should be doing. In this book we are certainly not providing any final answers to those questions, but we hope to have been curating a smörgåsbord of Nordic tidbits that give a flavor of how Nordic consumer culture exists at the nexus of the state, the market, and the consumers. And, like all smörgåsbords, we have aspired to satisfy those craving the intellectually savory, without having neglected those lusting after something sweet.

References

Adams, S. (2011). *Castoriadis's Ontology: Being and Creation*. New York: Fordham University Press.

Asplund, G., Gahn, W., Markelius, S., Paulsson, G., Sundahl, E., & Åhrén, U. (1931). *acceptera*. Stockholm: Tiden.

Berggren, H., & Trägårdh, L. (2015). *Är svensken människa? Gemenskap och oberoende i det moderna Sverige*. Stockholm: Norstedt.

Bode, M., & Østergaard, P. (2013). 'The Wild and Wacky Worlds of Consumer Oddballs': Analyzing the Manifestary Context of Consumer Culture Theory. *Marketing Theory, 13*(2), 175–192.

Bouchet, D. (2018). Beyond Reductionism, Constructivism and Arbitrary Sampling in Consumer Research Thanks to Castoriadis. In S. Askegaard & B. Heilbrunn (Eds.), *Canonical Authors in Consumption Theory* (pp. 258–265). London: Routledge.

Bowles, S., & Gintis, H. (2000). Reciprocity, Self-Interest, and the Welfare State. *Nordic Journal of Political Economy, 26*(1), 33–53.

Brown, J. D. (1955). Sin & Sweden. *Time, 65*(17).

Castoriadis, C. (1975 [1987]). *L'institution imaginaire de la société*. Paris: Seuil. [English Translation: *The Imaginary Institution of Society*. Cambridge: Polity Press, 1987].

Castoriadis, C. (1986a). L'imaginaire: La création dans le domaine social-historique. In *Domaines de l'homme* (pp. 219–237). Paris: Seuil.

Castoriadis, C. (1986b). Nature et valeur de l'égalité. In *Domaines de l'homme* (pp. 307–324). Paris: Seuil.

Chelekis, J. A., & Figueiredo, B. (2015). Regions and Archipelagos of Consumer Culture: A Reflexive Approach to Analytical Scales and Boundaries. *Marketing Theory, 15*(3), 321–345.

Clastres, P. (1974). *La société contre l'état*. Paris: Minuit.

Mauss, M. (1950 [1923]). Essai sur le don. In *Sociologie et anthropologie* (pp. 143–179). Paris: Quadrige/OUF.

Morin, E. (1956). *Le cinéma ou l'homme imaginaire*. Paris: Minuit.

Østergaard, A. (Director). (2006). *Gasolin'* [Documentary Film]. Denmark: Cosmo Film.

Østergaard, P., Linnet, J. T., Andersen, L. P., Kjeldgaard, D., Bjerregaard, S., Weijo, H., et al. (2014). Nordic Consumer Culture: Context and Concept. In *Research in Consumer Behavior* (Vol. 16, pp. 245–257). Bingley: Emerald.

Wilk, R. R. (1997). A Critique of Desire: Distaste and Dislike in Consumer Behavior. *Consumption, Markets and Culture, 1*(2), 175–196.
Žižek, S. (1992). *Looking Awry: An Introduction to Jacques Lacan Through Popular Culture*. Cambridge, MA: MIT Press.

Part I

Nordic Consumer Culture and the State–Market Nexus

2

Democracies of Taste Ruled by the Law of Jante? Rudiments of a Nordic Sociology of Consumption

Henri A. Weijo

What do Nordics consume? The simple answer would be to rattle off Nordic culinary staples like rye bread, wild berry sauces, gravlax, and pickled herring, or brand names from product categories like furniture, home electronics, and fashion that exemplify the idea of "Nordic cool." But how do these things relate to one another? What is, say, a hearty reindeer stew compared to an aesthetically spectacular dish in a nouveau Nordic restaurant? What is an IKEA recliner compared to a wooden dinner table from the latest Danish design talent? What is a weekend getaway at a summer cottage compared to one spent in one of the increasingly cosmopolitan Nordic capitals? Furthermore, how do Nordics consume? Is there a way of doing taste that would qualify as distinctly Nordic? For instance, does the undeniably egalitarian and conformist cultural mood of Nordic culture (Berggren and Trägårdh 2010) give a distinct flavor to Nordic consumption practices?

H. A. Weijo (✉)
Aalto University School of Business, Helsinki, Finland
e-mail: henri.weijo@aalto.fi

S. Askegaard, J. Östberg (eds.), *Nordic Consumer Culture*,
https://doi.org/10.1007/978-3-030-04933-1_2

This chapter explores these "what" and "how" questions by introducing a sociological perspective on Nordic consumption. Sociology of consumption investigates how a society's class and status groups are organized around or through consumption (e.g., Weber 1978; Corrigan 1997; Warde 2015). Such investigations (this chapter is no exception) often build on the theoretical oeuvre of Pierre Bourdieu (Corrigan 1997; Warde 2015; Arnould and Thompson 2018). Within the Bourdieuan analytical tradition, there is a paradigmatic split that maps onto these questions of what and how things are consumed. The greater field of sociology favors large swatches of statistical or survey data and concentrates on what different social classes are wont to consume (e.g., Bryman 1984; Peterson and Simkus 1992). A primary focus in this line of research has been to compare consumption categories in relation to one another to uncover how these categories serve as markers of distinction for different social groups (e.g., DiMaggio 1987; Lamont 1992). Conversely, consumer culture researchers prefer the "how" side of things and have made greater use of methods like ethnography and deep interviews (e.g., Holt 1997; Coskuner-Balli and Thompson 2013; Arnould and Thompson 2018). I will draw from both analytical traditions to outline what I believe are distinctly Nordic patterns of consumption, concentrating first on the "what" and then on the "how."

The rest of this chapter unfolds as follows. I begin by briefly outlining Bourdieu's sociological approach to the study of consumption. This section also elaborates how Bourdieu's theories have been used to study national taste patterns and relations between consumption categories. The following section builds on these macro-level studies to illuminate what Nordics consume. I will argue that in this regard our region does not differ much from other European countries and regions, save for markedly more omnivorous taste patterns. The subsequent section concentrates on how Nordics consume and explains how the cultural norms of conformity and the ethos of egalitarianism provide a macro backdrop for Nordic consumption praxis. The chapter concludes with a discussion of future research possibilities and speculation on where Nordic taste might be heading next.

Sociology of Consumption and National Patterns of Taste

Bourdieu's (1984, 1986) sociological approach foregrounds endowments of cultural, social, and economic capital (in simplified terms: what you know, who you know, and what you have) as the key determinants of class positions. Bourdieu saw these capital endowments accruing gradually through one's upbringing and resulting in socialized dispositions that make people with similar stocks of capital gravitate toward certain consumption fields over others. In other words, children of similar class backgrounds acquire habituated skills and aesthetic preferences through immersion in similar hobbies, vacation plans, and educational paths all the way up to higher education. For Bourdieu, taste is thus intertwined with societal structures of power, both historically and institutionally. If people with similar stocks of capital do indeed share a homological identification ("birds of a feather flock together"), then this explains, amongst other things, why social classes can appear so rigid across the decades or even the centuries.

Bourdieu's work begat a stream of research on how national and macro-level characteristics produce relational patterns between cultural fields and categories. Many of these investigations have built on DiMaggio's (1987) dimensional framework that he originally developed for categorizing societal patterns for artistic production and consumption. These dimensions have since been further developed within more general and comparative studies of national taste structures (e.g., Lamont 1992; van Venrooij and Schmutz 2010). The dimensions are *differentiation*, *hierarchy*, *universality*, and *strength of symbolic boundaries*. I review each of these and illuminate them with examples from well-known past studies.

Differentiation denotes the heterogeneity of cultural categories and to what degree categories break down into more refined or complex subgenres. Societies with a high degree of differentiation are usually socio-economically and ethnically diverse, offer more and better educational opportunities for their citizens, and have more tolerance for social role divergence (especially relating to sex and gender). Strong differentiation animates cultural production in Britain: the country's post-colonial immigration flows have spawned a host of subcultures whose field and capital logics do not mimic or become subjugated to those favored by the cultural elites (Gelder 2005). Thornton's (1996) famous study of club cultures illuminated this differentiation: electronic music genres break down into seemingly endless subgenres whose origins can often be traced to ethnic populations and communities (e.g., McLeod 2001). The USA as the proverbial melting pot is similarly diverse in terms of demographics, which supports the fragmentation of taste categories (Lamont 1992; Peterson and Simkus 1992).

Hierarchization means that cultural categories differ in their relative power and prestige, as opposed to being "different but equal." A society with a higher degree of hierarchization usually has a stable or widely shared system for social status, more income inequality, low social mobility, and a smaller and more exclusive political and educational elite. Bourdieu's (1984) study of 1960s France underlined the strict hierarchization of taste structures. For instance, classical music and other forms of "high art" favored by the elites were seen as more prestigious than those favored by the working classes, like folk music or *chansons*. Bourdieu also recounted how French cultural elites and political institutions judiciously reinforced this hierarchization. Differentiation enjoys a reverse correlation with hierarchization: stable taste hierarchies necessitate the type of cultural consensus that is difficult to sustain in diverse societies like the USA (Lamont 1992).

Universality denotes that the citizenry has a shared consensus on the content and relations between cultural categories. Universality thus suggests strong social cohesion, demographic homogeneity, higher social equality, and egalitarian educational opportunities. Quite logically, universality has a strong inverse correlation with differentiation, given the lack of cultural consensus in such societies. Yet, somewhat counterintuitively, universality does not usually support taste hierarchization. For instance, taste structures in Britain reflect the country's deep and historical class divide. As a result, the working classes have embraced a countercultural ethos to taste, which manifests in ignorance and open dismissiveness of the cultural categories favored by the elites, such as classical high culture (Thornton 1996; Bennett et al. 2009). France in the 1960s provides a notable exception, as strong class hierarchies coincided with relatively strong taste universality (Bourdieu 1984). This was once again a testament to how strongly cultural institutions can structure national patterns of taste.

Lastly, the strength of symbolic boundaries refers to the degree of difficulty for producers and objects to move between cultural categories, and how easily these categories can be contested or reinvented. In other words, strong symbolic boundaries mean that a cultural product from a category sitting at the bottom of the national taste hierarchy cannot shed its category origins, limiting the product's opportunities to gain prestige. Bourdieu's (1984) analysis of France in the 1960s underlined how the cultural elites, institutions, and other taste gatekeepers like cultural critics or the media jealously and systematically guarded the boundaries between symbolic categories. The USA, on the other hand, represents a polar opposite. America is a post-modern consumer culture par excellence—the movement of goods and producers between categories is uninhibited and rapid (Lamont 1992; Holt 1997). For example, a hip-hop artist in America can earn recognition as an artist of true excellence, even if hip-hop otherwise might enjoy less prestige than, say, jazz (van Venrooij and Schmutz 2010). Overall, strong symbolic boundaries have a negative correlation with high differentiation, low hierarchization, and low universality (Lamont 1992).

What Nordics Consume: Nordic Macro-Level Taste Patterns

This section uses the dimensional framework to shed light on Nordic taste patterns. Here I draw mostly from a recent large-scale inquiry into Finnish cultural capital and taste patterns led by a group of Finnish sociologists. The study remains one of the few similar-scale replications of Bourdieu's (1984) project, and certainly the only one conducted in the Nordics (for the final project report, see Purhonen et al. 2014). Spatial limitations prohibit covering all the interesting nuances that the study identified and many of the insights remain unique to the Finnish context. I will highlight issues in the study that I believe have relevance to the entire Nordic region. I will also draw from other studies conducted in the Nordics when appropriate.

Table 2.1 Dimensions of taste structures in selected countries

	France in the 1960s[a]	The USA in the 1980s and 1990s[b]	Britain in the 2000s[c]	Pre-EU Finland[d]	Finland in the 2000s[e]
Differentiation	Neutral	Stronger	Stronger	Weaker	Neutral
Hierarchization	Stronger	Weaker	Neutral	Weaker	Stronger
Universality	Stronger	Weaker	Weaker	Stronger	Neutral
Strength of symbolic boundaries	Stronger	Weaker	Neutral	Stronger	Neutral

[a]Bourdieu (1984)
[b]DiMaggio (1987), Lamont (1992), van Venrooij and Schmutz (2010)
[c]Bennett et al. (2009), Purhonen and Wright (2013)
[d]Mäkelä (1985)
[e]Purhonen et al. (2014)

Mäkelä (1985) had originally dismissed Bourdieu's applicability in the Nordic context. He saw Bourdieu's theories as mostly incompatible with Nordic welfare societies, where demographic homogeneity and a history of egalitarianism deter taste conflict and competition.[1] Some authors had also speculated that pre-European Union (EU) Nordic countries lacked access to consumption objects with which distinctions could be created (combined with higher levels of taxation and income distribution), at least in a truly hierarchical fashion (Østergaard 1997; Rahkonen 2008). Table 2.1 summarizes these differences in taste structures as either stronger, neutral, or weaker tendencies within that particular dimension. I have also included some of the studies mentioned in the previous section to give context to the interpretation (see the notes for sources that have presented similar categorizations). The table reveals a notable shift in Finnish taste patterns, with the most dramatic change taking place in the hierarchization of taste.

Virtanen (2007) writes that contemporary Nordic taste structures do not differ much from their European counterparts. In fact, Nordic marketplaces have in many ways become more globalized than those of other

[1] Rahkonen (2008) speculates that Mäkelä's hostility toward Bourdieu may have also been ideologically motivated. Bourdieu's ideas of rigid and invisible forces creating social division did not jibe well with the strong leftist zeitgeist of the 1980s.

European countries, where local production still enjoys greater preference (e.g., Østergaard 1997; Gottlieb 2004; Kjeldgaard and Östberg 2007; Giddens 2013; Østergaard et al. 2014). These global influences explain the growth in differentiation and the decline in symbolic boundary strength. The simultaneous growth in hierarchization in Finland runs counter to DiMaggio's (1987) model, but I believe this is also consistent with these global influences. For example, Giddens (2013) speculates that globalization has degrading effects on the solidarity and monocultural tendencies of Nordic societies. Other writers argue that growing differentiation and weakening category boundaries are logical consequences of societies becoming more post-modern, at least in the western world (Lamont 1992; Holt 1997; van Venrooij and Schmutz 2010).

Purhonen et al. (2014) singled out two categories where change has been more dramatic than others. The ascendant taste hierarchization was particularly evident in music, which again mapped onto similar trends across the western world (van Venrooij and Schmutz 2010). The strongest change had occurred in food tastes, which had become polarized between modern, ethnic, and light food favored by educated, young, and urban populations, vis-à-vis traditional and hearty food preferred by rural, older, and less educated populations. This revealed a robust hierarchization of food consumption, coupled with stronger symbolic boundaries and an erosion of taste universality. Much of this change can be explained by the drastic increase in variety within the food market following Finland's entry to the EU (Østergaard 1997; Weijo et al. 2018). These changes also align with findings elsewhere highlighting changing Nordic preferences for food due to global influences (Askegaard and Madsen 1998; Kjeldgaard and Östberg 2007; Purhonen and Gronow 2014). They accord too with studies on cosmopolitanism and global nomads that recount growing tensions between local and global tastes (e.g., Bardhi et al. 2012). My own research into the Restaurant Day food culture movement similarly recounted the growing desires of educated, young, urban, and globalist Finns to draw stronger distinctions between "good" and "bad" food in a competitive fashion (Weijo et al. 2018).

Despite these growing similarities to other western countries, the Nordic region remains distinct in one particular area: the pervasiveness of omnivorous taste patterns. Omnivorous consumption was originally conceptualized as a tendency of certain elite consumer groups in the West to consume across a multitude of cultural categories, anything from the high arts to low popular culture (Peterson and Simkus 1992). Subsequent studies have exposed omnivorousness as a mirage, as omnivorous consumers usually maintain only fleeting and experimental engagements in fields outside their natural taste dispositions (e.g., Holt 1997; Warde et al. 2007). Yet Purhonen et al. (2010, 2014) argue that Nordic omnivorousness is special. It is more pervasive and egalitarian, with all social classes consuming across a variety of cultural categories and in ways that can no longer be considered merely experimental or fleeting (see also Prieur et al. 2008). Virtanen (2007) similarly shows that these omnivorous tendencies are a distinct Nordic trait: the average populational proportion of omnivores in the 15 EU countries under study was 13%, but for Denmark and Finland almost double that (24% and 23%), and for Sweden almost triple (33%). Purhonen et al. (2010) also underline that univores—consumers refusing to venture outside familiar taste categories—were markedly rare in Finland, both among lower classes (to whom univore taste is a way of showing upper-class resentment) as well as elite groups (to whom univore taste is a means for snobbery). This prompts them to speculate that Finland might be a "democracy of taste" (van Eijck and Knulst 2005) because "nowhere else—at least as far as we have more systematic information—are cultural snobs as rare and the all-encompassing omnivorous taste combination as usual as in Finland" (Purhonen et al. 2010, p. 293). Purhonen et al. (2014) similarly write that the omnivore–univore dynamic makes Finland still something of a "monoculture" (Bennett 2007), by which they mean that the entire population consumes from certain taste categories (usually local and traditional, like foods), though not necessarily always in the same way. These omnivore–univore tendencies may thus slow down the decline in taste universality that might otherwise follow growing differentiation and waning symbolic boundaries under postmodernity. The democratic kind of omnivorousness may also explain the recent rise in hierarchization in Finland, as it suggests that the population agrees on which cultural categories enjoy more esteem than others.

The Nordic education system was built on strong egalitarian ideals (Sampson et al. 1994), which disseminate cultural capital more equally amongst the population and promote taste universalism. Virtanen (2007) attributes the higher levels of cultural participation and especially the aversion to both high- and lowbrow distinctions in the Nordics to the countries' high-quality and egalitarian educational systems. Purhonen et al. (2010, 2014) concur that omnivorousness in the Nordics correlates with education levels, though not as strongly as in other regions. Virtanen (2007) also identifies higher state expenditure in subsidizing culture as a key contributor to omnivorousness—the proportional size of cultural budgets in the Nordics is about three times bigger compared to other EU countries, giving even the less well-off at least the opportunity to experience a broader array of taste categories. However, it is clear that the higher classes are usually more likely to take advantage of such state sponsorship. Nordic countries also have more generous budgets for recreational sports, which have been established for similar egalitarian purposes (Kahma 2012). These governmental investments and inclusion in school curricula may explain why Nordics rather universally value leisure reading and recreational sports (Virtanen 2007; Kahma 2012).

The universality of Nordic welfare programs reconfigures their public perceptions and supports taste universalism. Political scientists describe the "paradox of redistribution" as the condition where universal welfare programs—equally available for rich and poor alike—are often the most effective in aiding those they are chiefly intended to, namely the less well-off (Korpi and Palme 1998). The universalism of these programs also ensures their broad political support. This allows for their continuous development and also reduces the stigmatization of service patrons. For example, many public services in the USA, like public transit, carry a risk of stigma because they are considered first and foremost social programs (Stromberg 2015). In the Nordics, a service like public transit is a taken-for-granted part of city infrastructure and a matter of great convenience. You see a similar dynamic of universalist attitudes with libraries: the Nordics are by far the most active library patrons in Europe, and these patterns hold across social classes (Virtanen 2007). This level of popularity in all likelihood could not be maintained without a social consensus on the necessity of these services.

How Nordics Consume: Conformity and Muted Distinctions under the Law of Jante

Holt (1997) writes that the aforementioned classification of taste categories is necessarily limited and, more importantly, often masks important aspects of taste patterns (see also Warde et al. 2007; Atkinson 2011). He underlines that America's egalitarian and populist laissez-faire ethos ensures that everyone is in a sense "entitled" to consume across all cultural categories. Holt's own analysis revealed that the true logic of distinction in America revolves around differences in consumption *practices* across the social classes. This focus on practice over object categories has since become a central linchpin for cultural consumer research in the study of taste and distinction (Arnould and Thompson 2018).

Is there a "how" to Nordic taste practices? After a deep dive into the literature, I believe we can answer in the affirmative, at least tentatively. I identified two distinct features of Nordic taste practices, which I call *the double bind of conformity* and *muted displays of distinction*. I emphasize that they do not illuminate differences between social classes, unlike Holt's (1997) analysis. They work similarly to the aforementioned egalitarian laissez-faire ethos in the USA and provide a macro backdrop for Nordic taste practices. I also emphasize that they are my own interpretive propositions and thus somewhat speculative. Future research should interrogate these features across Nordic countries, especially across different social classes.

The Double Bind of Conformity

Nordic culture is undoubtedly conformist (Berggren and Trägårdh 2010). There is a fair amount of historical evidence that the cooperative communal traditions of coping with agricultural difficulties in the harsh northern climate, peasant taboos of wealth-flaunting, and a lack of strong aristocracies have together forged a Nordic embrace of egalitarianism through *commonness*, which manifests in social classes from top to bottom striving to portray themselves as belonging to one "big middle" (e.g., Gullestad 1992, 2013; Byrkjeflot 2001; Berggren and Trägårdh 2010).

The most famous expression of this Nordic idealization of commonness is the Law of Jante, or Janteloven, originally put forth by Danish-Norwegian author Aksel Sandemose (1899–1965). Janteloven bears similarities to other folk concepts like "tall poppy syndrome" in Anglo-Saxon societies and "the nail that stands out gets hammered down" in China (Belk 2011; Cappelen and Dahlberg 2017). It bears reminding that Sandemose was a fiction writer; Janteloven was not a result of rigorous anthropological inquiry. However, its popularity across the Nordics speaks to its cultural resonance as a shorthand for Nordic egalitarianism and conformity (Trotter 2015). One phrase in particular is associated with Janteloven: "You shall not imagine you are better than us." However, this is actually one of several laws. The full coda reads:

> You shall not believe you *are* anything.
> You shall not believe you are as much as *us*.
> You shall not believe you are wiser than *us*.
> You shall not imagine you are better than *us*.
> You shall not believe you know more than *us*.
> You shall not believe you are more than *us*.
> You shall not believe *you* are good for anything.
> You shall not laugh at *us*.
> You shall not believe anyone cares about *you*.
> You shall not believe you can teach us anything. (Sandemose 1999 [1933], p. 653; via Trotter 2015, emphasis in original)

The Nordic inertia "toward the middle" as expressed by Janteloven has a double effect for Nordic consumers. It admittedly disciplines what is perceived as too eager status-hunting, pulling these consumers down. But it also affects those who would rather opt out of the distinction game altogether, pulling these consumers up. Miller (2008) reviews Gullestad's (2013 [1992]) study of Norwegian home decoration and observes this double effect when he remarks that Gullestad's informants were mindful of "two crimes to be avoided." The first crime was creating an impression of a person with social ambitions and a desire to seek distance from peers through taste displays. Linnet's (2011) inquiry similarly found that Danish middle-class consumers were quick to brand those who seemed too preoccupied with status-chasing as soulless and joyless. This stands in contrast with the competitive and refined displays of capital that the French appreciate (Bourdieu 1984). The second crime Miller (2008) identified was not keeping up with common standards of taste and care for the home. As Gullestad (2013) writes, "One of the worst things one can say about somebody's home is that it is impersonal (*upersonlig*) and without ambience (*uten atmosfære*)" (p. 147). Toeing the line between the two crimes is a nuanced affair: one must "as fashions change, keep up with the times but don't try to be any kind of vanguard" (Miller 2008).

Belk's (2011) work on benign envy similarly remarks on Janteloven's effect of simultaneously pulling up as well as down, though Belk saw the effect of pulling up as weak. The earlier examples suggest that the power of pulling up is stronger than Belk gives it credit for. It is also possible that the effect of pulling up shields those in the middle from feelings that they are better than those "below" and maintains a sense of egalitarianism. By disciplining others to keep up, those in the middle gain more room for their status displays. Perhaps we need an addendum to Janteloven: "You shall not imagine you are better than us, but you shall not make us feel that we are better than you, either."

Muted Displays of Distinction

Nordic culture does not erase distinctions, but it does make them subtler and more inconspicuous. More specifically, Nordics can show distinction when it is not perceived as directed to others, as showing off or putting others to shame. This issue was raised a while ago in the Consumer Culture Theory Facebook group, when a non-Nordic commentator offered that Nordic consumption should be studied from the point of view of collectivism or communism. This was quickly protested by Nordic scholars. Danish anthropologist Jeppe Linnet provided an erudite response:

> Even if Scandinavian society looks quite homogenous because of the economic leveling, normatively it is in this sense quite fragmented—or free, some would say (the socialdemocratic kind of freedom that a welfare state

> provides, e.g. being able to take a weird and risky education because one's parents have no say or financial involvement). However, this does not hold if others start to challenge us and suggest that they are "better" or have more worth—hence the Jante Law saying "you should not believe that you are better than us"—it has to do with a mutual sheltering of each other's subjective sphere. (Linnet 2013)

Linnet likens the Nordic idea of commonness to a shared mythology that requires collective buy-in and performative reification. This mythology collapses if consumption is seen as accentuating or communicating our differences—hence the imperative to balance individualistic desires with the "mutual sheltering of each other's subjective sphere," as Linnet so astutely put it. In other words, Nordic egalitarianism demands conformity toward the middle, but also *within* the middle. Our displays of taste should not be seen as a challenge to others or as a statement of how others should define themselves or live their lives through consumption.

Lindstén (2017) provides an example of such muted distinctions with her historical ethnography of coffee consumption in rural communities in Finland. In such communities, coffee was consumed daily and in a ritualistic fashion. On the face of it, these seemed like wholly egalitarian and even quiet affairs. Yet Lindstén's analysis identifies a great deal of stratification and inconspicuous signaling underlying these rituals. The home was cleaned up and prepared in direct proportion to the importance of the guests, such as when the local priest or head of the municipality came to visit. The presence of such esteemed guests meant that more, fresher, and a greater variety of biscuits were served. The coffee was brewed slightly stronger and the "good" plates and cutlery were pulled out from the drawer. When the coffee was served, the most honored guest always got the first pour. The coffee for this guest was usually served from a tray, unlike the others. The obligatory suggestion to "please, dig in" was always directed to the most esteemed guest; nobody lifted their cup until that person did. The other guests also took their cues for how many refills or extra biscuits they should take from the esteemed guest.

Lindstén's analysis found that those partaking in these coffee rituals were often oblivious to the rituals' hierarchical considerations. Lindstén speculates that these hierarchies were so naturalized and deeply ingrained that they had become pre-discursive. Even in cases when these hierarchical considerations were made apparent or verbalized, participants would often rush to deny these meanings. Unmasking this status dance within the coffee ritual collapsed the myth of egalitarianism and brought great discomfort. This links to Gullestad's (1992) characterization of Nordic culture as embracing *differences that do not constitute differences.* In plainer terms, Nordic consumers will gladly acknowledge their differences in interests, personalities, or passions, but not in a way that would reveal or underline their differences in social status (as in Janteloven). To borrow from Goffmanian vernacular, differences in social status recede to the back stage in Nordic consumption practices, and it is rarely acceptable to bring them back to the front stage.

There are, of course, status differences that Nordics accept and are even willing to explicitly acknowledge. Trotter (2015) translates the logic of Janteloven into Bourdieuan vernacular and argues that status displays are legitimate among Nordic consumers if they seem *disinterested* in taste competition. In other words, under Janteloven, one can only accrue symbolic capital within a particular field if it is presented as, to paraphrase Trotter, not as an attempt to stand out from the field but as standing *for* the field. This is similar to what consumption community literature identifies as symbolic capital gained by selfless and dutiful laboring on the community's behalf (e.g., Muniz and O'Guinn 2001). Another way of seeing this is that Nordics treat extrinsic motivations for field engagement as suspicious and intrinsic motivations as acceptable. Trotter (2015) singles out professional athletes as people Nordics are willing to grant status to, provided they present themselves as being driven by passion for the sport or representing the motherland. Gullestad (2013) also touches on this dynamic between intrinsic versus extrinsic when she contrasts "passive" and "active" home decoration: one can have nice things in the home if they are regularly and enthusiastically used in, say, hobbies. Creating an impression of disinterestedness in taste competition can also help mask actual status aspirations. Gullestad (2013) found that some of her informants made substantial and aesthetically impressive improvements to their houses during renovation projects. These projects were justified as serious economic necessities, such as maintaining the value of the home, which also provided a convenient shield from accusations of status-hunting.

The muting of status displays further presents temporal restrictions to when and how distinction can be claimed. As McCracken (2008) writes, the continuous reinvention of identity through experimentation with new consumption fields is like a national sport for middle-class Americans. When writing this chapter, I often found myself reflecting back to the three years I spent living in the USA. One thing I remember finding peculiar and even humorous was how quickly my American peers "claimed" new consumption fields as parts of their identities. For example, if an American friend had taken an interest in yoga, I found that they could declare themselves "a yogi" after buying a yoga mat and practicing their asanas for a few months. Yet it would not be uncommon for a Nordic person with years of dedicated yoga practice to balk at ascribing the "yogi" label to themselves and to self-deprecatingly insist that they are not that good at yoga. In other words, Nordic consumers are more careful with their identity reinvention projects, due to fears of social costs from perceived identity inconsistencies (cf. McAlexander et al. 2014). Arnould and Hartmann's dialogue-form chapter in this volume hints at this when they discuss Jantzen et al.'s (2006) work on Danish women's underwear consumption. Arnould's observation is astute:

> something that ... I associate with Nordic consumer culture is a concern for symmetry. That is the women were quite unhappy with mismatched underwear. They were quite concerned with mismatches between the public and the private. The front stage and the back stage. Exposing a gap between the front stage and the back stage was something that they found monstrous that they wanted to avoid ... I do think that's a Nordic thing, because in the US we would be quite ... so in the North American context we would be quite happy if the front stage was well managed. We could give a crap about the back stage as long as nobody sees it, because it's a facade. The facade is all important. (pp. 300–301)

This "concern for symmetry," as Arnould put it, suggests that Nordic consumers are less able to play the "unruly bricoleurs" and free identity experimenters compared to their North American brethren (Holt 2002). Gullestad (2013) similarly identifies that Norwegians consider the "wholeness" of their homes as an important orienting principle, and that this is not merely a question of aesthetic consistency. Linnet (2011) remarks along the same lines that wholeness is an important value for Danes, and that it means being consistent in one's presentation of the self to others as well as consistent to personal ideas of the self. Any new consumption field or interest must match a person's long-term identity narrative and will take a longer time to establish itself within it.

Concluding Remarks: Where Is Nordic Taste Going?

I conclude this chapter with speculative pontification on the future of Nordic taste. I begin by reviewing two outlier cases that may illuminate what the future holds.

The first case is Heikkilä and Rahkonen's (2011) study of upper-class Swedish-speaking Finnish women and their taste distinctions. Two things stood out from their findings. For one, the women they interviewed were not at all shy about declaring their own taste preferences as superior to others and drew specific boundaries, especially toward the general Finnish-speaking population. The women eschewed the Law of Jante—they damn right thought they were better than the rest of us. Second, the women avoided playing the taste game amongst themselves during the group interview. In fact, Heikkilä and Rahkonen recount that the women deferred and complimented each other's tastes almost to a fault. This stands in stark contrast to typical group interviews with high-status informants where taste conflict is often quick to emerge (Fern 2001).

What explains this atypical taste behavior? For one, Swedish speakers are not your typical minority. They remain economically privileged, at least comparative to national averages, and this may explain the group's sense of superiority in taste. Swedish speakers are also a small minority in Finland, less than 6% of the overall population. This number has been shrinking as more and more Swedish speakers are becoming bilingual or embracing Finnish as their primary language. These strong displays of distinction might reflect an awareness of increasing demographic marginality, even an existential threat to a way of life. Here we are reminded of

Gullestad's (1992) remarks that Nordic culture, with its expectations of conformity, monocultural tendencies, egalitarianism, and demographic homogeneity, has a dark side. Nordic culture can create a sense of exclusion for those not identifying with the big middle. At times, it can be even used to "justify" racism in the name of the common good. As Nordics become increasingly diverse, we can expect more atypical status displays when, for example, immigrants or refugees adapt their identities and consumption practices to their new Nordic surroundings (cf. McAlexander et al. 2014). I believe this offers a highly fruitful avenue for future research.

The second outlier case is Östberg's (2007) study of the so-called Brats phenomenon that jumped into public awareness in the late 1990s and early 2000s, when the media began chronicling the life in the fast lane of the young, pretty, and rich debutantes of Stockholm, and especially their nightlife escapades on Stureplan. These Brats were brash, youthful, loud, and, most important of all, not shy about being conspicuous in their consumption behavior. They religiously kept up with trends. They wore impressive designer clothes and matched them with expensive watches. They ordered copious amounts of champagne (sometimes even remembering to drink the stuff). Their biggest fear was to end up as your average Svensson—if they had a rallying cry, it probably would have been "fuck your Janteloven, thank you very much."

Östberg (2007) writes that some of this performative ostentatiousness was driven by resentment. Some Brats were from families where the parents had relinquished their noble status in the 1960s or 1970s in conformity with the social democratic zeitgeist of Sweden. Östberg speculates that Brat culture may thus represent a pendulum swing of sorts, a generational rebellion at this mistake of the past. But perhaps it is more than that. Brat culture is no longer tied merely to Stockholm; it is emulated by wannabe "stekares" across Sweden and even other Nordic countries. Conspicuous consumption is indeed markedly more normal in the Nordics now compared to just a few short decades ago, especially in Sweden (see Sofia Ulver's chapter on statist individualism in this volume). We also see this in the evolution of markets and industries. My home university was named after famed Finnish designer and architect Alvar

Aalto, whose design philosophy celebrated simplistic aesthetics and a staunch dedication to egalitarian ideals—he insisted his designs be affordable to all (Markoutsas 1985). Similar design philosophies were espoused by other Nordic design greats like Børge Mogensen, the designer behind the aptly named "People's Chair." This egalitarian design philosophy still permeates IKEA's brand DNA, though it is now more used in marketing communications than judiciously performed (Kristoffersson 2014; Skou and Munch 2016). These changes may tie into the global trends and influences mentioned earlier in this chapter. Whatever the reason behind the rise of Nordic conspicuousness, it, too, merits further inquiry from consumer researchers.

Many of the works cited in this chapter reveal that the home is sacred for Nordic consumers. It shelters us from the harsh elements, but it also creates a private sphere wherein we escape the gaze of others (Purhonen et al. 2010; Linnet 2011). As Gullestad (2013) states, Nordic homes' exteriors are "often lacking in decorations, detail and any visual stimuli" (p. 146), while the insides reveal a flurry of creative and often impressive taste experimentation. The ongoing proliferation of digital media is making the boundaries between public and private spheres increasingly blurry or difficult to discern (Scott 2016). This presents another fruitful avenue for future research, particularly from a sociological perspective. What do these changes mean for Nordic homes, or the Nordic sense of homeyness (McCracken 1989)?

Nordics are ripe with paradoxes (Byrkjeflot 2001; Berggren and Trägårdh 2010). We are simultaneously conformist and individualistic. We regulate our markets with a keen eye, but also cherish markets and entrepreneurship as sources of prosperity. We are cosmopolitans who hold dear our native and common cultures. We celebrate our differences, yet fear exposing differences that truly matter. We are self-deprecating, but respond harshly to criticism from outsiders (Booth et al. 2014). I hope this glimpse into what and how Nordic consumers consume will prove useful in making at least some sense of the peculiarities of our beloved region. For those who did not find this chapter useful, I leave you with this popular (and quite Jantean) Finnish idiom: "You ain't shit, but neither am I."

References

Arnould, E. J., & Thompson, C. (2018). Consumer Culture Theory: A Short History of a Young Subdiscipline (Or the Tale of the Rebellious Offspring). In F. F. Wherry & I. Woodward (Eds.), *Oxford Handbook of Consumption*. Oxford: Oxford University Press.

Askegaard, S., & Madsen, T. K. (1998). The Local and the Global: Exploring Traits of Homogeneity and Heterogeneity in European Food Cultures. *International Business Review, 7*(6), 549–568.

Atkinson, W. (2011). The Context and Genesis of Musical Tastes: Omnivorousness Debunked, Bourdieu Buttressed. *Poetics, 39*(3), 169–186.

Bardhi, F., Eckhardt, G. M., & Arnould, E. J. (2012). Liquid Relationship to Possessions. *Journal of Consumer Research, 39*(3), 510–529.

Belk, R. (2011). Benign Envy. *AMS Review, 1*(3–4), 117–134.

Bennett, T. (2007). Habitus clivé: Aesthetics and Politics in the Work of Pierre Bourdieu. *New Literary History, 38*, 201–228.

Bennett, T., Savage, M., Silva, E. B., Warde, A., Gayo-Cal, M., & Wright, D. (2009). *Culture, Class, Distinction*. London: Routledge.

Berggren, H., & Trägårdh, L. (2010). The Autonomous Child and the Moral Logic of the Swedish Welfare State. In H. Mattson & S.-O. Wallenstein (Eds.), *Swedish Modernism: Architecture, Consumption and the Welfare State* (pp. 50–65). London: Black Dog Publishing.

Booth, M., Price, A., Bolsø, A., Bergmann, E., Stubb, A., & Trägårdh, L. (2014). 'The Grim Truth Behind the Scandinavian Miracle' – The Nations Respond. *The Guardian*. Retrieved September 10, 2018, from https://www.theguardian.com/world/2014/feb/05/scandinavian-miracle-denmark-finland-iceland-norway-sweden.

Bourdieu, P. (1984). *Distinction: A Social Critique of the Judgement of Taste*. London and New York: Routledge.

Bourdieu, P. (1986). The Forms of Capital. *Cultural Theory: An Anthology, 1*, 81–93.

Bryman, A. (1984). The Debate About Quantitative and Qualitative Research: A Question of Method or Epistemology? *British Journal of Sociology, 35*, 75–92.

Byrkjeflot, H. (2001). The Nordic Model of Democracy and Management. In *The Democratic Challenge to Capitalism: Management and Democracy in the Nordic Countries* (pp. 19–45). Copenhagen: Copenhagen Business School Press.

Cappelen, C., & Dahlberg, S. (2017). The Law of Jante and Generalized Trust. *Acta Sociologica, 61*(4), 0001699317717319.

Corrigan, P. (1997). *The Sociology of Consumption: An Introduction.* London: Sage.

Coskuner-Balli, G., & Thompson, C. J. (2013). The Status Costs of Subordinate Cultural Capital: At-Home Fathers' Collective Pursuit of Cultural Legitimacy Through Capitalizing Consumption Practices. *Journal of Consumer Research, 40*(1), 19–41, https://doi.org/10.1086/668640.

DiMaggio, P. (1987). Classification in Art. *American Sociological Review, 52*, 440–455.

Fern, E. F. (2001). *Advanced Focus Group Research.* London: Sage.

Gelder, K. (Ed.). (2005). *The Subcultures Reader.* Hove: Psychology Press.

Giddens, A. (2013). *The Third Way: The Renewal of Social Democracy.* London: John Wiley & Sons.

Gottlieb, H. (2004). Subtitles and International Anglification. *Nordic Journal of English Studies, 3*(1), 219–230.

Gullestad, M. (1992). *The Art of Social Relations: Essays on Culture, Social Action and Everyday Life in Modern Norway.* Oslo: A Scandinavian University Press Publication.

Gullestad, M. (2013). Home Decoration as Popular Culture. Constructing Homes, Genders and Classes in Norway. In *Gendered Anthropology* (pp. 140–173). London and New York: Routledge.

Heikkilä, R., & Rahkonen, K. (2011). 'IT IS NOT A MATTER OF TASTE…' Cultural Capital and Taste Among the Swedish-Speaking Upper Class in Finland. *European Societies, 13*(1), 143–163.

Holt, D. B. (1997). Distinction in America? Recovering Bourdieu's Theory of Tastes from Its Critics. *Poetics, 25*(2–3), 93–120.

Holt, D. B. (2002). Why Do Brands Cause Trouble? A Dialectical Theory of Consumer Culture and Branding. *Journal of Consumer Research, 29*(1), 70–90.

Jantzen, C., Østergaard, P., & Vieira, C. M. S. (2006). Becoming a 'Woman to the Backbone': Lingerie Consumption and the Experience of Feminine Identity. *Journal of Consumer Culture, 6*(2), 177–202.

Kahma, N. (2012). Sport and Social Class: The Case of Finland. *International Review for the Sociology of Sport, 47*(1), 113–130.

Kjeldgaard, D., & Östberg, J. (2007). Coffee Grounds and the Global Cup: Glocal Consumer Culture in Scandinavia. *Consumption Markets & Culture, 10*(2), 175–187.

Korpi, W., & Palme, J. (1998). The Paradox of Redistribution and the Strategy of Equality. *American Political Science Review, 63*(4), 661–687.

Kristoffersson, S. (2014). *Design by IKEA: A Cultural History*. London: Bloomsbury Publishing.

Lamont, M. (1992). *Money, Morals, and Manners: The Culture of the French and the American Upper-Middle Class*. Chicago, IL: University of Chicago Press.

Lindstén, H. (2017). *"Olkaa hyvä ja ottakaa. Pankaa sekaan ja kastakaa". Kahvinjuonti suomalaisten maaseutukotien arjessa ja juhlassa 1920-luvulta 1960-luvun lopulle*. Turku University Publication Series.

Linnet, J. T. (2011). Money Can't Buy Me Hygge: Danish Middle-Class Consumption, Egalitarianism, and the Sanctity of Inner Space. *Social Analysis, 55*(2), 21–44.

Linnet, J. (2013). *Comment*. Retrieved July 10, 2018, from Consumer Culture Theory Facebook Group at https://www.facebook.com/groups/213134458706536/permalink/675505949136049/.

Mäkelä, K. (1985). Kulttuurisen muuntelun yhteiso¨llinen rakenne Suomessa. *Sosiologia, 22*, 247–260.

Markoutsas. (1985). Retrieved from http://articles.chicagotribune.com/1985-02-17/news/8501090933_1_alvar-aalto-design-wood.

McAlexander, J. H., Dufault, B. L., Martin, D. M., & Schouten, J. W. (2014). The Marketization of Religion: Field, Capital, and Consumer Identity. *Journal of Consumer Research, 41*(3), 858–875.

McCracken, G. D. (1989). Homeyness: A Cultural Account of One Constellation of Consumer Goods and Meanings. In *Interpretive Consumer Research* (Vol. 16). London: Association for Consumer Research.

McCracken, G. D. (2008). *Transformations: Identity Construction in Contemporary Culture*. Bloomington, IN: Indiana University Press.

McLeod, K. (2001). Genres, Subgenres, Sub-Subgenres and More: Musical and Social Differentiation Within Electronic/Dance Music Communities. *Journal of Popular Music Studies, 13*(1), 59–75.

Miller, D. (2008). Marienne Gullestad (1946–2008). *Material World Blog*. Retrieved July 13, 2018, from http://www.materialworldblog.com/2008/03/marienne-gullestad-1946-2008/.

Muniz, A. M., & O'Guinn, T. C. (2001). Brand Community. *Journal of Consumer Research, 27*(4), 412–432.

Östberg, J. (2007). The Linking Value of Subcultural Capital: Constructing the Stockholm Brat Enclave. In *Consumer Tribes* (pp. 93–106). Oxford: Elsevier/Butterworth-Heinemann.

Østergaard, U. (1997). The Geopolitics of Nordic Identity: From Composite States to Nation-States. In Ø. Sørensen & B. Sträth (Eds.), *The Cultural Construction of Norden* (pp. 25–71). Oslo: Scandinavian University Press.

Østergaard, P., Linnet, J. T., Andersen, L. P., Kjeldgaard, D., Bjerregaard, S., Weijo, H., et al. (2014). Nordic Consumer Culture: Context and Concept. In *Consumer Culture Theory* (pp. 245–257). Bingley: Emerald Group Publishing Limited.

Peterson, R. A., & Simkus, A. (1992). How Musical Tastes Mark Occupational Status Groups. In M. Lamont & M. Fournier (Eds.), *Cultivating Differences* (pp. 152–186). Chicago: University of Chicago Press.

Prieur, A., Rosenlund, L., & Skjott-Larsen, J. (2008). Cultural Capital Today: A Case Study from Denmark. *Poetics, 36*(1), 45–71.

Purhonen, S., & Gronow, J. (2014). Polarizing Appetites? Stability and Change in Culinary Tastes in Finland, 1995–2007. *Food, Culture & Society, 17*(1), 27–47.

Purhonen, S., & Wright, D. (2013). Methodological Issues in National-Comparative Research on Cultural Tastes: The Case of Cultural Capital in the UK and Finland. *Cultural Sociology, 7*(2), 257–273.

Purhonen, S., Gronow, J., & Rahkonen, K. (2010). Nordic Democracy of Taste? Cultural Omnivorousness in Musical and Literary Taste Preferences in Finland. *Poetics, 38*(3), 266–298.

Purhonen, S., Gronow, J., Heikkilä, R., & Kahma, N. (2014). *Suomalainen maku: kulttuuripääoma, kulutus ja elämäntyylien sosiaalinen eriytyminen [The Finnish Taste: Cultural Capital, Consumption and the Social Stratification of Lifestyles]*. Helsinki: Gaudeamus Helsinki University Press.

Rahkonen, K. (2008). Bourdieu in Finland: An Account of Bourdieu's Influence on Finnish Sociology. *Sociologica, 2*(2).

Sampson, P., Samuel, V., & Sugden, C. (1994). *Faith and Modernity*. Oxford: OCMS.

Sandemose, A. (1999[1933]). *En Flyktning Krysser Sitt Sport: Fortellingen om en Morders Barndom [A Fugitive Crosses His Tracks: The Story of a Murderer's Childhood]*. Oslo: Aschehoug & Co.

Scott, L. (2016). *The Four-Dimensional Human: Ways of Being in the Digital World*. London: Random House.

Skou, N. P., & Munch, A. V. (2016). New Nordic and Scandinavian Retro: Reassessment of Values and Aesthetics in Contemporary Nordic Design. *Journal of Aesthetics & Culture, 8*(1), 32573.

Stromberg, J. (2015). The Real Reason American Public Transportation Is Such a Disaster. *Vox*. Retrieved July 10, 2018, from https://www.vox.com/2015/8/10/9118199/public-transportation-subway-buses.

Thornton, S. (1996). *Club Cultures: Music, Media, and Subcultural Capital*. Middletown: Wesleyan University Press.

Trotter, S. R. (2015). Breaking the Law of Jante. *Myth and Nation, 23*.

van Eijck, K., & Knulst, W. (2005). No More Need for Snobbism: Highbrow Cultural Participation in a Taste Democracy. *European Sociological Review, 21*, 513–528.

van Venrooij, A., & Schmutz, V. (2010). The Evaluation of Popular Music in the United States, Germany and the Netherlands: A Comparison of the Use of High Art and Popular Aesthetic Criteria. *Cultural Sociology, 4*(3), 395–421.

Virtanen, T. (2007). *Across and Beyond the Bounds of Taste: On Cultural Consumption Patterns in the European Union*. Turku School of Economics, Series A-11.

Warde, A. (2015). The Sociology of Consumption: Its Recent Development. *Annual Review of Sociology, 41*, 117–134.

Warde, A., Wright, D., & Gayo-Cal, M. (2007). Understanding Cultural Omnivorousness: Or, the Myth of Cultural Omnivore. *Cultural Sociology, 1*, 143–164.

Weber, M. (1978). *Economy and Society: An Outline of Interpretive Sociology* (Vol. 1). Oakland, CA: University of California Press.

Weijo, H. A., Martin, D. M., Arnould, E. J., & Ger, G. (2018). Consumer Movements and Collective Creativity: The Case of Restaurant Day. *Journal of Consumer Research, 45*(2), 251–274.

3

Market Wonderland: An Essay about a Statist Individualist Consumer Culture

Sofia Ulver

Who would have thought that the citizens of a Nordic, historically profound social democracy would wind up as hyper-individualists? This chapter takes its departure from Henrik Berggren and Lars Trägårdh's *Is the Swede Human? Community and Autonomy in Modern Sweden* (2015; first released in 2006), a book which has had an unusually visible political, media, and cultural influence in Sweden, not least through its idea of Sweden as a *statist individualistic* society—a construct whose meaning I will elaborate on later. As a Swedish researcher on consumer society and culture, and fascinated by the academic, political, media, and intellectual popularity of this idea, I can't help wondering: What characterizes consumer culture in such a statist individualist context? What does it harness, celebrate, and encourage? For instance, might the market myth of

S. Ulver (✉)
Lund University, Lund, Sweden
e-mail: sofia.ulver@fek.lu.se

S. Askegaard, J. Östberg (eds.), *Nordic Consumer Culture*,
https://doi.org/10.1007/978-3-030-04933-1_3

Sweden as a Mecca in terms of the fast diffusion of consumer trends,[1] and therefore also an excellent market for corporations to test trends and innovations in, have anything to do with statist individualism? In this chapter I will audaciously ponder on this and other examples, by highlighting consumer culture in Sweden in general and some specific consumer lifestyle trends in particular, through the theoretical lens of Henrik Berggren and Lars Trägårdh's statist individualism.

Statist Individualism

The Nordic "character" has been thoroughly debated throughout history, and still is. For instance, the curious may want to take a look at the fierce debate about the Nordics in *The Guardian* (Booth 2014; Booth et al. 2014), or the reception of Anu Partanen's (2016) book on the advantages of the Nordic model in the American press (Moynihan 2016). The topic is without a doubt charged with tension.

Moreover, the character of the Swede specifically has been molded and dissected from various historical angles and themes, where most descriptions entail less complimentary descriptive nouns like austerity, coldness, and loneliness. Not a very cozy country, it seems. And indeed, in the age of multiculturalism, one may wonder why anyone would even consider coming to Sweden. The answer is (of course) the welfare state.

Berggren and Trägårdh's seminal *Is the Swede Human? Community and Autonomy in Modern Sweden* (2015) is a praised social history book presenting a "Swedish theory of love." In fact, this Swedish theory of love has not only had an impact academically, but also in pop culture, through a film by Eric Gandini featuring Swedish citizens' anecdotal experiences, Lars Trägårdh himself, and even Zygmunt Bauman. More importantly, politically the ruling parties in government between 2006 and 2014—the Alliance—used the central concept of the book—namely, statist individualism—as a point of departure for their communication and strategies, and also employed

[1] Trigger warning for sensitive readers! "Trend" is often used by pop management consultants for commercial purposes, but is here reappropriated.

one of the authors, Professor Lars Trägårdh, as commissioner in their so-called Framtidskommisionen (the Commission of the Future), which was created to identify and report important expected societal challenges between 2020 and 2050. In the media the book was highly reported on and Trägårdh especially became a frequent guest on televised panel debates and so on. Culturally the book was not only a bestseller but, as mentioned earlier, also the object of and inspiration for the documentary movie by Gandin called *The Swedish Theory of Love*. All and all, the book, with its literary, historical, and institutional analysis, had an unusually large—for quite an academic book—impact on Sweden's various types of institutions.

What might make the thesis so compelling, both academically and popularly, is its revelation of conspicuously strong ideological contradictions absorbed and governed in the state model. At first blush these contradictions seem to be irreconcilable, but through Berggren and Trägårdh's historical exposition of influential ideas promoted by national icons amongst authors, poets, historians, and politicians, it nevertheless becomes comprehensible how these contradictions have managed to coexist and co-work under the same national model. Moreover, being able to absorb and assuage ideological contradictions characterizes all Nordic countries, according to political scientist Byrkjeflot (2001), which to some part should make this book relevant to understanding the "Nordic model" as a whole. Furthermore, as Berggren and Trägårdh's exposition provides ideological explications for the Kantian and Simmelian classical tension between the social and the unsocial, it proves especially relevant in this time and age, when the meta level of cultural, political, social, and historical influence, and "the context of context" (Askegaard and Linnet 2011), has come to attract increasing interest among researchers of social science, rather than merely individual experiences. Sanctioned community and independence form the alluring paradox of the social contract in the welfare state.

So what does Berggren and Trägårdh's (2015) idea of statist individualism hold specifically? At a theoretical level (the less abstract level will be illustrated later by general examples from my years of research), three themes emerge as most important: *elitist social equality*, *individual freedom* (from other humans), and finally *the state as prime partner*. Berggren

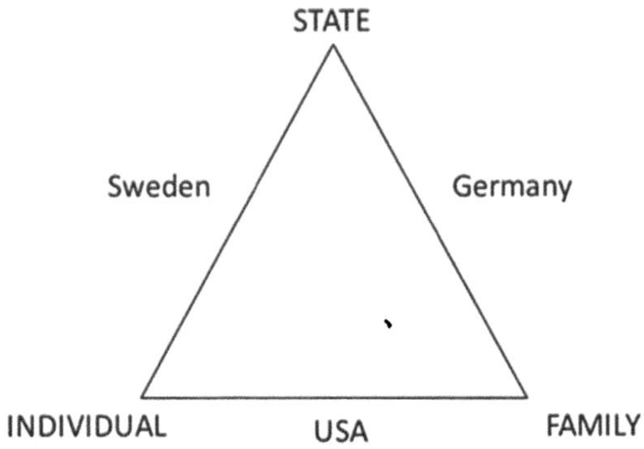

Fig. 3.1 Berggren and Trägårdh's (2015) sociopolitical triangle drama. Reprinted with permission

and Trägårdh make an ideal-typical classification of the most important units in society in their juxtaposed sites (Sweden, the USA, and Germany). They portray three results of a "sociopolitical triangle drama" (p. 79) where in Germany the state and family unite against the individual, in the USA the individual and family unite against the state, and in Sweden the state and individual unite against the family (see Fig. 3.1). In other words, a statist individualist society.

According to this model, for this welfare society to be realized, citizens must be emancipated from their (historically) clan-like family dependencies, and achieve equal value in relation to the rational and objective unit of the state. Instead of grandfathers and mothers deciding your fate by being the sole providers of your safety and survival, the state gives you as an individual the same right to decide your fate by providing you with what you need. Therefore, you no longer have to kiss up to your evil uncle, but in return must stay in a good relation with various national institutions; hence, freedom from forced personal relationships but not from the state. This influences the way Swedish people relate to each other in general. For example, who should put in an effort if someone is in urgent need of help? The state, of course, where the social acceptance of different kinds of dependencies look different than for instance in the USA (p. 81). In the American context, expectations are higher that relatives will take care of the weak, and the stigma is lower about accepting it. In Sweden, the expectation on relatives is low and the stigma of acceptance of their donations is high. On the other hand, the stigma is much lower when accepting aid from the state and vice versa: the expectation and social acceptation of the same are both high. This is a sort of "institutionalized care" where "the state's abduction of traditional interhuman, relational duties drives the development towards a more cold and loveless society" (p. 85). One critique stipulates that "It replaces the bonds between people that have been the precondition for intimacy and being close"; another that "autonomy in relation to other people has come to a huge price," namely "the surrendering of power to the state," where we actually have quite weak rights toward the state. Modern Swedish society has been shaped out of a social contract that "provides the individuals maximal emancipation with minimal moral consequence" (p. 86), which according to Berggren and Trägårdh also leads to a curiously individualistic view of love relationships: *The Swedish Theory of Love*. There, the ideal-typical statist individualist views his or her love as the most pure form of love, as it is in no way arranged, but solely based on true romance and intimacy. Probably due to this relative freedom from traditional family pressure, Sweden has more single households (p. 441) and the highest percentage of divorces in the world (and the other Nordic countries don't come far after). In theory, we can expand the scope of relationships to involve general, volitional friendships, the pursuit of which is made possible by the benevolent state.

How did we end up in this peculiar, unique model of (in)dependence and welfare culture, according to Berggren and Trägårdh? They bring forth many culture-historical and political reasons for this, where some historical intellectual influencers from the nineteenth and twentieth centuries are especially emphasized. Among these the national poet, philosopher, and history professor Erik Gustaf Geijer stands out. In 1838 he wrote about the "Yeoman farmer" (*Odalbonden*), who became a normative archetype for at least as rugged an individualist as the American frontier myth archetypes of mountain men, cowboys, and action heroes (Holt and Thompson 2004; Belk and Costa 1998), but one more concerned with nature and equality. Most importantly, instead of freedom from a state, Geijer's yeoman farmer and Viking idealization rather celebrated freedom from other individuals and the freedom that a society, state, and rule of law could give: the safety and security to be independent. Everyone is indeed part of a kinship, but one's fate is completely personal; "the individual is on his own," as historian Guretvitj states (in Berggren and Trägårdh 2015, p. 101). Another national influencer contemporary with Geijer was the author Carl Jonas Love Almqvist, who also emphasized the strong, individualist Swedish character as coming out of poverty, most ideally typified by the poor croft farmer. Yet another example was "Nietzsche's Swedish profet" (p. 159) Ellen Key, who like the national author August Strindberg celebrated Nietzsche in terms of radical individualism but, like Almqvist, with a touch of matriarchy. Her society model of rational Übermensch individuals, who deservingly would be emancipated as autonomous through thinking, were women (although by nature they were still regarded as more connected to the children and the home) and also children. Geijer, Almqvist, Strindberg, and Key were all proponents of human equality, not least between women and men, but in varying ways. What they had in common was their problematization of community and individualism, "a fusion between an individualistic view on man and a strong tradition of equality" (ibid., p. 167), from which modern Sweden in turn could develop.

This history of ideas came to lay cultural ground for the approaching era of social engineering in Sweden. Without this ground, the Social Democratic theorist, diplomat, and Nobel Peace Prize winner Alva Myrdal would perhaps not have been able to reach through with her ideas on common child care, women's right and duty to work, and so on; and Per Albin Hansson, the Social Democratic Prime Minister, would perhaps not have been able to announce and realize the idea of the new welfare Sweden as a relatively classless *Folkhem* (transl. "home of the people"). It is typically to the era of Folkhemmet that one refers in common speech when "misunderstanding" (as Berggren and Trägårdh see it) Sweden as collectivistic. The communality of Folkhemmet would never have been realized, they say, if it weren't for Sweden's hyper-individualist cultural roots, and it appears to be collectivist because everyone relates to one and the same agent—the state—but not to each other.

Next I will conceptually explore the statist individualist Sweden from a perspective of consumer culture; or rather, consider a few selected events, trends, and myths in Sweden's consumer culture and market through the theoretical lens of statist individualism. I will use empirical observations from more than one and a half decades of consumer cultural research in Sweden as illustrations.

Consumer Culture and Statist Individualism

Consumer trends and phenomena are both concepts commonly used to describe how certain consumption patterns flash by, diffuse, or get established in a consumer market. In this chapter I will use the word trend not as a scientific but as an emic concept—that is, how these events and patterns have been talked about in Swedish consumer culture and media. None of these trends exists solely in Sweden, far from it, but they have a disproportionally wide or fast penetration compared to other markets. Conversely, these do not constitute an exhaustive account of Swedish consumer culture, but are important (from my subjective point of view) changes that reveal something about Sweden, and perhaps—at least to some degree—about Nordic consumer culture as a whole. Therefore, I here use Sweden as a case to reflect on what makes it such an apt context for these trends—or the idea of these trends—to thrive.

First, a prevailing myth in business circles is that Sweden makes the perfect market to test an idea, as it either spreads really fast or it doesn't spread at all. Hence, the test cost would be significantly lower than if one tested the idea in another market where potential diffusion would take a much more complicated route and thus require a longer time to produce test results. The common rationale is that the Swedish people are relatively homogeneous and prefer to look and behave in the same way in order not to stand out from the crowd. Berggren and Trägårdh ask the rhetorical question of whether "the Swedish state protestant conformism," coming out of a strong farming class in alliance with the king or the state against the nobility, is the antithesis to "breaking one's own paths, deviating, thinking independently, yes even being aristocratic and eccentric?" (p. 54). The answer is evidently no. With a historically strong farming class, religious homogeneity (protestantism), and relatively egalitarian family culture (p. 95), this unique conformism may rather be precisely the answer to why (if the myth holds any truth to it) the Swedish consumer market would so quickly be penetrated, albeit saturated, by new innovations.

A complementary reason to these way-back-in-history understandings may be Sweden's road to becoming a welfare regime (p. 263) of citizen-consumers. In the first half of the twentieth century, social political decisions were made to depart from the stigma of verification of requirements to get social benefits *in natura* (food, clothes, or the like), and instead everyone should get general benefits in cash (such as the folk pension in 1913) to encourage "free consumer choice" (p. 264) in order for the citizen-consumer to consume what she or he—and not the state—preferred. This market orientation and "consumer power" ideology (pp. 354–355), in combination with a democracy built on popular unions on the one hand and a state-dominated corporative political order (p. 349) on the other, ending in a very broad middle class apt for everyday status competition, very likely paved the way for a consumer market particularly sensitive to consumer trends.

So, what consumer and market trends have been particularly influential in the Swedish consumer market during the last 20 years, and how can we understand their popularity from a statist individualist perspective? Next I will discuss five trends which revolve around Swedes' (1) swashbuckling body performances, (2) raging start-up fever, (3) swanky brat culture, (4) interior design frenzy, and (5) heroic foodism. I begin with the sweating body performances of the Swedish version of Robinson Crusoe.

Robinson Crusoe on the Run

During the past decade, the streets of rural and urban Sweden have seen more and more runners, more or less austere looking, some with backpacks with weights on their backs. In traditional and social media, a large focus has been given to running, not least to the more extreme versions: marathons and other endurance running events that often are combined with other branches like biking and swimming (e.g., Ironman). In various large surveys commissioned by organizations connected to the Swedish government, such as Riksidrottsförbundet and Svensk Friidrott, the interest in running has increased by almost 70% since 2007, and between 2004 and 2014 the number of organized runs doubled. Today, almost every fourth adult in Sweden runs at least once a week. In a PhD dissertation by Janet Johansson (2017), this trend is explored specifically among top managers, a group in which endurance and ultrarunning appears to have become a growing imperative, requirement, and norm over the past years, at least if one wants to be seen as a "strong leader." Cederström and Thanem (2018) calls this "fitness leadership" and exemplify it with the CEO and self-titled "head coach" who runs the Swedish sport fashion brand Björn Borg like a "cross-fit gym". In the meantime, the types of organized training, climbing, and endurance running have become more and more extreme and absurd, where pain is to be maximized, something Scott et al. (2017) as well as Carys Egan-Wyer (forthcoming) explore in their research on "Tough Mudders" and endurance runners.

Through the lens of statist individualism, the success of this competition in endurance and suffering is not so peculiar. Berggren and Trägårdh (2015, p. 41) write: "The ideal state for a Swede is to live like Robinson Crusoe in nature, as an independent individual, free from the mutual dependence and collective consideration forced by close community with others." As the quote testifies, the Swedish national character literature conveys a heroic, hard-suffering, self-sufficient archetype best portrayed by Robinson Crusoe, who thrives in rough nature with scarce resources. And he (of course) makes it. This idealization of loving and thriving from poverty and nature corresponds with Geijer's yeoman and Almqvist's croft farmers, and latches on to the radical individualism they preached. Yet, as Berggren and Trägårdh also state in relation to the dream of the Robinson Crusoe hero, it is tragically not possible. The persistence of Swedish nation and culture requires from its solitary inhabitants that they form social bonds in the form of an abstract community. They need to leave nature and enter modern society. But today, within the safe confines of modern society, the freedom-seeking inhabitants have finally found a way to solve this conflict. In these endurance sports they can both be solitary and together; a crowd of solitary Robinson Crusoes struggling together.

A similar pattern can be observed in Iceland, where a disproportionally huge number of successful athletes are produced. As in other Nordic contexts, the readiness for this can be understood through rough climate and terrain, and in turn the limited choice of leisure activities half the year (leading to indoor sports), but also through archetypes in folklore and myths (Itu 2018). In Swedish culture, there has also been a readiness which, according to Berggren and Trägårdh, is historically grounded in the "reliable, protestant self-help philosophy" (p. 262) that permeated Swedish culture at the turn of the nineteenth century. Self-help culture was strongly anchored in working- and lower middle-class culture for the majority of the twentieth century through local popular folk movements, where health (e.g., sobriety) and sports made common themes. Little did one know that one day these unification efforts would fragmentize into solitary Tough Mudders and stone-hard Ironmen.

A Unicorn Culture

Besides being amongst the world's most internet broadband–connected countries, Sweden is, according to a Wharton article in 2015, second only after Silicon Valley in multibillion-dollar tech companies—so called Unicorns—produced per capita. More generally, according to OECD research, Sweden has 20 startups per 1000 employees, compared to the USA's mere 5. Maliranta et al. (2012) argue that the Nordics—despite their "cuddly capitalism" (higher overall tax burden and more generous safety nets)—have generated at least as much innovation activity as the "cut-throat" capitalist USA, and reached matching levels of productivity and innovation in important parts of the economy. What from a statist individualist perspective has produced such an apparent hotbed for entrepreneurs?

The Swedish self-sufficient individualist celebrated by Geijer and Almqvist (pp. 89–177) became perhaps even more potent via the narcissistic molding of the Swedish version of the (Nietzschean) Übermensch by Strindberg and Key. As Geijer stated, "every genius is practical" (p. 98). Hence, being academic or refined was not the highest virtue, but getting things done.

Also according to Berggren and Trägårdh, the nineteenth-century French sociologist Frédéric Le Play stated that Sweden had a family form which encouraged a strong sense of the individual power of initiative, as children generally were trusted with a lot of autonomy (p. 72). Later on, erasing the image of the allodial farmer as the national archetype, during the construction of Folkhemmet as a welfare model for the world led by Per Albin Hansson, the Swedes were often called "The Future People" (p. 232). Earlier, in 1916, Ludvig Nordström had already talked about "the excellent Swedish race," who far better than any other people knew the art of engineering, progressive functionalism, and hard work; the Swedes were rational and futuristic.

All and all, a hard-working, progressive, practical (technological), hyper-individualist, and grounded grass-roots culture most likely made a perfect breeding ground for Unicorns, who often specialized in digital products organically entangled in consumer culture (e.g., Spotify, Skype, and King).

A Fashion of Equality Backlash

In the mid-1990s, unusually conservative-looking but colorful (male) flaneurs with pilot sunglasses and waxed slicked-back hairstyles began to appear on the streets of Stockholm. This style was called "brat" or "stekare," and referred to a casual but conspicuous upper-class look which Östberg (2005) termed the "brat enclave." He explained their emergence in Sweden as upper-class teenagers' revenge for their parents' voluntary disclaim of noble privileges in the 1970s. If we are to believe Berggren and Trägårdh (2015), the revenge may go deeper and further back than that. It may be a revenge for the centuries of "stigma" of being noble in a country where the nobility was seen as the enemy by both the king and the farmers. Early Swedish democracy occurred before urbanization started for real, and was usually exemplified by healthy farmers portrayed in opposition to the indolence, idleness, and laziness of the upper class.

In the 1800s, unlike in the more capitalist-developed countries of Europe or in the USA, in Sweden the bourgeoisie was very weak and liberal political movements were actually constituted by the largest group: the farmers. In fact, 80% of all citizens lived by agriculture and only 15% were somewhat urbanized at this time (today it is the other way around; Statistiska Centralbyrån (2010)). Hence, the culture lived by farmers had an immense influence on what later has been talked about as "Swedishness," or "Nordicness" for that matter. Not theoretical or "educated" (*bildade*), only pragmatic (pp. 187 and 211), "The Nordic enlightenment was not utopic but took form from a pragmatic rationality anchored in the farmer society" (Berggren and Trägårdh 2015, p. 98), and paved the way for a vision of social rather than noble aristocracy (p. 167).

Under such circumstances, nobility was not appreciated. So, when Stockholm's upper-class youth saw its chance, it took it. Like peacocks, they took over club and restaurant culture with typical St. Tropez party behavior (drinks tables, *helrör*, champagne, etc.) in their pink shirts, Panerai watches, and club jackets. The fashion traveled fast to other Swedish towns and the phenomenon was established as a whole industry (e.g., Stureplansgruppen). This can paradoxically be interpreted as a result of the Swedish celebration of equality in combination with the Nietzschean belief in the Übermensch. As announced by Ellen Key at the beginning of the twentieth century (p. 165), *everyone* should be allowed to be an Übermensch, which hints at an elitarianism on a *national* rather than social group level. The brat enclave was a symbolic trial to invert this logic. We are still to see if it started a larger cultural process or if it backfired.

The gender equality backlash in this trend was also evident. Östberg (2005) notes that this enclave of brats was dominated by a male-chauvinist masculinity (although sometimes packaged as gentlemanly in its upper-class flair), where women were merely boat bunnies and trophies, often in conspicuously objectified erotic styles. This was a time where half-naked pinup girls became popular again on the covers of new lifestyle magazines like *Café* and *Slitz*, and silicon breasts became a much more common sight in the popular media. This (from a feminist standpoint) backlash seems to be a right provocation against all gender equality struggles in Swedish history. It stands out and doesn't seem to correspond with any of the national fathers' or mothers' preaching in Berggren and Trägårdh's diligent review. Neither does it seem to have resonated as much in the other Nordic countries as it did in Sweden. But perhaps this is exactly what the revenge was all about, targeting the most holy of values in

Swedish cultural history: the social equality virtue in general, and the gender equality virtue in particular.

The Perfect Home

When foreigners look at Sweden's largest homes-for-sale website Hemnet, a common reaction to the interior furnishing is: "Wow, all homes are so modern! And they all look the same!" Even Swedes themselves have the critical self-distance to note the same thing, I learnt during my empirical research on taste in home aesthetics (Ulver-Sneistrup 2008). Like in many countries, during the 1990s the Swedish real estate and home market started a giant value trip that has not yet stopped (at the time of writing), which has led to enormous profits for some, and an impossible home market to get into for others. But it also latched on to the global-western trend of interior decoration (Arsel and Bean 2012), where the consumption of interior decoration became the most expansive of all consumption categories in Sweden (Fuentes 2016). This could not least be observed in the plenitude of magazines, television programs, websites, designer brands, and stores that emerged at this time—and by just taking a glance at Hemnet.

Regardless of social position, the "home" is seen as special, even sacred, in the Nordic cultures; and improving the home is even viewed as a lifetime project which gives meaning to life (Gullestad 1997). Words like "kos" (Norwegian), "hygge" (Danish), and "mysigt" (Swedish) have—not least under the severe outdoor conditions throughout history—implied ideas of warmth, beauty, peace and quiet, solidarity, and protection against the outside world (be it institutions, factory work, or later the market). Grant McCracken (1989) found similar connotations of "homeyness" in the American context, but understood this use of the word as more particular to the working class than the middle class.

In Sweden specifically, historians and ethnologists have often described the home as that very special place where one displays one's "decency," not least in rural areas (e.g., Frykman and Löfgren 1987). Perhaps it is then not so strange that the entrepreneurial Ingvar Kamprad came up with the idea of IKEA—now a furniture retail giant—in the Småland countryside around Älmhult. The success story of IKEA runs so deep in the collective memory that one could perhaps say it has become part of Swedishness itself, outside Sweden too.

During my PhD studies I did a multisited ethnography (Sweden, USA, and Turkey) looking at aesthetic taste in the homes of the urban middle class (Ulver-Sneistrup 2008). IKEA was a constantly recurring topic (me being Swedish) and was brought up by every respondent, no matter where in Turkey or the USA they came from. However, the modern, functionalistic furniture of IKEA meant completely different things depending on site and cultural capital (Holt 1998; Bourdieu 1984). Representatives of the cultural elite in the USA could appreciate IKEA's personal tone of voice, but looked down on its products for lacking authenticity and disliked its industrial, large-scale commercialism; whereas the corresponding group in Turkey highly appreciated IKEA's modern break with the clearly normative interior tradition they were used to, and socially pressured by their surroundings to follow. In Sweden, on the other hand, IKEA was taken for granted as the provider of household basics, and curiously respected as if it were a saint and international proof of national excellence.

Indeed, in Sweden, the home was often represented as something like "Society's elementary school for social virtues" (Berggren and Trägårdh 2015, p. 274), by for example Alva Myrdal and Ellen Key at the beginning of the twentieth century. In the 1960s, the feminist Eva Moberg criticized this loudly. But nevertheless, in the social engineering of Folkhemmet, Alva Myrdal amongst others—not least architects—normatively proclaimed functionalistic, modern interior architecture and styles for the rural and working classes to become part of the upcoming middle class. Hence, long before IKEA started making modern, affordable furniture "for the many people," there was an established common assumption in Sweden that character and virtue could be decoded from the way your home was arranged and styled (Berggren and Trägårdh 2015; Frykman and Löfgren 1987; Ulver-Sneistrup 2008). Home was a micro cosmos of Folkhemmet, where the negotiation of ideological contradictions took place, because in many of the early visions for a modern Sweden, the public *became* the domestic (p. 154). Geijer's Lutheran standpoint was that women were indeed politically equal to men, but their natural place was the home; Almqvist was a proponent of matriarchy and state-governed responsibility for children; and to Strindberg the home was the battleground for the equality struggle, and women had exactly the same right of self-fulfillment as men, as long as their motives weren't trivial. Furthermore, early influential feminists like Ellen Key and Alva Myrdal, and later Eva Moberg's rebellious Group 222, Annika Baude, Maj-Britt Sandlund, Siv Thorsell, and Barbro Backberger, one of the eight in Group 8, never shared a common view of who would be the main one responsible for the home or the children. Unlike what many foreign observers usually assume, the versions of feminism varied widely, from conservative, liberal, to left wing, and from complementary, biological, to social constructionist views. However, the political synthesis nevertheless took a route from the internationally hegemonic joint taxation of families to individual taxation, which made the home a shared but not an economically unified space of socialization. Perhaps this economically individualized, but physically shared, relationship to space, together with other social political gender equality reforms, paved the way for not only one (the woman) but two (the woman and the man) consumers of interior home decoration and aesthetics. Considering also that children and teenagers in middle-class Sweden often had their own rooms and, as mentioned by Ellen Key for example, were regarded as autonomous with their own rights, the home encapsulated more than two such individualist consumers. The more the merrier.

Bearded, Climate-Friendly Foodies

Similar to, and contemporary with, the increased flurry of interior decoration in the 1990s, and continuing far after the turn of the millennium, a hype around food, cooking, and eating appeared, and to many the preferred way to express one's global middle-class identity was to become a *foodie* (Johnston and Baumann 2010). Considering that the cuisine had never been part of the Swedish, or even Nordic, national pride—quite the opposite—it was certainly not a given that this trend would take off as the home decoration trend had, but it sure did. Between 2004 and 2017, the interest in and consumption of food increased radically amongst Swedish people; the number of restaurants increased more than threefold; Michelin stars started to sprinkle on Swedish, Danish, Finnish, and Norwegian chefs; and the "New Nordic" cuisine became a household brand in fine dining all over the world (Ulver 2017, 2019; Leer 2016). How could this trend become so wide, strong, and persistent in the Nordics, so historically poor in gastronomic refinement? The explanations are many, but if we view this from a statist individualist perspective and use Sweden as a case, what do we see?

Foodie culture, which is said to have emerged from the mid-1990s onward, celebrates "authenticity" in terms of natural, organic, crafted, small-scale, and non-industrial produce (Ulver and Klasson 2018; Ulver 2017, 2019; Ulver-Sneistrup et al. 2011; Johnston and Baumann 2010). This of course fits like a glove with the celebration of nature that we could see in nineteenth-century tales of the Swedish character's excellence and even superiority amongst Geijer, Almqvist, and Strindberg, but also the nationalist Rudolf Kjellén. It applies not least to the adoration of the farmer which, as elaborated on earlier, also had political and structural meaning, where farmers and the state shared a common enemy in nobility. Subsequently, Jante Law–loyal farmers had, relative to other countries in Europe, a very strong cultural and political position, which was a contrast class-wise to the more refined, gentlemanesque bourgeoisies on the continent. If this, as Berggren and Trägårdh (2015) argue, came to be a reason for later self-loathing and national bitterness during the eighteenth and nineteenth centuries—when Swedes were often accused of being impolite, uneducated, asocial, and uncivilized—through foodie culture this rural legacy could finally scent the fresh morning air. Farmer values were back, kicking the provocative nobility-worshiping brats off stage.

When we speak of "farmers' markets," we usually refer to the conjoining of some small-scale farmers and their partners at a small town square in some late capitalist country, selling their locally produced and ecological products directly to the town's benign consumers. However, when reading about the emergence of Swedish statist individualist culture, it becomes very clear that the whole of Sweden itself was a metaphorical farmers' market, judging by its historical constitution of stances as seen earlier. Hence, foodie culture, with its climate-friendly, locally produced, and from-scratch cooking imperative, could easily take root in such prepared soil.

The celebration of terroir and merroir from the soil, oceans, and forests has not least been visible at world-praised restaurants and in iconic television series like *Chef's Table*, as analyzed by Ulver and Klasson (2018), where, for instance, the renowned chef Francis Mallmann travels the world with his "band of gipsies" (*metranza*) and practices pit cooking over an open fire out in the wilderness. According to Berggren and Trägårdh (2015), Geijer saw two kinds of pagan religions: "fire," which was the active elevating us to the divine, and "water," which was the passive descent into dissolution of the individual. Not surprisingly, Geijer preferred the fire version of this Norse paganism: "war-like fire is also the life of human, which in struggle and combat seeks air, and birth in the death at the battlefield" (own translation from quotation in Berggren and Trägårdh 2015, p. 99). It probably does not leave a doubt that this is a celebration of traditionally "masculine virtue, bravery and harshness," as expressed by Berggren and Trägårdh (ibid., p. 99). And this obsession with rugged masculinity may be another route to understanding why foodie culture attracted such success in Sweden.

Despite today being the most gender equal country on earth, as the common tale and the United Nations have it, Sweden also has been a truly patriarchal society. As researched by Klasson and Ulver (2015) and Ulver (2015), this cultural legacy continues to thrive even in contexts where the immediate appearance states the opposite. Male foodies have now in some sense occupied the traditionally feminine space of the home, the kitchen, and made it into a stage for everyday performance and social identity construction. This has on the one hand encouraged a more equal distribution of mundane, unpaid household labor, but has also meant that *hegemonic masculinity* (Connell 2005) has taken over in terms of what practices and cultural codes are rewarded in the kitchen (Klasson and Ulver 2015), and where the interpretive prerogative for what is good taste is given to the one with "social magic": the man (Ulver and Klasson 2018; Neuman 2016). In other words, perhaps centuries of gender struggles have opened up for men to enter feminine spaces, and thereby particularly welcomed new consumption patterns and trends—such as foodie culture—that have invited them to do so.

Market Wonderland

As part of a wider Nordic model, but from the specific perspective of statist individualism, Swedish consumer-citizens need to stand alone next to, rather than within, the interdependent communality among co-consumers. This corresponds well with the *Gesellschaft*-like and Rousseauian "perfect independence" *from* other *citizens* that governs individualism in the Swedish context, instead of de Tocqueville's freedom from the state, and leads us to understand that communality does not automatically mean sociality. The social aspect may very well be absent from the state-sanctioned community, an insight that is often ignored in the "traditional" community literature in consumer culture research (e.g., Muniz and O'Guinn 2001), but acknowledged in more recent literature on crowds and publics (Arvidsson and Caliandro 2015), although usually referring specifically to the digital, more or less anonymous world.

Drawing from the consumer trend examples in this chapter, they all communicate very intimately with the main paradox of statist individualism; that is, the combination of freedom from interpersonal dependency, naturalized state dependency, and elitist equality. People compete for status in an otherwise stagnant and "obese" middle class, historically provided for by the welfare state, as solitary runners, unicorns, foodies, brats, and home stylists. In the line of independence all is done in an individualistic, competitive manner to stand out, but in line with isomorphism (DiMaggio and Powell 1983) it all turns out the same in the end (for more insights on status competition in the Nordics, see Chap. 10 in this volume). In an elitist equality sense, they all deserve to have and be the very best, and that is how progress progresses in a statist individualistic society. As so well put by Berggren and Trägårdh, modern Sweden doesn't come out of warm solidarity (as perhaps has been popularly promoted), but out of a "chilly" merger of the ideals of individualism and equality (p. 167). Perhaps this is why Sweden is particularly apt to absorb what the sociologist Eva Illouz (2007) calls *emotional capitalism* with all its "cold intimacies."

Beyond the scope of this text, but as a potential route for future research, I would like to offer a short reflection on the importance of societal units, as brought up earlier in Fig. 3.1. For a consumer cultural researcher, one of the first things that stands out is (of course) the relative lack of a "market" in Berggren and Trägårdh's model. The market is sometimes mentioned in the book—especially in the second part—but, as we saw in Fig. 3.1, the major institutional units of the USA's, Germany's, and Sweden's societies are represented by the family, individual, and state, yet not the market. I argue that by adding the market as a unit we could much better understand what forces are at hand in our society, which to a large extent can be considered a consumer society. Without the market as a central institutional unit, many important aspects will get lost in any social analysis. Although the following thoughts do not include what each society unites *against* (as Berggren and Trägårdh's excellent model did; e.g., individual and state *against* family as in Sweden's case), an initial step to include the market as a potential unit would be to acknowledge it at all. Throughout Berggren and Trägårdh's text, each national context highlights three units as the most important: (1) Sweden: state, individual, and market; (2) USA: market, individual, and family; and (3) Germany: family, state, and market (see Fig. 3.2).

Viewing the national contexts from that perspective, perhaps it now makes perfect sense that Swedish people conform so quickly and neatly to movements in their surroundings: visions of growth and progress provided by the market and the state, coupled with the solitary farmer's need to closely follow where the rain falls, sun shines, and wind blows.

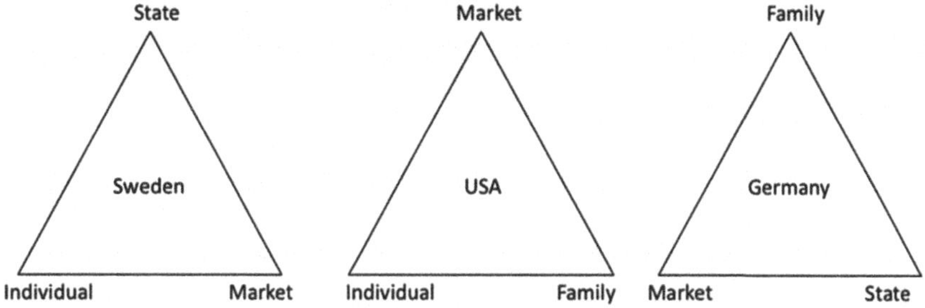

Fig. 3.2 Sociopolitical units of importance with the market, modified from Berggren and Trägårdh (2015). Reprinted with permission

References

Arsel, Z., & Bean, J. (2012). Taste Regimes and Market-Mediated Practice. *Journal of Consumer Research, 39*, 899–917.

Arvidsson, A., & Caliandro, A. (2015). Brand Public. *Journal of Consumer Research, 42*(5), 727–748.

Askegaard, S., & Linnet, J. T. (2011). Towards an Epistemology of Consumer Culture Theory: Phenomenology and the Context of Context. *Marketing Theory, 11*(4), 381–404.

Belk, R. W., & Costa, J. A. (1998). The Mountain Man Myth: A Contemporary Consumer Fantasy. *Journal of Consumer Research, 25*(3), 218–240.

Berggren, H., & Trägårdh, L. (2015). *Är Svensken Människa? Gemenskap och oberoende i det moderna Sverige*. Stockholm: Norstedts Förlag.

Booth, M. (2014, January 27). Dark Lands: The Grim Truth About the 'Scandinavian Miracle'. *The Guardian*, Online. Retrieved from https://www.theguardian.com/world/2014/jan/27/scandinavian-miracle-brutal-truth-denmark-norway-sweden.

Booth, M., Price, A., Bolsø, A., Bergmann, E., Stubb, A., & Trägårdh, L. (2014, February 5). The Grim Truth Behind the 'Scandinavian Miracle' – The Nations Respond. *The Guardian*, Online. Retrieved from https://www.theguardian.com/world/2014/feb/05/scandinavian-miracle-denmark-finland-iceland-norway-sweden.

Bourdieu, P. (1984). *Distinction*. London: Routledge.

Byrkjeflot, H. (2001). *The Democratic Challenge to Capitalism: Management and Democracy in the Nordic Countries* (H. Byrkjeflot, S. Myklebust, C. Myrvack, & F. Seijersted, Eds.). Copenhagen: Copenhagen Business School Press.

Cederström, C., & Thanem, T. (2018, March). The Swedish CEO Who Runs His Company Like a Cross-Fit Gym. *Harvard Business Review*, Online. Retrieved from https://hbr.org/2018/03/the-swedish-ceo-who-runs-his-company-like-a-crossfit-gym.

Connell, R. W. (2005). *Masculinities* (2nd ed.). Cambridge: Polity Press.

DiMaggio, P. J., & Powell, W. W. (1983). The Iron Cage Revisited: Institutional Isomorphism and Collective Rationality in Organizational Fields. *American Sociological Review, 48*(2), 147.

Egan-Wyer, C. (forthcoming). PhD Thesis in Progress, Lund University Press, Lund, Sweden.

Frykman, J., & Löfgren, O. (1987). *Culture Builders: A Historical Anthropology of Middle-Class Life*. New Brunswick, NJ: Rutgers University Press.

Fuentes, M. (2016). Hemmets kommersialisering driver inredningskonsumtionen. In M. Roos (Ed.), *Konsumtionsrapporten 2016* (pp. 41–52). Gothenburg: Göteborgs Universitet.

Gullestad, M. (1997). The Home as an Expressive Statement. In H. Mackey (Ed.), *Consumption and Everyday Life*. London: SAGE.

Holt, D. B. (1998). Does Cultural Capital Structure American Consumption? *Journal of Consumer Research, 25*(1), 1–25.

Holt, B. D., & Thompson, C. J. (2004). Man-of-Action Heroes: The Pursuit of Heroic Masculinity in Everyday Consumption. *The Journal of Consumer Research, 31*(2), 425–440.

Illouz, E. (2007). *Cold Intimacies – The Making of Emotional Capitalism*. Cambridge: Polity Press.

Itu, A. (2018, September). Talent in the Land of Fire & Ice – What Makes the Icelandic Athletes So Good? *Boxrox*, Online. Retrieved from https://www.boxrox.com/crossfit-strongman-icelandic-athletes/.

Johansson, J. (2017). *Sweat Is Weakness Leaving the Body – A Study of the Self-Presentational Practices of Sporty Top Managers in Sweden*. PhD Dissertation, Department of Business Administration, Stockholm University.

Johnston, J., & Baumann, S. (2010). *Foodies*. New York: Routledge.

Klasson, M., & Ulver, S. (2015). Masculinising Domesticity: An Investigation of Men's Domestic Foodwork. *Journal of Marketing Management, 31*(15–16), 1652–1675.

Leer, J. (2016). The Rise and Fall of the New Nordic Cuisine. *Journal of Aesthetics and Culture, 8*(1), 1–12.

Maliranta, M., Määttänen, N., & Vihrlälä, V. (2012). Are the Nordic Countries Really Less Innovative than the US? *VOX*, CEPRS Portal Online. Retrieved from https://voxeu.org/article/nordic-innovation-cuddly-capitalism-really-less-innovative.

McCracken, G. (1989). 'Homeyness': A Cultural Account of One Constellation of Consumer Goods and Meanings. In E. C. Hirschman (Ed.), *Interpretive Consumer Research* (pp. 168–183). Provo, UT: Association of Consumer Research.

Moynihan, M. (2016, July 8). Stockholm Syndrome. *The Wall Street Journal*, Online. Retrieved from https://www.wsj.com/articles/stockholm-syndrome-1468008681.

Muniz, A. M., & O'Guinn, T. (2001). Brand Community. *Journal of Consumer Research, 27*(4), 412–432.

Neuman, N. (2016). *Stories of Masculinity, Gender Equality, and Culinary Progress: On Foodwork, Cooking, and Men in Sweden*. PhD Dissertation, Uppsala University, Sweden.

Östberg, J. (2005). The Linking Value of Subcultural Capital: Constructing the Stockholm Brat Enclave. In B. Cova, R. V. Kozinets, & A. Shankar (Eds.), *Consumer Tribes* (Vol. 2007, pp. 93–107). Oxford: Elsevier/Butterworth-Heinemann.

Partanen, A. (2016). *The Nordic Theory of Everything: In Search of a Better Life*. New York: HarperCollins.

Scott, R., Cayla, J., & Cova, B. (2017). Selling Pain to the Saturated Self. *Journal of Consumer Research, 44*(1), 22–43.

Statistiska Centralbyrån. (2010). Tätorter 2010 Befolkningsstruktur-Befolkning, ålder och kön.

Ulver-Sneistrup, S. (2008). *Status Spotting – A Consumer Cultural Exploration into Ordinary Status Consumption of the "Home" and Home Aesthetics*. PhD Dissertation, Lund Business Press, Institute of Economic Research, Lund.

Ulver, S. (2015). Encouraged Intrusion and the Entering of a Subordinate Consumption Field – Exploring Changing Gender Distinctions in the *Foodie* Consumer Culture. *NA – Advances in Consumer Research, 43*, 415–420.

Ulver, S. (2017). Restaurangens nya guldålder. In M. Roos (Ed.), *Konsumtionsrapporten 2017* (pp. 31–46). Gothenburg: Göteborgs Universitet.

Ulver, S. (2019, January). From Mundane to Socially Significant Consumption: An Analysis of How Foodie Identity Work Spurs Market Formation. *Journal of Macromarketing*, 1–18.

Ulver, S., & Klasson, M. (2018). Social Magic for Dinner? The Taste Script and Shaping of Foodieness in Netflix's Chef's Table. In Z. Arsel & J. Bean (Eds.), *Taste, Consumption and Markets: An Interdisciplinary Volume*. New York: Routledge.

Ulver-Sneistrup, S., Askegaard, S., & Kristensen, D. B. (2011). The New Work Ethics of Consumption and the Paradox of Mundane Brand Resistance. *Journal of Consumer Culture, 11*, 215–238.

Unicorn Articles. Retrieved from https://techsavvy.media/in-the-north-everyone-lacks-behind-swedish-fintech/; http://knowledge.wharton.upenn.edu/article/how-stockholm-became-a-unicorn-factory/.

4

Why Can't They Behave? Theorizing Consumer Misbehavior as Regime Misfit between Neoliberal and Nordic Welfare Models

Diane M. Martin, Frank Lindberg, and James Fitchett

Consumer misbehavior is well known in the tourist industry: the ugly American bemoaning the heat in Rome, the drunk Australian littering a Balinese beach, the European trampling over majestic Majorca. These tourist stereotypes are labeled rude and insensitive, seeming to willfully destroy idyllic natural and cultural treasures. Welcomed for their economic stimuli, reviled for their behavior, and yet accepted as part of a mature tourist industry, they come and they spend. Local cash registers ring. Yet, when holidaymakers encounter the Nordic hybrid nature-based marketplace, some unintentionally misbehave in ways that violate the

D. M. Martin (✉)
RMIT University, Melbourne, VIC, Australia
e-mail: diane.martin@RMIT.edu.au

F. Lindberg
Nord University Business School, Bodø, Norway
e-mail: frank.lindberg@nord.no

J. Fitchett
University of Leicester School of Business, Leicester, UK
e-mail: jaf30@leicester.ac.uk

S. Askegaard, J. Östberg (eds.), *Nordic Consumer Culture*,
https://doi.org/10.1007/978-3-030-04933-1_4

broad social contract that characterizes the Nordic countries (World Economic Forum, Davos 2011). Recently, topics like "Tourists camping in the graveyard," "Parking chaos in Lofoten," "The forest of shit," and "Tourists invade private property" (www.nrk.no/nordland, 2016/17) have been the headlines in the Norwegian media. One may wonder: Why do consumers misbehave?

Consumer misbehavior is defined as behavioral acts which "violate the generally accepted norms of conduct in consumption situations, and thus disrupt the consumption order," with consequences of either material loss and/or psychological damage affecting marketers, marketing institutions, and other consumers (Fullerton and Punj 2004, p. 1239). Misbehavior usually involves shoplifting, vandalism, financial fraud, aggression, or sexual harassment (Yagil 2008), which affects firms, service employees, and other consumers (Faber et al. 1995), and compulsive consumption (ibid.) or substance addiction (Hirschman 1992), which affects consumers themselves. However, some level of misbehavior is tolerated by suppliers, acknowledged as part of the financial and social costs of doing business.

This psychological approach to consumer misbehavior (Fisk et al. 2010) leaves explanations of misbehavior in cross-cultural contexts under-theorized. Taking a cultural lens to misbehavior, we extend the findings that "many of the driving forces of legitimate consumer behavior have simultaneously been stimulants of consumer misbehavior" (Fullerton and Punj 2004, p. 1244). While social systems of different cultures may share many similarities, the differences as they arise in consumer behavior can be profound. Invoking Foucauldian reasoning, we employ "governing" and "modes of thought" which indicate that it is impossible to study "technologies of power without an analysis of the political rationality underpinning them" (Lemke 2001, p. 191). Our attention is directed toward the co-presence of heterogeneous norms, values, and morals, or what we refer to as regimes, and how consumer misbehavior can be explained in the midst of several higher-order justification principles (Corvellec and Hultman 2014). Behavioral justification is then conventionalized with underlying values and rules that govern consumers' beliefs about why certain acts are normal and good (Biggart and Beamish 2003) or "right" or "wrong" in a specific social context.

We investigate consumer misbehavior under conditions of two competing forms of regimes, the neoliberal and Nordic welfare state regimes. We do so through analyses of stakeholders' views, including media headlines that report tourist misbehavior such as those described earlier, and discuss how such stories can be an unintended consequence of exacerbating competing values and norms which originate in structures outside the consumption context. This chapter contributes to a novel framework for understanding consumption misbehavior, the role of social order in a Nordic context, and tensions that appear when the neoliberal consumption regime meets a competing Nordic marketplace logic. In other words: How can tensions among consumption regimes help explain consumer misbehavior in a tourism context?

The context of our study is one of the iconic tourist destinations of Norway, the Lofoten Islands. While Norway's visitor population at commercial accommodation grew 27% between 2000 and 2014, Lofoten's grew 50% (Eilertsen 2016). Promoted as "The world's most beautiful islands" (Lofoten Travel Guide 2014), tourists come to enjoy experiences among mountain ranges rising from the sea under the summer midnight sun and the winter northern lights. They arrive by plane, passenger boat, coastal steamer, or with a car or camper on a ferry. However, not all are on their best behavior. The head of the Lofoten Destination Marketing Organization (DMO) fears that the tourism industry will end up becoming an "industry of conflicts," and the chair of Lofoten's Outdoor Recreation Council argues that tourist misbehavior is a problem that needs solving: "Lofoten's a big headache—we need to take control" (Eilertsen 2016). Lofoten residents want to know: Why can't the tourists just behave?

Perceptions of Misbehavior

Shopkeepers and service providers grant consumers a form of impersonal trust; that is, having faith in people whom one does not know personally. Consumer conduct is implicitly allied with a social contract (e.g., Steiner et al. 1976) and acts of consumer misbehavior violate this contract and its underlying trust. Consumers who drift into this realm engage in variations of misbehavior such as shoplifting, vandalism, financial fraud, and physical or verbal abuse of other consumers and of employees. Some misbehavior is premeditated and deliberate. For example, the intent of an act of vandalism could be to show defiance toward a large, commercial institution (e.g., Baron and Fisher 1984), or to enjoy a thrilling experience (e.g., Katz 1988), or maybe to gain the approval of peers (e.g., Sutherland 1947).

However, other acts labeled as deviant by the labeler may not necessarily be unethical or even illegal. Instead, they violate a normalized morality. Such behavior is an unintended consequence of the marketing activities of firms, which seek to promote a philosophy of consumption so that consumers will buy more. Fullerton and Punj (1998) argue that "widespread misbehavior by consumers … is inevitable given the dynamics of (neo-liberal) consumer culture" (p. 408). They identify 35 types of misbehavior, ranging "from the intricacy of insurance fraud and database theft on the one hand, to mindless thuggery in mall parking lots on the other" (p. 409). Three of these values related to morality and the calculation of opportunism are evident amongst misbehaving tourists. The first, the Absence of Moral Constraints, explains that "when the urges of the self are paramount—especially amidst a prevailing ethos of abandon and excitement—moral constraints against misbehavior are weakened" (p. 404). Likewise, an Openness of Exchange Environment suggests that "some environments are so powerfully designed, so exciting to consumers, that they become 'sensually endowed and miraculously constituted perfectly for the emergent project in deviance'" (Katz 1988, p. 56 in Fullerton and Punj 1998, p. 404). A combination of Hedonism and Deviant Thrill-Seeking "misbehavior enables some thrill-crazed consumers to fulfil their cravings in an exciting way, adding to the exhilaration of the consumption experience" (p. 404). Tourists escape the mundane conventions of city life to enjoy the powerful freedom of nature. A homogeneity of values and socially accepted morality underscores each of these pathways to unintended misbehavior. The tourist, by definition, is removed from the familiar and seeks experiences in the wider world, but might not be aware of the social contract of the region they are visiting.

The Neoliberal Regime: Consumer-Tourist

Neoliberalism in social theory has long been a focus of academic study and we don't intend to fully review its versions and critiques here. We are interested in consumption models under the condition of neoliberalism. Neoliberalism "proposes that human well-being can best be advanced by liberating individual entrepreneurial freedoms and skills within an institutional framework characterized by strong private property rights, free markets, and free trade" (Harvey 2010, p. 2), with the state's role mainly enforcing the conditions for the free market to thrive. Neoliberal consumerism is a way of life and a realm within which the power relations of contemporary society are played out (Yngfalk 2015, p. 3). Consequently, the ideal markets would be those that are competitive and that commodify nearly everything, including not only the economic spheres but also the cultural and social spheres of public and private life (Dwyer 2018). The allegedly necessary "freedom" of the economy thus consists of a freedom from responsibility and commitment to society (von Werlhof 2008). This version of "deep-neoliberalism" operates through "a multiplicity of governing networks, nodes and modes that allow for far greater levels of contingency and context-specific variation" (Venugopal 2015, p. 170).

In contemporary (western) consumer culture, people live under various forms of neoliberal regimes within which consumers become subject to indirect forms of power that are exercised by institutional frameworks and various organizations in the management of populations (Yngfalk 2015). This involves, amongst other things, the delineation of concepts, the specification of objects, and the provision of arguments and justifications related to the marketplace.

We use the concept of consumer-tourism to characterize the consumption role associated with market-oriented neoliberal regimes. First, consumer-tourism is situated in the relationship between private firms and consumers. In global markets the consumer-tourist has the freedom to travel and is encouraged to spend time away from home for an enriched lifestyle and increased well-being (Shankar et al. 2006). Second, the model is distinctive in the manner in which consumers choose and receive goods and services. The relationship between the firm and the consumer is transaction oriented and instrumental, with a focus on individual interests and need satisfaction. The third aspect, particularly relevant here, concerns the legitimate conduct of the exchange situation. Engaging in transactions, consumer-tourists expect the provider to protect and serve them. In a Ritzerian optic, the consumers would engage in pre-scripted and pre-packaged holidays (Ritzer 1996) that industry stake-holders carefully plan and execute to ensure hedonic experiences for the consumer-tourist, but ultimately economic growth, jobs, and rising incomes at the destination. The conduct of the consumer-tourist in neo-liberal regimes is not very demanding at a destination, because the firms expect little from the individual other than payment for the product.

Consumer and tourism research shows how consumer-tourists seek antistructure (Turner 1969), often at a distance from everyday urban structures, that results in hedonic experiences distinguished by the com-munion of shared liminality and sacredness (e.g., Arnould and Price 1993; Kozinets 2002; Sharpe 2005). Many consumer-tourism practices entail a "gazing" tourist role, which is how people learn to consume places through organized tourism under neoliberal conditions (Lash and Urry 1994; Perkins and Thorns 2001; Urry 1990, 2002; Urry and Larsen 2011). When consumer-tourists encounter the Nordic welfare state regime, neoliberal conditions may not fully apply.

Nordic Welfare State Regime: Citizenship-Tourism

Through a Foucauldian lens, consumers are often objectified and subjec-tified within the neoliberal ideology, which means that governmentality both acts on people *and* makes them empowered subjects. Through this dialectic the agent may act "freely" in a field of action that is structured by a certain truth (Denegri-Knott et al. 2018). Although critical tourism movements suggest alternatives such as slow tourism, transformative tourism, and socially responsible tourism, the neoliberal mindset and taken-for-granted assumptions are so established that it creates a powerful incentive within people to continue to adopt or accept prior behaviors, choices, or tools in global tourism (Dwyer 2018).

In certain Nordic markets, especially at rural tourist destinations, we think that visiting tourists might "meet" consumption regimes that depart from the prevailing neoliberal regime to a certain extent. This does not mean that Nordic consumer culture can be thought of as homogeneous (Østergaard et al. 2014), because global capitalism and individualism are accepted in the midst of structures such as state intervention and egalitarianism. Consumption and market configurations between cultural regions can be quite different (Cova 2005). In order to provide some normative and moral grounding for Nordic regional specificities, we draw on the work of the historian Trägårdh's (2010) theorization of the Nordic welfare state.

In contrast to Anglo-American welfare models, the Nordic model is based on social (democratic) citizenship, which was developed in the twentieth century and characterized by the way in which fundamental entitlements, such as education, health care, child care, and pensions, have been granted universally to individuals on the basis of citizenship (Trägårdh 2010). The main difference depends on the individuals' acceptance of state intervention or not. According to Berggren and Trägårdh (2010), there is a general antipathy toward state intervention in the USA, whereas the social-democratic influence in the Nordic countries means there is much greater acceptance of the alliance between the state and the individual citizen. Ideally, in Anglo-American contexts the individual citizen should provide for him- or herself in the field of the market and trusting the goodwill of the family and the community, whereas the social citizenship of Nordic state regimes reflects an ideal of mutual autonomy between individuals and an ambition to "liberate the individual citizen from all forms of subordination and dependency in civil society" (Berggren and Trägårdh 2010, p. 13), for example the poor from charity, the workers from their employers, wives from their husbands. Deeply held values are often referred to as relatively open markets, strong welfare systems, egalitarianism (Østergaard et al. 2014), and, as a consequence, social capital, trust, and welfare-based individual autonomy (Trägårdh 2010; Wollebaek et al. 2012).

The Nordic welfare state regime contrasts with the neoliberal regime in important ways. First, in the neoliberal regime civil society, often referred to as the non-profit sector, is regarded as prior to, distinct, and autonomous from the state. In this narrative, Trägårdh (2010, p. 231) argues, "the state is always seen as harboring a potential for domination, intervention, regulation, collectivism and positive law imposed arbitrarily from above," which also has an impact on the market (profit) sector. Ideally, however, the market must be freed from the state so that choices are made available to consumers. This division of state–civil society–market does not harmonize well with the Nordic model. Instead, the state plays a major role in most affairs of the region, resulting in high levels of taxes and a large public sector, but also social equality and a linked governance structure between the state, the civil sector, and the market. For example, a tourist destination would be one dependent on state priority and protection, often through direct payments (e.g., entrepreneurial support) and indirect investments (e.g., infrastructure), whereas the development locally would be viewed as a governance alliance between the state (local/regional government), civil society, and the corporate world. The marketplace then consists of stakeholders from all three sectors of society, and state intervention and citizen democratic influence go "hand in hand" with private firms.

Second, the Nordic welfare model has consequences for the social contract. While social citizenship grants universal benefits and thus social equality and egalitarianism, the consequence is, according to Trägårdh (Berggren and Trägårdh 2010; Trägårdh 2010), increased individual autonomy. Whereas individualism under the neoliberal regime signifies empowerment of the freedom to choose (Shankar et al. 2006), the logic under the Nordic state regime is rather different: "active interventionism on the part of the state to promote egalitarian conditions is not a threat to individual autonomy but rather the obverse: a necessary prerequisite to free the citizens from demeaning and humbling dependence on one another" (Berggren and Trägårdh 2010, p. 16). The state–individual alliance can be seen as dialectical, where the state takes care of individuals who at the same time are freed from dependencies (cf., rights of children, women, elderly, disabled, consumers). According to Trägårdh, and not without historical reference to a lack of feudal institutions and strong peasant and fishing cultures, the most important moral codes are self-sufficiency and independence, or fear of becoming subservient and unequal. The social contract relies on conformism, democratic participation, equality, and being law-abiding on the one hand, and property rights norms, high trust (interpersonal and governmental), self-improvement (education, work; Trägårdh 2010), and the ideal of the well-behaved and wholesome worker (Trägårdh and Svedberg 2013), along with little respect for authority, on the other.

Third, state interventionism and the somewhat paradoxical social contract have consequences for how the marketplace works in the Nordic model. The regime's morality, mostly through a tacit mindset, implies that social rights have to be earned by attending to duties and responsibilities. For citizens this means three demands: labor-market participation, social respectability, and social responsibility—including oneself and one's family (Lundberg and Åmark 2001). In rural Nordic regions, the citizenship-tourism model implies that consumption is not merely a right by transaction, but rather a right by citizenship participation.

The citizen-tourist is expected to earn social rights through active involvement in local activities and experiences, and to behave well according to the moral codes of the social contract. Those who do not live up to the citizenship involvement contract are deemed unworthy and undeserving, and may become subject to harsh and unsentimental treatment by actors in the marketplace.

Method

We employ heterogeneity as a useful way to study consumer misbehavior. While maintaining the frame of the neoliberal regime, we can also examine alternatives found in the Nordic welfare state regime. Whereas neoliberalism and the state (Bauman 2001) intersect on the large scale at modes of public governance and administration in western contexts, for instance as discussed related to Nordic practices of food consumption (Draper and Green 2002) and food labeling (Yngfalk 2015), we investigate consumption heterogeneity when international tourists visit a remote tourism area in Norway's Lofoten Islands. We focus on local and regional stakeholders' interpretations of heterogeneity during instances when consumers' misbehavior "is inevitable given by the dynamics of (neo-liberal) consumer culture" (Fullerton and Punj 1998, p. 408). The social contract of such a market is paradoxical due to the co-presence of multiple values and morals, and ongoing disputes about how to consume the place prevail in the media.

This study privileges the "context of the context" (Askegaard and Linnet 2011) rather than consumers' lived experiences. Within the context we find important actors—that is, DMOs, residents, tourism providers—all holders of cultural values foundational to the Nordic welfare state regime. This research also relies on multiple methods of data collection, whereas socio-historical data, much of it retrieved through online resources, and ethnographic-inspired fieldwork (Arnould and Wallendorf 1994) constitute the main sources. In addition, three research seminars were organized among the researchers during the interpretive process. Participant observations in Lofoten and interviews with various stakeholders on site are the main sources of primary data.

Stakeholder Data

The participants for the in-depth interviews were selected based on the results of an initial interview with an informant employed by the Northern Norway DMO who had exhaustive knowledge of the Lofoten destination: its socio-historical development, its present and future challenges, and which stakeholders would provide knowledge of market formation dynamics. This recruitment process allowed for the selection of participants who either played a significant role in the market formation of the destination or had insights and opinions about such processes. We contacted the participants through e-mails and phone calls and made appointments with citizens, business managers, DMOs, consultants in tourism and regional development, and advisors at the county level. This resulted in the participants listed in Table 4.1.

Table 4.1 Stakeholder participants

Role	Stakeholder	Age	Sex
Manager	DMO, Northern Norway	Mid 40s	Female
Manager	DMO, Lofoten	Late 40s	Female
Insurance agent	Citizen	Late 30s	Male
Insurance agent	Citizen	Mid 60s	Male
Student	Citizen	Early 20s	Male
Student	Citizen	Mid 20s	Male
Consultant	Tourism and regional development	Early 40s	Male
Manager	Museum	Early 50s	Male
Owner	Experience provider	Mid 40s	Male
Manager	Hotel	Mid 40s	Male
Owner	Experience provider	Early 40s	Female
Owner	Experience provider	Early 50s	Female
Senior advisor	County	Early 60s	Male
Manager	County	Mid 50s	Female
Senior advisor	County	Early 40s	Male

Most of these interviews (10) were conducted in English, and the research team visited the participants in their offices. The rest of the interviews (5) were conducted in Norwegian and later translated into English.

All interviews were taped and transcribed. Inspired by hermeneutic interpretation (Alvesson and Sköldberg 2009), we attained analytical scrutiny through spiral interplay between the various empirical texts, the cultural-historical meaning of Lofoten, and the meso/macro dimensions related to market formation of this destination; that is, through interpretive processes of zooming in and out (Gherardi 2006). Since we aimed at studying processes of consumption in contested places, it was important to follow challenges between views and practices and the impact on the development of Lofoten as a market. Thus, we tried to identify what happened, and how and why it happened, from various stakeholder viewpoints (Kvale and Brinkmann 2009). To complement such interpretations, we took advantage of being an international research team and organized ex post research discussions after the interviews to improve the interpretive scrutiny in the midst of historical, cultural, and textual meanings. These research team discussions were also taped and transcribed.

Results: Misbehavior between Neoliberal and Nordic Welfare State Regimes

Generalities of what constitutes serious misbehavior remain uncontested, for instance shoplifting versus fraud. Yet violation of the spirit of the Nordic regime is also labeled misbehavior by Lofoten residents, the keepers of the cultural values and norms. They take exception to tourists' activities that violate the values underlying particularly Nordic concepts of authenticity, uniqueness of the location, and every man's (sic) right to access the land. Two themes contribute to the tensions that underpin regime misfit, and in particular the Nordic value of every man's right to access the land.

The first theme is tourists' misinterpretation of the collective rights of the culture. While the beauty of the islands can be gazed at from a chair in front of a café, the rugged nature of the landscape means that trained mountain guides are often required for more adventurous activities. As one hotel manager explains: "You have to know the archeology and to know that the mountains, where to go, the weather … it's not that easy to take the guests out into the nature here." Industry providers take measures toward a balance between the desires of international guests and the rigor of mountain hiking. The manager continues:

> When we get a lot of international guests—if it's a couple or just two people coming we will send them—we look at them and see how they are dressed and … what kind of shoes they have. We will point out hiking trips for them, if they are alone. If there is a big group then we try to use (local adventure provider) XX Lofoten or some other company to run the trip for them so we are assured of the security.

Tourists who forgo the services of guides often take shortcuts on dangerous mountain routes, putting their own lives and the fragile mountainside flora at risk. In the fishing village of Reine, locals complain that "tourists go everywhere," as the hotel manager explains:

> some places in Lofoten … the paths are ruined because there are too many people walking there … we have one path that has been there for centuries

and when it's wet people just try to get another path and you get the grass.... Erosion. The small rocks start to fall. Which is a big problem now....

A representative of a community consulting firm concurs:

Every year tourists die or are injured because the mountains here, are not—for me—I mean, I grew up here so I know how to handle those mountains, but Russian tourists from Moscow have never done that before. You need tourists that ask you if you can go there and then it's like "No. Go back the way you came! <laughs> You're not equipped to go up that mountain!"

Damage from erosion and "forests of shit" spoil the experience for others. Yet it is among these tourists that DMOs find the iconic images of Lofoten's extreme adventure lifestyle that provides appeal to others, including "soft-adventure" and gazing tourists:

DMO:	The best ones for us is not extreme sport tourist, but they give us the best image. They... bring other people to us. They made Lofoten cool. It is young, it is powerful, it is extreme. But they have no—this is not the people who use the money here.
Interviewer:	Okay, they don't stay in the hotels...
DMO:	No, they could buy a beer or something but they are out and they do a lot of old crew and stuff.
Interviewer:	But they work for you and...
DMO:	They sent picture in social media ... and they felt "this is beautiful. You have to come here and take a look."

The community consultant concurs:

Some of them don't leave much money behind. They stay in tents and there is some ripple effects on like—they buy some food and they drink some beer and that's it. They're very important for the social economy, though. And couch surfers and people like that. Many of those in that young segment has Lofoten and the surfing in Lofoten as like, on their bucket list.

Stakeholders (i.e., domestic tourists, county officials, regional DMOs) argue that trust, trustworthiness, respect, and responsibility are central tourist values. However, county officials and DMOs note that many tourists fail adjusting to the citizenship-tourism model. Many tourists misbehave, for example by littering and invading private property, and this is referred to as unworthy, disrespectful, and irresponsible toward the collective ethos of Lofoten cultural values.

The inherent paradox here is related to how tourists misinterpret the state-provided benefits of Nordic citizenship. The benefit of moving freely in nature ("public access law"), parking, and tenting almost anywhere are collective rights, which means that tourists are granted the same rights and "become" citizens the moment they enter Lofoten. The problem is that many do not understand the responsibility that comes with Nordic social citizenship. The egalitarian freedom comes at the cost of respectability and social responsibility, and not just monetary costs.

The second theme is touristic non-authentic gazing. Lofoten was a nexus for visitors of a very different sort for decades: the fishermen came for the Arctic cod every winter, staying in small cottages and fishing the icy waters. They brought economic value to the small villages in the archipelago and returned to the mainland at the end of the season. Today these cottages are rented to tourists. They have been updated to suit modern tourists' aesthetics, while also maintaining markers of Lofoten's cultural heritage. These tourists visit the local cod fishing and Viking museums, eat traditional Norwegian meals in the local restaurants, and hire local guides for a modern-day fishing adventure. The DMO explains:

> people from forty-plus … or forty through sixty … these people came here, they used their money in the restaurants and the hotel and they want to eat well and sleep well. They will pay for activities and they will not go by their own. They want to go kayaking, fishing with dream boats and other things. They want to watch the seagulls … and they pay for everything. They pay for everything.

These are the desired tourists. Some stakeholders believe that visitors should be interested in culturally authentic experiences or just stay away. One Samee reindeer farmer wants to attract tourists who will pay for authentic encounters and so she maintains her prices high to keep "the gazing tourists away.... She wants exclusive culturally interested people that really ask questions about the Samee way of living and the reindeer and all that kind of thing" (field notes discussion). Many of these gazing tourists add little to the economy:

Interviewer:	We saw one thing—these Germans turning up—
DMO:	Ugh.
Interviewer:	—in the big campers and—
DMO:	Middle-aged ... fifty plus.
Interviewer:	They're arriving there in this big truck and then sitting outside and watching this thing going by.
Interviewer:	When we're traveling around we see people camping and we see people with...
Consultant:	Mmm! Yeah. I forgot the campers because the caravans are not the most popular group of tourists.
Interviewer:	People with trucks and caravans...
Consultant:	Yeah.
Interviewer:	So, they are popular or not so popular?
Consultant:	I don't know because often ... before they brought sort of everything from Sweden or Germany or wherever they came from. They stop here and then they dump their toilet in the roads on the side and don't really leave as much money as they leave trash.

Debates on local media underscore the tensions around grazing tourists: "There are a lot of international tourists that act as if they are in an amusement park" (NRK TV). One county official notes: "They do not understand they're visiting a living society. It is as if they are visiting Disneyland." From these stakeholders' perspective, tourists act as if they were "consumers" who have paid a price for the "right" to consume. These actions are deemed misbehavior if they relate to violations of centrally held values. Another county official suggests more oversight from the state, arguing that "policy makers should decide the structure of tourism," regulating tourism and private businesses so that Lofoten maintains carrying capacity and develops legitimacy as a "trustworthy" destination.

A manager concurs, arguing that increased governmental regulation is necessary:

> That's my nightmare—that so much people are coming here and there's no regulations. You can throw your garbage away, and you can do whatever you like. You can fish as much as you like. Today I know about six fishing companies from Eastern Europe that sell trophy fishing in this region to their home market.

Not only do these tourists fail to convey the youthful extreme-adventurousness of photogenic backpackers, they also demonstrate self-sufficiency and contained needs, adding little to the commons of the Nordic. They visit the place not as visitors but as "gazers," who regard Lofoten as an amusement park which can be experienced from a distance. Or, as a recent headline in the local newspaper indicates: "The tourists know their rights in nature, but not the responsibilities" (Lofoten Post, October 2, 2018). The local stakeholders deem such behavior unworthy and undeserving, misbehaving according to the spirit of the Nordic welfare system.

Discussion

This study contributes to consumer misbehavior research (Fullerton and Punj 1997, 1998, 2004) and conceptualizes regime misfit as tensions between the Nordic welfare and neoliberal models. Taking a socio-cultural approach, we extend consumer misbehavior theory beyond the individualized frame of reference. We also illuminate the origins of tensions between neoliberal consumption and Nordic state-based consumption models that originate both within and outside the marketplace. Thus, we enlarge the interpretive framework for how to understand misbehavior and tensions during consumption. We argue that the consumption conflict is not necessarily between consumers or between consumers and producers, or between marketplace dynamics, but rather between structural regimes at play when globalized consumerism meets the social order of a local Nordic marketplace.

In the Nordic model, the individual is a citizen, with the morality of the commons, and the expectations are that civil society along with the state are the major arbiters to maintain egalitarian rights. In the neoliberal model, the individual is a consumer and civil society is based on the morality of the individual and expectations of limited involvement by the state as an arbiter for the free market. Market interactions between buyers and sellers are familiar to both. However, the case of Lofoten illuminates the gulf between moralities and expectations of appropriate social behavior, privileging the commons for the Nordic model and the individual for the neoliberal model. These tensions, combined with increasing numbers of tourists (Eilertsen 2016), put pressure on the infrastructure and access to nature and try the patience of stakeholders in the tourist market.

Media and stakeholders' reports of tourist misbehavior in Lofoten underscore the ways in which consumer misbehavior is unintentionally stimulated by heterogeneity between regimes co-present in the marketplace. The hybrid Nordic model includes the freedom of choice found in the neoliberal model, alongside the values of a social safety net and shared access to the land. What consumer-tourists seem to miss is the nuances of citizenship behavior expected of them. A cultural lens illuminates these missteps and suggests extension of the misbehavior concept to accommodate heterogeneous moralities. We submit that consumer misbehavior is not only a psychological construct, but also relative to context. Contrasts between the Lofoten Islands as a culturally rich homeland and a Disneyesque destination exemplify the divide between the Nordic welfare state and neoliberal logics.

Our cultural analysis extends several concepts of consumer misbehavior. For instance, the Absence of Moral Constraint under the Nordic welfare logic exacts a lower degree of selfishness, "when the urges of self are paramount" (Fullerton and Punj 1998, p. 404), to constitute misbehavior; that is, leaving trash and camping adjacent to an inhabited home. In misbehavior according to the Openness of Exchange Environment typology, the "environments are so powerfully designed, so exciting to consumers, that they become 'sensually endowed and miraculously constituted perfectly for the emergent project in deviance'" (Katz 1988, p. 56 in Fullerton and Punj 1998, p. 404); the combination of Hedonism and Deviant Thrill-Seeking “misbehavior enables some thrill-crazed consumers to fulfil their cravings in an exciting way, adding to the exhilaration of the consumption experience” (p. 404), and is evident in consumer-tourists’ disregard for proper pathways, proper waste disposal, and over-use erosion on the mountain paths. While life-long Lofoten residents, such as the consultant cited earlier, understand the danger to both nature and visitors and make efforts to guide the misbehaving toward better and safer paths, the neoliberal model has little room for a deep appreciation of nature as a place of commons, or for the relationship between common access and common responsibility.

Fullerton and Punj (1997) suggest two control techniques for consumer misbehavior. The first of these is an educational effort to inform tourists of the values of the Nordic social system, and relies on the majority of consumers exerting informal sanctions against miscreants. The underlying assumption is that misbehaving tourists will curb their ways when faced with information and informal public disapproval. The second technique is deterrence, which includes both formal and informal sanctions while also limiting the opportunity for misbehavior to occur, employing surveillance and increased possibility of punishment. The authors are careful to note that control strategy effectiveness varies among different consumers. Fullerton and Punj (1997) claim that both education and deterrence control techniques have low to moderate likelihoods of reaching misbehaving consumers who display an Absence of Moral Constraint, are enticed by an Openness of Exchange Environment, and exhibit Hedonism and Deviant Thrill-Seeking behaviors.

Incongruence between the Nordic welfare state citizenship-tourism and the neoliberal economic logic of consumer-tourism represents a source of regime conflict between notions of “rights and responsibility” on the one hand and “rights to access” on the other. Global tourism legitimizes access based on the ability to pay, with the expectation that all externalities and costs (including environmental and social costs) can be adequately accounted for through a commodity mechanism in which the only requirement for tourists is to pay toward the costs associated with these impacts, which are duly factored into the costs of tourist products, services, and experiences via market mechanisms.

Without appreciation of the role of civil society as distinct from the state and foundational morality of the Nordic commons, writ broadly, consumer-tourists only see the "rights to access." They don't participant in the Nordic welfare system as residents and as such have little to do with the "rights and responsibilities" of citizenship. This is not to say that it is not incumbent on consumer-tourists to be made culturally aware.

Of greater concern is that the fissure between the Nordic welfare state and the neoliberal economic logic may be widening. Limited communal responsibility, once familiar in western democracies, has been diluted by what Giesler and Veresiu (2014) call increased consumer responsibilization. They argue that rather than an "influence of moralistic governance regimes on consumer subjectivity ... responsible consumption requires the active creation and management of consumers as moral subjects" (Giesler and Veresiu 2014, p. 840). Where the responsibility for moral behavior sits with neoliberal consumer-tourists, they must manage themselves within the regime of the Nordic model. The issue is a matter of expectations and opportunity. According to the World Economic Forum Davos Nordic report, "the Nordic countries ... are characterized by a broad social trust extended beyond the intimate sphere of family and friends to include other members of society (World Economic Forum 2011, p. 16).... In addition to putting a strong emphasis on individual self-realization these countries are characterized by a high degree of social trust: well over 50% of respondents claim to trust other people, including strangers" (p. 17). Applying Giesler and Veresiu's (2014) theorizing, it seems that misbehaving tourists are operating *according to* their individualized moral positions. With the neoliberal system effectively outsourcing morality to consumers, "the consequences of the action are borne by the subject alone, who is also solely responsible for them" (Lemke 2001, p. 201). Consequently "consumers are reconstructed as free, autonomous, rational, and entrepreneurial subjects who draw on individual market choices to invest in their own human capital, such that the need for top-down intervention into the (neo-liberal) market is rendered obsolete" (Giesler and Veresiu 2014, p. 841) Thus, according to the nuanced Nordic moral citizenship guidelines inherent in the norms of Nordic civil society, there is an increasing likelihood that consumer-tourists will misbehave. When these consumers find themselves in this new form of governmentality, with a competing basis of moral behavior, they break no actual laws, but violate the spirit of the law. This puts at risk the resident/tourism relationship balance.

Efforts to curb the issue are outlined in strategy documents, interviews, and the media. The "Strategy Plan for Lofoten Tourism (2017–2022)" calls attention to how Lofoten can reject the expectations of tourists and instead facilitate soft adventure tourism (Steen 2017, p. 4). Several stakeholders, especially DMOs and businesses, work toward designing (guided) experience products to cope with non-authentic gazing tourists, while the municipality and regional advisors work with infrastructure improvements (e.g., rest rooms, information) to cope with misinterpretations of the collective rights of the place. For example, the "hiking sign project" and communicating "Lofoten codes of conduct" to tourists are expected to educate tourists on how to act responsibly and in a trustworthy manner. Extending Fullerton and Punj (1997), the Lofoten community efforts rely on redirecting product offerings and infrastructure improvements, in addition to the theorized education efforts. Further research is however needed to shed light on the efforts to cope with the tensions between competing regimes of the marketplace.

While DMOs, tour providers, and officials work toward a solution, the tourists continue to come to Lofoten, adding to the economy, posting iconic photographs of the "world's most beautiful islands," and misbehaving.

This chapter introduced the concept of "regime misfit" to explain how consumer misbehavior is unintentionally stimulated by tensions between values co-present in the marketplace. We relied particularly on local stakeholder perspectives, exposing the ways visitors misbehave in the context of the Nordic welfare regime. The regime misfit we theorized was one between the neoliberal and Nordic welfare state regimes. More research is needed to understand the values and morality that underlie such tensions and misbehavior. Finally, one may wonder how regime misfit may explain consumer misbehavior in highly neoliberal contexts. Future research is needed to understand the extent to which visitors are aware of misbehaving, particularly in cross-cultural contexts.

References

Alvesson, M., & Sköldberg, K. (2009). *Reflexive Methodology. New Vistas for Qualitative Research* (2nd ed.). London: Sage.

Arnould, E. J., & Price, L. L. (1993). River Magic: Extraordinary Experiences and the Extended Service Encounter. *Journal of Consumer Research, 20*(1), 24–45.

Arnould, E. J., & Wallendorf, M. (1994). Market Oriented Ethnography. *Journal of Marketing Research, 31*(November), 484–504.

Askegaard, S., & Linnet, J. (2011). Towards an Epistemology of Consumer Culture Theory: Phenomenology and the Context of Context. *Marketing Theory, 11*(4), 381–404.

Baron, R. M., & Fisher, J. D. (1984). The Equity-Control Model of Vandalism: A Refinement. In C. Levy-Leboyer (Ed.), *Vandalism: Behavior and Motivations* (pp. 63–76). Amsterdam, NY: North-Holland.

Bauman, Z. (2001). *The Individualized Society*. Cambridge: Polity Press.

Berggren, H., & Trägårdh, L. (2010). Pippi Longstocking: The Autonomous Child and the Moral Logic of the Swedish Welfare State. In H. Mattsson & S.-O. Wallenstein (Eds.), *Swedish Modernism: Architecture, Consumption and the Welfare State* (pp. 50–65). London: Black Dog Publishing.

Biggart, N. W., & Beamish, T. D. (2003). The Economic Sociology of Conventions: Habit, Custom, Practice, and Routine in Market Order. *Annual Review of Sociology, 29*, 443–464.

Corvellec, H., & Hultman, J. (2014). Managing the Politics of Value Propositions. *Marketing Theory, 14*(4), 355–375.

Cova, B. (2005). Thinking of Marketing in Meridian Terms. *Marketing Theory, 5*(2), 205–214.

Denegri-Knott, J., Nixon, E., & Abraham, K. (2018). Politicising the Study of Sustainable Living Practices. *Consumption, Markets & Culture, 21*(6), 554–573.

Draper, A., & Green, J. (2002). Food Safety and Consumers: Constructions of Choice and Risk. *Social Policy & Administration, 36*(6), 610–625.

Dwyer, L. (2018). Saluting While the Ship Sinks: The Necessity for Tourism Paradigm Change. *Journal of Sustainable Tourism, 26*(1), 29–48.

Eilertsen, H. (2016). *Lofoten's Big Headache – We Need to Take Control.* Retrieved from High North News: http://www.highnorthnews.com/lofotens-big-headache-we-need-to-take-control/.

Faber, R. J., Christenson, G. A., De Zwaan, M., & Mitchell, J. (1995). Two Forms of Compulsive Consumption: Comorbidity of Compulsive Buying and Binge Eating. *Journal of Consumer Research, 22*(3), 296–304.

Fisk, R., Grove, S., Harris, L. C., Keeffe, D. A., Daunt, K. L., Russell-Bennett, R., et al. (2010). Customers Behaving Badly: A State of the Art Review, Research Agenda and Implications for Practitioners. *Journal of Services Marketing, 24*(6), 417–429.

Fullerton, R. A., & Punj, G. (1997). Can Consumer Misbehavior Be Controlled? A Critical Analysis of Two Major Control Techniques. *ACR North American Advances, 24*(1), 340–344.

Fullerton, R. A., & Punj, G. (1998). The Unintended Consequences of the Culture of Consumption: An Historical-Theoretical Analysis of Consumer Misbehavior. *Consumption, Markets and Culture, 1*(4), 393–423.

Fullerton, R. A., & Punj, G. (2004). Repercussions of Promoting an Ideology of Consumption: Consumer Misbehavior. *Journal of Business Research, 57*(11), 1239–1249.

Gherardi, S. (2006). *Organizational Knowledge: The Texture of Workplace Learning*. Oxford: Blackwell.

Giesler, M., & Veresiu, E. (2014). Creating the Responsible Consumer: Moralistic Governance Regimes and Consumer Subjectivity. *Journal of Consumer Research, 41*(3), 840–857.

Harvey, D. (2010). *The Enigma of Capital and the Crisis of Capitalism*. New York, NY: Oxford University Press.

Hirschman, E. C. (1992). The Consciousness of Addiction: Toward a General Theory of Compulsive Consumption. *Journal of Consumer Research, 19*(2), 155–179.

Katz, D. R. (1988). *The Big Store*. New York, NY: Penguin.

Kozinets, R. V. (2002). Can Consumers Escape the Market? Emancipatory Illuminations from Burning Man. *Journal of Consumer Research, 29*(1), 20–38.

Kvale, S., & Brinkmann, S. (2009). *Interviews: Learning the Craft of Qualitative Research Interviewing* (2nd ed.). Los Angeles: Sage.

Lash, S., & Urry, J. (1994). *Economies of Signs and Space*. London: Sage.

Lemke, T. (2001). 'The Birth of Bio-Politics': Michel Foucault's Lecture at the Collège de France on Neo-Liberal Governmentality. *Economy and Society, 30*(2), 190–207.

Lofoten Travel Guide. (2014).

Lundberg, U., & Åmark, K. (2001). Social Rights and Social Security: The Swedish Welfare State, 1900–2000. *Scandinavian Journal of Social History, 26*, 157–176.

Østergaard, P., Linnet, J. T., Andersen, L. P., Kjeldgaard, D., Bjerregaard, S., Weijo, H., et al. (2014). Nordic Consumer Culture: Context and Concept. In J. W. Schouten, D. M. Martin, & R. Belk (Eds.), *Consumer Culture Theory, Research in Consumer Behavior* (Vol. 16, pp. 245–257). Bingley: Emerald Group Publishing Limited.

Perkins, H. C., & Thorns, D. C. (2001). Gazing or Performing? Reflections on Urry's Tourist Gaze in the Context of Contemporary Experience in the Antipodes. *International Sociology, 16*(2), 185–204.

Ritzer, G. (1996). *The McDonaldization of Society: An Investigation into the Changing Character of Contemporary Social Life*. Thousand Oaks, CA: Pine Forge Press.

Shankar, A., Cherrier, H., & Canniford, R. (2006). Consumer Empowerment: A Foucauldian Interpretation. *European Journal of Marketing, 40*(9/10), 1013–1030.

Sharpe, E. K. (2005). Delivering Communitas: Wilderness Adventure and the Making of Community. *Journal of Leisure Research, 37*(3), 255–280.

Steen, T. (2017). *Strategiplan – Lofoten som reisemål 2017–2022 (Strategy Plan – Lofoten as Destination 2017–2022)*. Svolvær, Lofoten: Destination Lofoten and Lofoten Council.

Steiner, J. M., Hadden, S. C., & Herkomer, L. (1976). Price Tag Switching. In *Criminology Between the Rule of Law and the Outlaws* (pp. 173–185). Dordrecht, NL: Springer.

Sutherland, E. H. (1947). *Principles of Criminology*. Philadelphia, PA: Lippincott.

Trägårdh, L. (2010). Rethinking the Nordic Welfare State Through a Neo-Hegelian Theory of State and Civil Society. *Journal of Political Ideologies, 15*(3), 227–239.

Trägårdh, L., & Svedberg, L. (2013). The Iron Law of Rights: Citizenship and Individual Empowerment in Modern Sweden. In A. Evers & A.-M. Guillemard (Eds.), *Social Policy and Citizenship: The Changing Landscape* (pp. 222–256). Cary, NC: Oxford University Press.

Turner, V. W. (1969). *The Ritual Process: Structure and Antistructure*. Ithaca, NY: Cornell University Press.

Urry, J. (1990). *The Tourist Gaze. Leisure and Travel in Contemporary Societies*. London: Sage.

Urry, J. (2002). *The Tourist Gaze*. London: Sage.

Urry, J., & Larsen, J. (2011). *The Tourist Gaze 3.0* (3rd ed.). London: Sage.

Venugopal, R. (2015). Neoliberalism as Concept. *Economy and Society, 44*(2), 165–187.

von Werlhof, C. (2008). The Globalization of Neoliberalism, Its Consequences, and Some of Its Basic Alternatives. *Capitalism, Nature, Socialism, 19*(3), 94–117.

Wollebaek, D., Lundåsen, S. W., & Trägårdh, L. (2012). Three Forms of Interpersonal Trust: Evidence from Swedish Municipalities. *Scandinavian Political Studies, 35*(4), 319–346.

World Economic Forum, Davos. (2011). *Shared Norms for the New Reality: The Nordic Way*. Retrieved from https://www.globalutmaning.se/wp-content/uploads/sites/8/2011/01/Davos-The-nordic-way-final.pdf.

www.nrk.no/nordland, 2016/17.

Yagil, D. (2008). When the Customer Is Wrong: A Review of Research on Aggression and Sexual Harassment in Service Encounters. *Aggression and Violent Behavior, 13*(2), 141–152.

Yngfalk, C. (2015). Bio-Politicizing Consumption: Neo-Liberal Consumerism and Disembodiment in the Food Marketplace. *Consumption, Markets & Culture, 19*(3), 1–21.

5

Unacceptable Consumption: Conflicts of Refugee Consumption in a Nordic Welfare State

Maria Hokkinen

Globally, almost 66 million people have been forcibly displaced from their homes, over 22 million of them internationally (UNHCR 2017). Most of the world's refugee population lives in developing countries, but the prolonged conflicts in North Africa and the Middle East have escalated the refugee crisis in Europe too. In 2015, a record high number of asylum seekers and refugees arrived in the Nordic countries. The numbers of filed asylum applications varied by country: Sweden topped the list with 163,000 applications (Migrationsinfo 2016), whereas Finland received approximately 32,000 applications (Finnish Immigration Service 2016), Norway 31,000 (IMO Report for Norway 2017), and Denmark 21,000 (Library of Congress 2016). This movement changed the lives of those displaced as well as stirring unforeseen reactions from those born and raised in the Nordic countries. The newly arrived asylum seekers were not only receivers of different types of public services, but also active consumers whose presence in the marketplace was hard to ignore.

M. Hokkinen (✉)
Åbo Akademi University, Turku, Finland
e-mail: maria.hokkinen@abo.fi

S. Askegaard, J. Östberg (eds.), *Nordic Consumer Culture*,
https://doi.org/10.1007/978-3-030-04933-1_5

Most studies on multicultural consumers are focusing on immigrants who migrate for work, study, or family reasons, making their experience greatly different from that of refugees. The refugee experience can involve specific circumstances, such as changes in family setting caused by displacement, economic hardships, and trauma from past experiences in the home country or during the refugee journey (Kriechbaum-Vitellozzi and Kreuzbauer 2006). In addition, a loss of material possessions (Belk 1988) is often immanent, making it necessary to acquire a number of items when resettling in the new country. Simultaneously, refugees need to deal with the task of transforming their everyday life, navigating legal and societal complexities while being expected to actively learn a new language and integrate into a new culture. During this grand transformation phase, consumption is happening constantly. In other words, refugees as consumers and the implications of the refugee consumer status for relations to the locals still deserve more attention.

This chapter addresses a core dimension of the state–market nexus, certain consumers' legitimacy to consume, by looking into the reactions of the locals in a Nordic welfare state toward newly arrived Middle Eastern refugee consumers. In western societies, consumption is regarded as the norm; it is through consumption that people access a normal and happy life (Bauman 2007). The ways in which one is "allowed" to engage in this activity seem, however, to vary between different members of society. In Finland, some financial assistance is offered to applicants during the asylum process, and more so to those receiving a residence permit, enabling participation in the local consumer culture. The refugee crisis of 2015 showed that there are pre-conceived ideas of how refugees are supposed to consume. Their use of smartphones, the amount of money spent on the journey from the Middle East to northern Europe, as well as the mere appearance of the newly arrived asylum seekers stirred confused reactions in the media and public discussion (Pellander and Kotilainen 2017; O'Malley 2015).

I investigated what types of relational conflicts the introduction of refugee consumers into the Finnish socio-cultural environment stirred, and what these can reveal to us about the underlying values and attitudes toward consumption in a welfare state context. Based on a relational configuration analysis of indigenous responses to immigrant acculturation

(Luedicke 2015), this chapter explores the idea that the responses to refugee consumption stem from feelings of community erosion, challenged authority positions, expectations of equality matching, and micro–macro-level moral dilemmas. I argue that some of these relational tensions in the marketplace are emphasized in the Nordic welfare state context and with refugee consumers. In addition to the four conflicts identified by Luedicke (2015), I suggest a fifth dimension of mistrust in the fairness of the welfare system, which becomes evident in the Nordic setting.

This chapter also illustrates these phenomena by analyzing online discussion forum posts regarding refugee consumption in Finland in the aftermath of the 2015 peak year of refugee arrivals. The purpose of the examples from the online forums is not to provide a full-blown empirical analysis, but rather to illustrate my conceptual arguments regarding the position and legitimacy of certain consumers in the market by demonstrating these with excerpts. The study contributes to consumer acculturation research—specifically mutual acculturation literature—by deepening our understanding of the local community's reactions to new consumers on the market. I also suggest that the relational conflicts that emerged in the wake of the 2015 events in Finland have roots in the very foundations of the Nordic welfare model, as well as in the rising distrust in traditional state institutions.

First, a brief overview is provided of the existing acculturation literature, with a specific focus on inter-group relations in consumer settings. Second, the context that this conceptual framework is studied within is presented. Then, the empirical part follows with examples from online forums illustrating the conceptual arguments, followed by a discussion and implications for the current societal debate and future directions of research.

Theoretical Background

In the following, I aim to give a short overview of how consumer acculturation (Berry 1997; Askegaard et al. 2005; Luedicke 2011), in particular mutual acculturation (Bourhis et al. 1997) and ethnic conflicts in consumption settings (Luedicke 2015), is understood in the current literature. The subsequent analysis of the events following the 2015 refugee situation in Finland builds on the model by Luedicke (2015) about the conflicts between immigrant and indigenous consumers.

Acculturation and Consumption

When people are exposed to new cultures, for example when resettling in a new country, they undergo changes in self-identification. One of the classic models of this process is the acculturation taxonomy by Berry (1997). This psychological model is based on two dimensions: on the one hand, the individual's extent of identification with the culture of origin; and on the other hand, the desire to relate to the host culture. Because cultural differences and identity clashes often become visible in the marketplace, the acculturation of immigrants to the consumer culture of their new home countries attracted the interest of scholars early on. The early wave of consumer acculturation studies (Hirschman 1981; Reilly and Wallendorf 1987) explored the different acculturation outcomes and the extent of acculturation among immigrant consumers, laying the foundation for the systematic investigation of culturally specific aspects of consumer behavior. In older research, the acculturation process was seen as linear, moving gradually from identification with the culture of origin toward assimilation with the culture of the new home. More recently, the research focus has shifted from linear assimilation models toward *post-assimilationism* (Askegaard et al. 2005; Luedicke 2011). Assimilation, or gradual immersion into the host culture over time, is no longer taken for granted. Instead, myriad different identity outcomes and experiences have been identified, taking in consideration the contexts that shape acculturation processes (Peñaloza 1994; Peñaloza and Gilly 1999). Oswald (1999) studied Haitian immigrants in the USA, confirming that acculturation outcomes are not stable, but that consumers engage in "culture swapping" depending on the social context. Askegaard et al. (2005) added a third acculturative force to the mix: in addition to the culture of origin and the host culture, immigrants are also influenced by global consumer culture. An extensive body of literature about multicultural and immigrant-background consumers shows that people adapt and integrate to the consumer culture of their new country in different ways and at different paces (Peñaloza 1994; Luedicke 2011).

Mutual Acculturation

The underlying assumption of the early acculturation theories was the relative dominance of the local community (or "host culture") over immigrant groups. Immigrants were expected to adjust to the local customs and culture, often due to their minority position in the different domains of society (Bourhis et al. 1997). As a response to this, the model of interactive acculturation (IAM) was developed, aiming to consider both minority and host community acculturation in multicultural societies (Bourhis et al. 1997). This model takes into account the context in which the immigrant is acculturating and the expectations and responses of the receiving community regarding the acculturation process and identity outcomes. It is not always without conflicts that interactions and mutual acculturation between immigrants and locals play out. In the following, I provide a closer look at the possible relational conflicts between immigrants and locals in consumer settings, based on the relational configuration analysis developed by Luedicke (2015).

Mutual Acculturation on the Marketplace: Luedicke's Relational Configuration Analysis

Immigration requires the adaptation of existing social relations, cultural practices, and expectations by locals who have lived in the space before the immigrants' arrival, Luedicke (2015) points out. His study is set in a rural Austrian village and looks at the relationships between indigenes and Turkish immigrants through the lens of relational models theory (Fiske 1991). Luedicke (2015) points out that human interactions are often structured by expectations and relational rules (Fiske 1991), but that the role of consumption in ethnic group relationships has so far not been sufficiently studied. He applies the Fiskenian relational model to a market where immigrant consumers are present, identifying four sources of ethnic group conflict in the multicultural consumption setting.

First, Luedicke found out that the indigenous felt an *erosion of their community* as the immigrant consumers drew closer to the indigenes. For example, the locals were reluctant to sell their property to Turkish immigrants and opposed to marketers adding Turkish labels to grocery products. The indigenous felt that their community was vulnerable to change, especially when the perceived sellout was done with profit in mind. Second, *authority ranking relationships* were shaken up due to certain consumption practices of the immigrants. As Luedicke (2015) remarks, the locals' position of authority in the "host country" has been taken for granted in most of the acculturation literature until now. In Luedicke's interviews, Turkish immigrants driving BMWs were causing the locals to feel that the immigrants outperformed them, and their hierarchical position was threatened. Ownership of luxury items positioned the immigrant consumers symbolically above the locals. Immigrant consumption practices that challenge the established consumer hierarchy were interpreted as an ethnic takeover or uninvited change in status recognition rules. Another source of conflict in the Austrian setting (Luedicke 2015) is the perceived *violation of equality matching rules*. The locals compared the immigrants' and the locals' economic and socio-cultural contributions to society, perceiving certain immigrant behaviors as unearned privileges. As Luedicke (2015) points out, people do not usually have exact data about others' contributions to society or the benefits that they receive. Lacking exact statistical information, people tend to rely on visual cues of what others are consuming in their assessments of wealth and societal contribution versus exploitation. The Austrian locals suspected the Turkish immigrants of system abuse by, for example, adopting children in hopes of getting higher child-care benefits. Immigrants' ownership of higher-end cars spurred suspicions of exploitation of the Austrian system. The fourth and last ethnic group conflict identified in the Austrian-Turkish setting is called the *micro–macro moral dilemma*. The indigenous adhere to macro-level norms of equality, solidarity, and mutual respect amongst all members of the society. Simultaneously, however, the indigenous treat Turkish immigrants in their village as outsiders and fail to regard them as equal consumers and community members.

There seems to be a problem of transferring the high norms of equality and respect to everyday practice in the own local community.

Perceptions of Refugees

Luedicke's (2015) model of indigenes' responses to immigrant consumer acculturation excels at highlighting sources of ethnic group conflict in a multicultural marketplace. However, in a setting where the immigrants have a refugee background, some of the relational conflicts mapped out by Luedicke (2015) are likely to play out differently.

Before going forward and discussing the relational conflicts in markets receiving refugee consumers, it is necessary to clarify what is meant here by the term "refugee." The United Nations 1951 Refugee Convention (UNHCR 2010) defines a refugee as a person who flees their country in fear of political or other forms of persecution. The definition is declaratory, meaning that a person should be regarded as a refugee until their case has been determined (UNHCR 2018). However, many people who leave their countries through fear of violence and persecution have neither a determined status as refugees nor the authorization or documents to cross borders. Instead, the transit is often taken irregularly (IOM 2011) and with the help of smugglers and dangerous vessels. In 2015, over one million people arrived in Europe by irregular means, many across the Mediterranean sea, and almost 4000 are believed to have drowned (UNHCR 2015). In the European Union, the newly arrived refugees are usually called asylum seekers. The Refugee Council (2018) defines an asylum seeker as follows: "A person who has left their country of origin and formally applied for asylum in another country but whose application has not yet been concluded." This chapter deals with the refugee situation of 2015 in Finland, thus focusing mainly on the people who applied for asylum after their arrival in the country. However, for the sake of simplicity and out of respect to the declaratory definition of the UN, the term "refugee" is used in this chapter to denote both those whose asylum application is still being processed and those whose refugee status is already determined.

Apart from formal definitions, people tend to have their own preconceived ideas of who qualifies as a refugee and how a "real" refugee is supposed to be (Malkki 1996; Gibney 1999; Wright 2002; Haynes et al. 2004). Many of the presumptions of how refugees should look, behave, and consume seem to come from media representations of former refugee crises, more often than not distant in either time or space. According to Wright (2002), there are common elements in the portrayal of refugees in the media. The images serve to elicit the proper emotional reaction among viewers and to determine how we see refugees. For example, a typical image portrays people in a state of degradation, naked and stripped of their possessions (Wright 2002). When researching Hutu refugees in Tanzania, Malkki (1996) found that refugee administrators on site were prone to define "real" refugees based on their looks—reversely excluding certain people from the refugee category and assistance because they did not look or behave in a certain way. People who had freshly arrived and looked at their worst were deemed to be worthier of help than those whose visible signs of being a refugee had faded (Malkki 1996). The world's largest refugee populations live in Africa, the Middle East, and North Africa (UNHCR 2017). From the Nordic point of view, these locations may seem distant and unfamiliar. Gibney (1999) argues that people are more sympathetic to refugees whom they can relate to, and who come from geographically close locations. Media reporting, especially negative discourses, deepens the gap between local population and refugees and can heighten the sense of "us" and "them," treating refugees as the others (Haynes et al. 2004). For instance, metaphors of threat and natural disasters when reporting about refugee "floods," as well as the political discourse of a zero-sum game with refugees causing a financial burden to society (Grove and Zwi 2006), serve to deepen the gap between refugees and the local population.

Considering how refugees are presented and perceived in society, the relational conflicts are likely to evolve differently when the Luedickean model is applied to a setting with refugee consumers. For example, the natural disaster discourses in the media serve to heighten the worries of ethnic takeover and erosion of the local community. Moreover, when the receiving society is dominated by a strong, universalist social welfare system, the suspicions of benefit abuse and violations of equality matching are likely to intensify. I will now proceed to an analysis of how these dynamics unfolded in the context of the Finnish refugee situation in 2015.

Research Context and Method

When the refugee arrivals in Finland were at their peak in 2015, the situation was discussed in a lively way both online and offline. Politicians, the Finnish Immigration Service, grass-roots organizations, as well as the public were all involved in uttering their opinions, and the differing voices sometimes took an aggressive tone. In this chapter, I have chosen to analyze some of the local population's opinions of the refugee situation. The aim is not to provide a full empirical review of the sentiment toward refugee consumers in Finland, but rather to illustrate with examples how the relational conflict model by Luedicke (2015) played out in a specific setting. Before presenting excerpts from online forums where locals discuss the newly arrived refugee consumers, I will set the theoretical concepts in their context by briefly presenting the ideological foundations of the Finnish welfare state and the societal responses to the 2015 refugee crisis.

Foundations of the Nordic Welfare State

The term "welfare state" has been used since the 1930s, but still lacks one unified definition (Greve 2007). As Kananen (2016) points out, the Nordic welfare states, unlike their counterparts in continental Europe and the UK, developed in countries without a history of a totalitarian political regime or a strong class hierarchy. The Nordic model is characterized by universalism (rather than means-tested support targeted only at the poor), a high level of taxes, and low levels of wage differentiation (Greve 2007). Welfare states enjoy significant support from people. Bowles and Gintis (2000) claim that this support for redistributive policies comes not from seeking self-interest (as would be the case according to traditional theories of the selfish *homo economicus*), but rather from deeply held values of reciprocity and obligations to others. Interestingly, Bowles and Gintis also (2000) theorize that the support for egalitarian policies may lessen if there is a perceived social distance between the giver and the recipient. Economic inequality and racial and language differences would lead, Bowles and Gintis (2000) argue, to decreased motivation to help those in need. According to Barker (2017), the Nordic welfare states, although universalistic, do not always extend their humanitarian principles to outsiders and others. The ideology of the Nordic welfare states is based on ideas of all humans' worth of economic and social investments, but there has been a rising cynical view about income support recipients. Especially newer legislation in Finland seems to be occupied with avoiding benefit abuse and strengthening sanctions in case of non-compliance with rules (Kananen 2016). There seems to be an increasing conditionality regarding who is eligible for the benefits of the welfare state.

Nordic Responses to the 2015 Refugee Situation

All Nordic countries, except Iceland, were the top receivers of refugees in Europe in relation to their population (Etzold 2017). In the wake of the 2015 events, the Nordic countries seemed to keep a close eye on what their neighbors were doing and proposed stricter asylum laws one after another. Many of the legislative changes attempted to make these countries less attractive destinations in the eyes of potential refugees. The governments were quick to tighten their asylum politics and border controls were even implemented, a measure unheard of in the post-war Nordics that had been characterized by free movement since the 1950s. As Barker (2017) argues, the strict response was not only due to a claimed reception "system overload," but also stemmed from the need of the welfare state to preserve security for those on the inside (at the cost of causing insecurity for the "outsiders"). The Nordic welfare states thus had a conflict in upholding their humanitarian values and respecting the human rights of the refugees, while attempting to protect the national welfare state project (Barker 2017).

The 2015 Refugee Situation in Finland

In 2015, 32,476 asylum applications were filed in Finland, which was nearly tenfold the number in previous years (Finnish Immigration Service 2016). Most of the applicants, approximately 63%, came from Iraq. In addition to Iraq, typical countries of origin were Afghanistan (16%), Somalia (6%), and Syria (3%). The sudden increase in applications quickly overwhelmed the Finnish Immigration Service, responsible for processing asylum applications. Reception centers for housing asylum seekers were established around the country (their number increased from 20 to 140 in 2015), and during the busiest times people were housed in temporary facilities and even tents outside (Rautio and Juutilainen 2016). After the peak in autumn 2015, the arrival numbers started to decrease. European countries put up barriers and controls on their borders, thus stalling the northward movement.

Yet, tens of thousands of people remained in Finland waiting for their asylum decisions. During the asylum-seeking process, the seeker is not covered by the Finnish social security system. Instead, financial assistance is paid in the form of a reception allowance. This money is meant to cover necessities during the asylum process and is paid by the state of Finland. The reception allowance (Finnish Immigration Service 2018) for a single adult is €263.78 per month, or €75.36 per month if the asylum seeker lives in a reception facility where meal services are included. If the asylum seeker is granted international protection in Finland, they are covered by the same public social and health services as other inhabitants of the municipality (Ministry of Social Affairs and Health 2017). If the immigrant is registered unemployed and/or receiving financial support, an integration plan is drawn up by the municipal employment office and the immigrant (Act on the Promotion of Immigrant Integration, 1386/2010). The immigrant receives financial support while following the plan. The daily unemployment benefit for a single household is €32.40 per day for five days a week (KELA 2018). If the immigrant fails to participate in the integration measures defined in the plan, they lose the right to financial assistance (Act on the Promotion of Immigrant Integration, 1386/2010). In addition to this, the individual is typically eligible for social welfare benefits, such as housing allowance and income support from the local municipality to cover necessities. As these excerpts from the legislation show, the newcomers have the financial means to participate in the local consumption culture, with at least some degree of freedom in their consumption choices.

Data

The examples of online discussions regarding refugee consumption are taken from two Finnish discussion forums, Suomi24 and Hommaforum. Suomi24 is one of the biggest social media outlets in Finland, with around 20,000 new discussion entries about a range of topics published each week. Hommaforum, in turn, is a discussion forum solely focused on immigration-critical discussions. The data was collected by performing a search with Finnish keywords relating to refugees and consumption on the forums. The resulting discussion threads were sorted for relevance and thereafter 14 of them were chosen for closer scrutiny. The opinions expressed on these forums cannot be treated as representative of the whole population. However, they are efficient in painting a picture of the opinions of people who experience conflicts regarding refugee consumer behavior.

Data Analysis

The naturally occurring and unfiltered online data from the discussion forums was first coded manually using keywords and then categorized according to topics, following the four conflict types outlined by Luedicke (2015). Then, a thematic analysis (Aronson 1995) was performed, forming a picture of the discussion forum participants' opinions. The data analysis revealed critical sentiments toward refugees, mostly backed up by rumors or forum participants' firsthand experiences in consumption spaces or social welfare offices. Some also used official reports and statistics (e.g., of social welfare use by nationality) to justify their opinions.

Jealousy, distrust, and fear were recurring emotions in the entries, along with aggression.

The knowledge accrued from the discussion threads was applied to Luedicke's (2015) model of four sources of ethnic conflict, to study the relational conflicts experienced by the locals on the introduction of refugees to their familiar consumption spaces. When looking into the forum discussions, a fifth dimension, specific to the welfare state context, arose. I call this mistrust in the welfare system and discuss it after Luedicke's four conflict types.

Results

In the following, I will illustrate with the help of excerpts from online forum discussions how some of the conflicts identified by Luedicke (2015) were shaped in the Finnish context in 2015. I build on Luedicke's model and provide an additional perspective, a fifth conflict, to the existing theory.

Community Sellout

In 2015, centers for housing the newly arrived refugees were established throughout the country at a high pace. The centers brought the refugees, until then for many Finns known only from newspaper headlines, close to the home sphere. This spurred a discussion of community sellout. The main fear connected to the reception centers seemed to be similar to that observed by Luedicke (2015): the worry of cultural erosion. In addition, the economic aspects of receiving the refugees to the local community were treated negatively. Pseudonym "Kellere" writes in August 2015: "This is the last drop for our town, nothing can save it anymore." The author continues to lament how the town, seemingly struggling with financial scarcity, will now experience a drop in property values and an increase in crime. The sentiment reminds you of a "NIMBY" (not in my backyard) phenomenon (defined by the Merriam Webster dictionary (2018) as opposition to something considered undesirable in one's neighborhood) backed up by economic arguments, fear of crime, and general unwillingness to face the refugees in your community. Similar to Luedicke's findings, the indigenous community was aggravated by the idea of having to live close to the newcomers. The conflict was heightened by the notion of economic profit being made from the "reception center business," in towns and communities otherwise deemed to be struggling with economic hardships.

Challenged Authority Ranking Positions

In the Nordic welfare state context, as elsewhere, the authority position of locals seems to be uncontested compared to immigrants. The perceived conspicuous consumption of refugees is met on online discussion forums with aversion. Because the consumers in this setting are refugees, their consumption—especially if it is considered to consist of valuable items—is interpreted as proof that they are not really in need of international protection. The online forum participants express anger and envy toward the possessions of refugees, revealing a mismatch in their expectations of how a refugee should look like and behave. Small details in appearance, such as hairstyles, trigger resentment in locals, according to them proving that the young people with "gel in the hair" are not in need of asylum or humanitarian assistance, but in fact criminals. "You can see from a kilometer's distance that the crimi … poor gel-children hanging out in town are not here to respect or thank the local society. They are here to take it over" (pseudonym "Foobar," January 2018). As this comment shows, a fear of ethnic takeover by refugees is present, similar to Luedicke's findings. The pseudonym "ChewBacca," in turn, offers observations on the appearance of refugee youth on the forum in November 2015. The forum author notes that the refugees are using phones and headphones actively, and their school bags and clothes seem to be new from the store. "ChewBacca" also mentions that the charities were "begging" for donations for the refugees, implying that the brand new supplies might be handouts instead of purchases. As these forum posts signal, the possessions, purchases, and even donations used by the refugees triggered envious comments. As also noted by Luedicke, the locals try to regain their authority status in the market by claiming that the immigrant consumers did not earn their luxury goods themselves. In the context of Finland in 2015, the newcomers failed to adhere to the local population's expectations of how "real refugees" should look like. With their groomed appearance and unused school supplies, the refugees seemed to occupy a position in society not reserved for them.

Violation of Equality Matching

In the Finnish welfare state setting, the suspicions of benefit abuse and unearned privileges enjoyed by the refugees are a recurring theme in online discussions and political debates alike. Especially in the aftermath of 2015, accusations proliferated of people using false grounds for asylum with the sole purpose of accessing the welfare benefits in Finland. The Finnish government was planning major changes to the law regulating social security, with the aim to cut the welfare benefits for refugees for the first years after receiving asylum (Koivuranta 2015). However, the plan was found to be unconstitutional and later canceled (Kaija 2016). In Luedicke's context, the Austrian villagers used visible consumption as a cue to assess the Turkish immigrants' societal contribution versus exploitation. In the Finnish context, immigrant-looking people are grouped as refugees and their mere visit to Kela, the social insurance institution of Finland, is used as a proxy to confirm their violation of the equality matching principles. For example, pseudonym "Dvitamiini" writes in November 2017 that on visiting the social welfare office, most of the clients seem to be "refugees from Middle East or Africa." "Dvitamiini" continues to suspect that they are unwilling to work and instead cheat the welfare system, while harming those who are in real need of assistance. On the discussion forums, the argument was not only that refugees had not contributed enough to society to earn the social welfare benefits, but also more deep-rooted sentiments of inherited right to the social welfare system of the native country. "We should not offer foreigners the same and especially not better benefits than for Finns, because Finland is the country of the Finns and it should favor Finns in everything. It's not racism, it's our exclusive right" (September 2017, pseudonym "Kipusisko").

Unlike in the Austrian setting, where the claims of unearned privileges were only based on societal contribution versus exploitation, the Finnish discussion also brings up historical or inherited rights to the welfare benefits. The universalist principles of social welfare seem to not stretch to people who do not belong to the (here undefined) category of "Finns." Pseudonym "Kipusisko" continues their post by accusing immigrants of "reproducing uncontrollably," which in turn brings us back to the fears of ethnic takeover and outright racist sentiments.

Micro–Macro Moral Dilemma

In the Austrian village studied by Luedicke, locals and immigrants had lived side by side for decades. There were incidents of discrimination on the local micro level, while higher moral norms of every person's equality were adhered to on a macro level. In the situation of Finland in 2015, however, the refugees (in larger numbers) had recently arrived, and those locals who were not involved in voluntary efforts to help the refugees were likely to have had very few personal contacts with them. Instead, they appeared to be a faceless mass whose "flooding" into Finland should be stopped by any means possible, regardless of moral norms or international agreements. Pseudonym "Atte Saarela," writing in October 2015, summarizes these sentiments by suggesting that the immigrants be provided with low-quality food and housing in order to give a signal that they are not welcome in Finland. The political left and its human rights campaigns are met with repulsion. Unlike in Austria, in the context of Finland an adherence to high moral norms is not visible. Instead, the forum members seem to dwell on fantasies of cutting the existing social welfare benefits, while ridiculing international law and human rights. A moral dilemma between high norms and what is practiced locally is less obvious than in Luedicke's material.

Mistrust in the Righteousness of the Welfare System

When going through the discussion forum posts regarding these themes, an additional topic, not present in Luedicke's material, emerged: namely, many people were blaming the Finnish welfare system for "allowing" benefit abuse and handing out gratuitous support. The tangible aggression toward refugees was partly shifted toward the government and the social welfare institutions for allegedly favoring refugees and immigrants over the local population. New terms, such as the "magic wall" (referring to automated teller machines or ATMs), were invented to ridicule the refugee's right to monetary benefits. For instance, pseudonym "Kela_Platinum" claims in November 2015 that money is handed out to refugees while they are just slacking off. Interestingly, the author shifts the blame to the very foundations of the Finnish welfare system: "We can only blame our own stupidity, for having this utterly insane system, where all people of the world can be paid money without doing anything in return." As the post illustrates, the frustration is triggered by the refugees, but reveals an underlying discontent with the welfare system. In addition, many online discussion participants seemed to have a misconception about how benefits are distributed, claiming the existence of gratuitous benefits paid to everyone without any activity in return. Some authors seemed to exhibit a degree of sympathy mixed with irony, declaring that they would do the same if they were in a similar situation: "I'm not that good of a person that I would abstain from the free health care, education, apartment and disco money, if they were offered it to me on a golden platter" (pseudonym "Histon," January 2018). The refugees were also suspected of coming to a welfare state only to enjoy its benefits. The "disco money" was a recurring topic in the forums, referring to the forum participants' sightings of young refugee-looking youths spending free time in bars and cafés. Apart from this consumption practice, deemed unfit for refugees, health care and education were also considered unjustified for refugees.

Discussion and Conclusions

In this chapter, I have described the refugee situation that occurred in Finland in 2015, focusing on the relational conflicts that were triggered by refugee consumer behavior in the Finnish welfare state context. The examples from online forums illustrate how the Luedickean (2015) ethnic consumer conflicts played out in the aftermath of the 2015 refugee situation in the Finnish welfare state context.

In the Finnish context, where refugees had recently arrived in larger numbers and where the local social welfare system covers refugees and locals alike, some of the relational conflicts played out differently from Luedicke's theory. The sellout of the community also worried the Finnish locals, and the towns and nob-governmental organizations (NGOs) were accused of embracing the newcomers despite economic scarcity in the community. The authority ranking relationships were shaken when the refugees' appearance and possessions did not match the expected image of the "good refugee," spurring accusations of refugees not being in need of assistance. The third conflict, violation of equality matching, revealed underlying nationalistic attitudes, striving for a social welfare system only available to Finns themselves. Refugees' mere visits to the social welfare office were interpreted as benefit abuse. A micro–macro moral dilemma was not as obvious as the other three conflicts; instead, the discussion entries on the forums were preoccupied with ideas of closing the borders and cutting all of the benefits from non-indigenous people. The fifth and additional relational conflict deals with the mistrust expressed by the locals toward the social welfare system. Instead of merely blaming refugees for benefit abuse, the debaters shift their aggression toward a system that allegedly allows this. This is a novel finding that expands on the analysis presented by Luedicke.

These conflicts have roots in the very foundations of the Nordic welfare model. In societies with a strong welfare system, people tend to support the egalitarian system. However, if the social distance to the benefit recipients is large, the willingness to support tends to be lower (Bowles and Gintis 2000). In the case of refugee consumers, the benefit recipients are culturally distant and unfamiliar and thus treated as second-class citizens by many of the opinionated online forum participants. The 2015 refugee situation in northern Europe also challenged the pre-conceived image of the accepted appearance of a refugee—as a hungry, battered person in a distant location. Suddenly, the young, healthy-looking men with their neatly cut hairstyles, trendy clothes, and using their iPhones like any other twenty-something came to towns and villages in Finland. This triggered aggression and fear along with accusations of benefit abuse.

We do not know who the people in the forums discussing under the cover of pseudonyms are, and we lack information on their socio-economic situation and possible patronage of the social welfare institution. The frustration of the locals in the discussion forums seems to be propelled by a feeling of unequal treatment by the welfare system. This could indicate that the harsh attitudes toward benefit use by the refugees stem from people who themselves need to rely on the social welfare system for support. The style of writing differs by author, but for most debaters logical (however racist) reasoning and spelling seem not to be a problem, indicating that they are somewhat educated. An interesting direction for future research would be to contact some of the discussion forum participants (e.g., through private message on the forum) and interview them to get richer data on their backgrounds and attitudes.

The choice of discussion forums to be analyzed naturally affects the outcome: the people engaging in anti-immigration discussions online can be assumed to represent the most critical group in society, not suffering from moral dilemmas despite harsh words and ridicule of human rights. It is also theorized that people tend to be more aggressive online, behind pseudonyms, than in their face-to-face encounters with people (Suler 2004). These extreme examples serve a purpose of exemplifying underlying sentiments toward refugee consumers and help conceptualize the new situation in society. It would be interesting to explore whether and how the attitudes toward refugee consumption are different at the other end of the "opinion spectrum," namely among those locals who engaged in helping the refugees. In order to deepen our understanding of the prerequisites of consumption, it would also be interesting to extend the empirical material from refugees to other groups using the social welfare system, whose social distance to the locals is smaller (such as students and stay-at-home parents).

The analyzed material shows that the Finnish government and social insurance institution have failed in informing people about how the welfare system works. Despite the repeated efforts of official institutions to inform the public of the same levels for benefits for everyone, regardless of ethnic background, the Finnish discussion forum activists keep repeating the claims of gratuitous benefits and higher amounts of money being paid to refugees. The rumors of a social welfare system that unfairly benefits immigrants lack factual ground, but seem to feed each other and slowly emerge as "facts." The aversion is targeted toward both the social welfare system and the foreign-born individuals using it. The emergence of so-called alternative media and the increasing distrust in traditional news outlets and governmental institutions are partly responsible for heightening the spread of false information. In addition to mere misconception or ignorance, there are actors who purposefully spread false information in order to benefit their own political agenda. This type of propaganda is a feature of the post-truth society, where opinions are no longer based on tested facts but rather on personal beliefs and feelings. Media and political crisis discourse, emphasizing economic scarcity and the inability of the Finnish economy to support its own population, let alone the "floods of refugees," also plays a role in heightening the conflicts. Inequality and the feeling of being left out when social welfare benefits are distributed are bigger societal issues that mere information campaigns cannot solve.

References

Act on the Promotion of Immigrant Integration 1386/2010. Retrieved May 15, 2017, from http://www.finlex.fi/fi/laki/kaannokset/2010/en20101386.pdf.

Aronson, J. (1995). A Pragmatic View of Thematic Analysis. *The Qualitative Report, 2*(1), 1–3.

Askegaard, S., Arnould, E. J., & Kjeldgaard, D. (2005). Postassimilationist Ethnic Consumer Research: Qualifications and Extensions. *Journal of Consumer Research, 32*(1), 160–170.

Barker, V. (2017). *Nordic Nationalism and Penal Order: Walling the Welfare State.* Routledge.

Bauman, Z. (2007). *Consuming Life*. Cambridge: Polity.

Belk, R. W. (1988). Possessions and the Extended Self. *Journal of Consumer Research, 15*(2), 139–168.

Berry, J. W. (1997). Immigration, Acculturation, and Adaptation. *Applied Psychology, 46*(1), 5–34.

Bourhis, R. Y., Moise, L. C., Perreault, S., & Senecal, S. (1997). Towards an Interactive Acculturation Model: A Social Psychological Approach. *International Journal of Psychology, 32*(6), 369–386.

Bowles, S., & Gintis, H. (2000). Reciprocity, Self-Interest, and the Welfare State. *Nordic Journal of Political Economy, 26*(1), 33–53.

Etzold, T. (2017). *Refugee Policy in Northern Europe: Nordic Countries Grow Closer But Differences Remain*. Retrieved May 25, 2018, from https://www.swp-berlin.org/fileadmin/contents/products/comments/2017C01_etz.pdf.

Finnish Immigration Service. (2016). *Vuonna 2015 myönnettiin hieman yli 20 000 oleskelulupaa, uusia Suomen kansalaisia reilut 8000*. Retrieved July 11, 2018, from https://migri.fi/artikkeli/-/asset_publisher/vuonna-2015-myonnettiin-hieman-yli-20-000-oleskelulupaa-uusia-suomen-kansalaisia-reilut-8-000.

Finnish Immigration Service. (2018). *Reception Allowance*. Retrieved March 12, 2018, from http://migri.fi/en/reception-allowance.

Fiske, A. P. (1991). *Structures of Social Life: The Four Elementary Forms of Human Relations: Communal Sharing, Authority Ranking, Equality Matching, Market Pricing*. New York: Free Press.

Gibney, M. J. (1999). Kosovo and Beyond: Popular and Unpopular Refugees. *Forced Migration Review, 5*, 28–30.

Greve, B. (2007). What Characterise the Nordic Welfare State Model. *Journal of Social Sciences, 3*(2), 43–51.

Grove, N. J., & Zwi, A. B. (2006). Our Health and Theirs: Forced Migration, Othering, and Public Health. *Social Science & Medicine, 62*(8), 1931–1942.

Haynes, A., Devereux, E., & Breen, M. J. (2004). *A Cosy Consensus on Deviant Discourse: How the Refugee and Asylum Seeker Meta-Narrative Has Endorsed an Interpretive Crisis in Relation to the Transnational Politics of World's Displaced Persons*. Limerick: University of Limerick, Mary Immaculate College.

Hirschman, E. C. (1981). American Jewish Ethnicity: Its Relationship to Some Selected Aspects of Consumer Behavior. *The Journal of Marketing, 45*, 102–110.

IMO Report for Norway. (2017). *Immigration and Immigrants 2015–2016*. Retrieved May 25, 2018, from https://www.regjeringen.no/contentassets/5a

8e49d721ad456ea8bd698ea2d543ef/immigration-and-immigrants-20152016-complete.pdf.

IOM. (2011). *Key Migration Terms*. Retrieved March 27, 2018, from https://www.iom.int/key-migration-terms.

Kaija, J. (2016, November 24). Hallitus perui maahanmuuttajien sosiaaliturvan rajaamisen. *MTV Uutiset*. Retrieved July 9, 2018, from https://www.mtv.fi/uutiset/kotimaa/artikkeli/hallitus-perui-maahanmuuttajien-sosiaaliturvan-rajaamisen/6184180#gs.EBp5FZU.

Kananen, J. (2016). *The Nordic Welfare State in Three Eras: From Emancipation to Discipline*. Routledge.

KELA. (2018). *Amount of the Unemployment Benefit*. Retrieved July 11, 2018, from https://www.kela.fi/web/en/amount-of-the-unemployment-benefit.

Koivuranta, E. (2015, September 21). Ministeri Mäntylä sosiaaliturvan heikennyksistä: Vaikeiden tilanteiden edessä. *YLE Uutiset*. Retrieved July 9, 2018, from https://yle.fi/uutiset/3-8299513.

Kriechbaum-Vitellozzi, E., & Kreuzbauer, R. (2006). Poverty Consumption: Consumer Behaviour of Refugees in Industrialized Countries. *NA-Advances in Consumer Research, 33*, 435–444.

Library of Congress. (2016). *Refugee Law and Policy: Denmark*. Retrieved May 24, 2018, from https://www.loc.gov/law/help/refugee-law/denmark.php.

Luedicke, M. K. (2011). Consumer Acculturation Theory: (Crossing) Conceptual Boundaries. *Consumption Markets & Culture, 14*(3), 223–244.

Luedicke, M. K. (2015). Indigenes' Responses to Immigrants' Consumer Acculturation: A Relational Configuration Analysis. *Journal of Consumer Research, 42*(1), 109–129.

Malkki, L. H. (1996). Speechless Emissaries: Refugees, Humanitarianism, and Dehistoricization. *Cultural Anthropology, 11*(3), 377–404.

Migrationsinfo. (2016). *Hur många i Sverige är födda i ett annat land?* Retrieved from http://www.migrationsinfo.se/fragor-och-svar/hur-manga-utrikes-fodda-sverige/.

Ministry of Social Affairs and Health. (2017). *Social Security and Services of Asylum Seekers in Finland*. Retrieved November 20, 2017, from http://stm.fi/en/social-security-and-services-of-asylum-seekers-in-finland.

NIMBY. 2018. *Merriam-Webster.com*. Retrieved July 10, 2018, from https://www.merriam-webster.com/dictionary/NIMBY.

O'Malley. (2015, September 7). Surprised that Syrian Refugees Have Smartphones? Sorry to Break This to You, But You're an Idiot. *Independent*. Retrieved May 20, 2018, from https://www.independent.co.uk/voices/comment/surprised-that-syrian-refugees-have-smartphones-well-sorry-to-break-this-to-you-but-youre-an-idiot-10489719.html.

Oswald, L. R. (1999). Culture Swapping: Consumption and the Ethnogenesis of Middle-Class Haitian Immigrants. *Journal of Consumer Research, 25*(4), 303–318.

Pellander, S. & Kotilainen, N. (2017). *(Not) Looking Like a Refugee: Visual Memories of Refugeeness and the Figure of 'The iPhone Man'.* Retrieved May 20, 2018, from https://www.law.ox.ac.uk/research-subject-groups/centre-criminology/centreborder-criminologies/blog/2017/06/not-looking.

Peñaloza, L. (1994). Atravesando Fronteras/Border Crossings: A Critical Ethnographic Exploration of the Consumer Acculturation of Mexican Immigrants. *Journal of Consumer Research, 21*(1), 32–54.

Peñaloza, L., & Gilly, M. C. (1999). Marketer Acculturation: The Changer and the Changed. *The Journal of Marketing, 63*, 84–104.

Rautio, M. & Juutilainen, V. (2016, January 16). Näin Suomi muuttui – katso miten turvapaikkakriisi eteni ja näkyi vuonna 2015. *YLE News*. Retrieved June 29, 2018, from https://yle.fi/uutiset/3-8595369.

Refugee Council. (2018). *The Truth About Asylum: Who Is Who*. Retrieved from https://www.refugeecouncil.org.uk/policy_research/the_truth_about_asylum/the_facts_about_asylum.

Reilly, M. D., & Wallendorf, M. (1987). A Comparison of Group Differences in Food Consumption Using Household Refuse. *Journal of Consumer Research, 14*(2), 289–294.

Suler, J. (2004). The Online Disinhibition Effect. *Cyberpsychology & Behavior, 7*(3), 321–326.

UNHCR. (2010). *Convention and Protocol Relating to the Status of Refugees.* Retrieved March 20, 2018, from http://www.unhcr.org/3b66c2aa10.

UNHCR. (2015). *Over One Million Sea Arrivals Reach Europe in 2015.* Retrieved March 27, 2018, from http://www.unhcr.org/afr/news/latest/2015/12/5683d0b56/million-sea-arrivals-reach-europe-2015.html.

UNHCR. (2017). *Figures at a Glance.* Retrieved February 8, 2018, from http://www.unhcr.org/figures-at-a-glance.html.

UNHCR. (2018). *Emergency Handbook.* Retrieved March 20, 2018, from https://emergency.unhcr.org/entry/95331/refugee-definition.

Wright, T. (2002). Moving Images: The Media Representation of Refugees. *Visual Studies, 17*(1), 53–66.

6

Swedish Dads as a National Treasure: Consumer Culture at the Nexus of the State, Commerce, and Consumers

Susanna Molander, Jacob Östberg, and Ingeborg Astrid Kleppe

AC/DC roars out of the speakers in the crowded basement where two men are standing talking amongst dumbbells, barbells, boxing gloves and sweating bodies. One of them has a beard and a tight black t-shirt under which his powerful tattooed biceps can be discerned, the other one is beardless, with thinner arms and a somewhat looser black t-shirt. This is the personal trainer and his client who during the workout are discussing putting babies to sleep. Their conversation slips over to the problems with feeding and, later elaborates on the client's

S. Molander (✉)
Centre for Arts, Business and Culture, The Stockholm School of Economics Institute for Research, Stockholm, Sweden

J. Östberg
Stockholm Business School, Stockholm University, Stockholm, Sweden
e-mail: jacob.ostberg@sbs.su.se

I. A. Kleppe
Norwegian School of Economics, Bergen, Norway
e-mail: Ingeborg.Kleppe@nhh.no

S. Askegaard, J. Östberg (eds.), *Nordic Consumer Culture*,
https://doi.org/10.1007/978-3-030-04933-1_6

body and his family's annoying disinterest in the fact that it is now beginning to take shape—two Swedish men and fathers talking about everyday life. (Field notes, Fall 2015)

This vignette depicts two men in a crowded gym, but it also invokes an image of the two men in their most private, at home nurturing their small children, feeding them or putting them to sleep. Furthermore, it invokes an image of when these two spheres clash, when one of the men describes how he is flexing his hard-earned muscles in front of the family without getting the desired attention, or perhaps without even being seen. We believe this vignette captures some of the tensions and negotiations that surface when something as archaically masculine as fatherhood goes through as quick and thoroughgoing a transformation as it has in Sweden over the last couple of decades. We use Sweden as an illustrative example throughout this chapter. All the Nordic countries have, by international standards, fairly progressive gender politics, but Sweden stands out in this regard with a pronounced gender equality agenda or state ideology that is sometimes described as state feminism, to depict the large partisan agreements of basic ideas related to political visions of gender equality. As a case in point, the "Swedish Gender Equality Agency" was inaugurated in January 2018 with the explicit goal for "women and men to have the same power to shape society and their own lives" (Jämställdhetsmyndigheten 2018). While these developments toward gender equality started on a grass-roots, activist, and not least political level spearheaded by the Swedish state, we increasingly see how consumer culture itself has come to play an important role in perpetuating a gender equality agenda, both by consumers who increasingly engage in market-mediated identity work to negotiate this new subject position, and by companies jumping on the bandwagon in order to be connected to a social movement surrounded by positive connotations. The case of fatherhood in Sweden is thus a good context for gaining an understanding of how consumer culture evolves at the nexus of the (welfare) state, individual consumers' lived lives, and companies' marketing activities. Fatherhood, however, needs to be explored within the context of family.

Fatherhood under State Feminism

Previous consumer cultural research on families has established a dynamic relationship between the family sphere and the market (e.g., Coskuner-Balli and Thompson 2013; Epp and Price 2008; Epp and Velagaleti 2014; Moisio et al. 2004; Wallendorf and Arnould 1991). This research, however, is mostly based on a North American context, and when applying these theories in contexts like the Nordic it becomes apparent that the understanding of the state and its influence on consumer culture in general and the family in particular is under-theorized. The state usually remains in the background as a legislator, either setting up absolute limits or giving incentives, while its ideology-producing function is still under-theorized. This is also true when it comes to how the state can engage in the market to resolve (or reproduce) gender injustices and family dynamics (Hein et al. 2016), including the role of the father.

The field of masculinity studies provides a few instances where state policies influence fatherhood ideals and practice on a more ideological level (Gregory and Milner 2011; Hobson and Morgan 2002) by helping "to shape practice in ways which tackle specific configurations of rights and responsibilities, for example, by changing assumptions about the gendered nature of care in legal systems, by modifying working time regimes, and by tailoring targeted rights to leave" (Gregory and Milner 2011, p. 601). From these studies we know that when the ideological stance of the state appears unclear, as it does in, for example, France and the UK (Gregory and Milner 2011), this is reflected in both public discourse and popular culture representations, which subsequently appear scattered—for example via the parallel existence of both traditional and new types of fatherhood in popular media (Gregory and Milner 2011). These indications that the ideology-producing function of the state does matter is an exception to the rule, however, as this role of state legislation and policy is mostly ignored.

As we shall see in what follows, however, Sweden provides ample examples of how a distinct state ideology of gender equality has influenced consumer culture evolving at the nexus of the (welfare) state, individual consumers' lived lives, and companies' marketing activities. When we talk about ideology here, we follow Eagleton (1991) in referring to the different ways in which a worldview, value, or belief system of a group of people is continuously created and recreated through various types of reproduction strategies. More to the point, we refer to how the state propagates various normative ideas aimed at promoting certain ways of life. The Swedish context enables theorizing of the state as an involved actor with the legitimacy to influence individual citizens' lives and consumption choices (Berggren and Trägårdh 2006; Brandt and Kvande 2013). In this context, state policies define the conditions under which individuals and families organize their lives concerning child care, participation in the labor force, and consumption of market offerings. One example of this is the generous parental leave allowances that enable parents to stay at home with their children up to the age of 18 months. This parental leave allowance is gender neutral, in the sense that out of these 18 months, 15 can be taken by either the mother or the father. Even if fathers still take far less parental leave than mothers, there is an increasing political and social pressure for fathers to spend time at home with their children as the primary caretaker (Plantin 2015).

While the peculiarities of parental leave allowances are unique to the particular empirical context of this study, we suggest that the state's ideological influence on market negotiations is worthy of systematic attention, even in other contexts where the ideological influence might be subtler. Drawing on insights from a prolonged theoretical and empirical interest in issues of Swedish fatherhood ideals, the aim of this chapter is to discuss this as an interplay between the state, commercial actors, and individual consumers' identity projects. We start by a brief historical exposé of the Swedish state's gender ideology-producing function promoting specific fatherhood ideals. We then continue with how individual male consumers relate to these fatherhood ideals in their identity work. Finally, we address the commercial realm by discussing the commercial concept of Scandinavian Man, whereby Nordic/Swedish masculinity is used as a platform for selling Nordic design and fashion around the world.

The Swedish State's Gender Ideology-Producing Function: Three Historical Touch Points

The Swedish welfare state is characterized by an ethos of individualism, with "the overarching ambition to liberate the individual citizen from all forms of subordination and dependency in civil society: the poor from charity, the workers from their employers, wives from their husbands, children from parents (and vice versa when the parents have become elderly)" (Berggren and Trägårdh 2010, p. 13). This ambition clearly differs from both its continental European counterparts and the USA. In the USA there is a general resistance toward state interventions when it comes to both the individual and the family, who instead cooperate to keep the state out. In Europe state interventions are much more accepted, but while the state sponsors the family rather than the individual in most of them, in Sweden the state and the individual ally themselves against the family (Berggren and Trägårdh 2010, p. 13). In Sweden the individual in focus is the child, whose ability to flourish must be independent of class or gender. For individualism to fully bloom, egalitarianism and gender equality are key and have therefore been institutionalized via various laws and policies, of which parental leave is an important part. A large body of masculinity research has already shown how Swedish fatherhood ideals via pointed political efforts have changed over time (see for example Klinth 2002; Johansson and Klinth 2008; Plantin 2003). Here we will present how Sweden's shifting gender ideology over the years influenced fatherhood ideals with the help of three iconic fatherhood images, of which two were used as promotional tools by the state.

The Distant Breadwinner in 1932

During the agrarian society that dominated until the industrial revolution when people increasingly started working for a salary, the family worked together as a production unit. The father was then an integral part of the children's everyday lives and functioned as a work introducer

(Plantin 2003). The completely opposite fatherhood ideal, the distant breadwinner, took over during industrialization at the turn of the twentieth century and culminated during the 1950s with increased prosperity and the ideal of the housewife. While the mother was associated with the intimate sphere and primary parenthood, the father was active in the public and served as a distant role model who only spent time with his children on Sundays (Plantin 2003). The Swedish artist Bror Hjorth's "The Family" from 1932 illustrates this situation (Fig. 6.1).

The painting was considered groundbreaking at the time, when the family was hardly a common motif for male artists, as it was considered too mundane and uninteresting (Axelsson 2015). Using his own family as the motif, the artist seems to ironize over himself as a father, but also over the father role in a broader sense. While the woman holds her hands protectively around the child and signals care, the man in the background does not seem to know where to put his hands and instead sucks frenetically on his cigar, whose smoke appears to frame the painting. Indeed, the artist mirrors a time when male breadwinning was seen as forming the necessary framework for caregiving, while male hands-on care was presented as awkward (Axelsson 2015). But this was also a time when

Fig. 6.1 Bror Hjorth's "Familjen" [The Family], 1932. Reprinted with permission from Eskilstuna Konstmuseum. Photo: Lars Wallin/Bror Hjorths Hus

more progressive thinking in terms of gender equality started to influence the political debates in Sweden. The Social Democratic government, which was in power for the majority of the twentieth century, had just started to take a progressive stand in favor of women by questioning the hegemony of the existing male breadwinner model and starting to work toward the idea of a two-provider family (Hagemann 2002, 423). The artist's ironic stance signals change.

The Caring Father in 1974

Another groundbreaking illustration of fatherhood was presented some 40 years later as part of the Swedish state's gender equality efforts, promoting paternity leave with help of the weight lifter Lennart "Hoa-Hoa" Dahlgren smilingly holding a cheeky baby in his arms (Fig. 6.2).

Fig. 6.2 Lennart "Hoa-Hoa" Dahlgren. Reprinted with permission. Photo: Reio Rüster/Försäkringskassan

Feminism and labor needs made this a time when men had to make room for women in the public sphere, and when greater demands were placed on men's commitment to and time spent with their children (Plantin 2003). From the 1970s onward, the state's widely supported gender equality ideology (Klinth 2002; Johansson and Klinth 2008) allowed each family to negotiate how to distribute the fairly extensive parental leave between the mother and the father. The goal was to accomplish a "double emancipation," ensuring men and women the same opportunities in both work and family life. And the one who came to symbolize these efforts more than anyone else was Hoa-Hoa. The fact that the initiative was quite original globally and surrounded by national pride is hard to miss when studying Hoa-Hoa's T-shirt with the Swedish colors and Sweden's heraldic national symbol, the three crowns.

The image highlights a completely different type of father than Bror Hjorth's, namely one who knows how to care and who seemingly has a very close relationship with his child. This is accentuated by the absence of the mother in the picture. However, the image also demonstrates a man who does not compromise with his masculinity. Rather the opposite—the little baby makes the muscles beneath the tight T-shirt even more impressive. Hoa-Hoa's care for the baby seems effortless, and the image thereby also communicates that this effortlessness is something that should characterize men's commitment to child care overall. It expresses a type of commitment that allows the father to keep the right to choose when and how to care, although leaving the basic responsibility to the mother, not least when things get rough. While the image thus reflects a caring father, we also suggest that it reflects a typical case of what Aarseth (2013) calls "child oriented masculinity." This depicts instances when children become incorporated into their fathers' self-fulfillment projects rather than the fathers attending to the children's needs. The child emerges like a prop used to enhance the father's masculine features, rather than the child being the focus of the image. The father's effortlessness further suggests that this is a confident man who cares when he chooses to. The fact that the whole reform had been surrounded by choice rather than an obvious commitment was also something that the statistics confirmed. There were not many fathers who took their parental leave. In 1980, after

16 years of equal opportunity, women were still using 95% of the leave days (SCB 2010). Indeed, simply giving men the opportunity to care was not enough, as breadwinning and the demands of work life were still central to how Swedish masculinity was constructed (Mellström 2006).

The Everyday Father in 2015

Though preceded by an intense political debate (Klinth 2002), it was only in 1995, when some days began to be earmarked for each of the parents, that an actual change took place (Brandt and Kvande 2013). Today, about 20% of the allotted days are earmarked for each parent, and this has produced immediate results in fathers' take-up by increasing their share to 25% (SCB 2014), just a small percentage over the 20% of days that are earmarked to them. Breadwinning and the demands of work life are still central to how Swedish masculinity is constructed (Mellström 2006), but Swedish companies have become more positive toward men taking parental leave (Haas and Hwang 2009).

While Hoa-Hoa was the poster child for men who had a choice over the decades to follow, it was not until the Swedish state's support of the photo project *Swedish Dads* (Bävman 2015), presented some 40 years later, that a new groundbreaking imagery of fatherhood emerged. Indeed, the fathers featured in this imagery did not only spend their allotted 20% with their children, but shared parental leave more or less equally with their partners, just as the Swedish state envisioned when introducing the legislation. The photo exhibition has been traveling around Sweden and the world since 2015 and reflects a type of care characterizing parents spending an extended and intensive period of time together with their children (Johansson 2003). This was also noted in a Swedish chronicle:

> This is the short period in which the contemporary man lives a bit like the old housewife, inside the four walls, where he or she is not visible to the world. If the images in the "Swedish dads" tell a story it is not the story of the new man, but about the ethics of care. What happens in a relationship

> where one person's life is totally dependent upon the other's attentions? One in which one is entirely dependent upon the other.

Indeed, the imagery describes an involved parenthood that distinguishes it from other types of imagery and that therefore renders it both so provocative and so celebrated. Far from Hoa-Hoa's strong masculine man smilingly dancing around with his child in his arms, this is the everyday for a father on parental leave stuck in the home together with his toddler. The father in the photograph in Fig. 6.3 is not even smiling. Instead, he looks absently at the camera, while in the background we see

Fig. 6.3 Photograph from the "Swedish Dads" collection by Johan Bävman. Reprinted with permission

his toddler tirelessly pulling the balloon bouquets hung on the door. The atmosphere projected has a morning-after taste. The balloons are already a bit deflated and the father looks tired, worn out even. They have just finished the toddler's one-year birthday celebrations, and the well-informed observer can sense what has been going on. This is involved fathering representing a type of non-optional care where the father takes full responsibility. Rather than signaling men's participation as a voluntary commitment, it is here described in terms of necessity—these are fathers drawn into the wear and tear of everyday childcare that demands their full attention. While the fathers cross gender boundaries via the day-to-day activities exhibited in the photos, the accompanying text displaying their occupation and names reveals that they still keep a strong foothold in work life, a central aspect of what is expected from a father (Doucet 2006). By this the state signals the need for double emancipation—that society will benefit from loosening gender norms without forcing them to give up this important part of their identity. Indeed, society needs social equals sharing the burdens of both work life and child care. After having discussed the historical developments of the state ideology through representation, we now shift focus to the fathers' lived experiences.

Identity Work: It's a Man's Job

Many observers of contemporary society claim that today we have significantly higher degrees of freedom to choose our identity in comparison to before, when structural aspects such as gender, social class, occupation, and family relationships gave us a more or less pre-defined identity template to step into (Bauman 2007). When these formerly solid structures wither away, consumers are left with having to find other means than relying on tradition in constructing a coherent life project. For example, men trying to carve out an identity position as an involved father can rarely look at their own fathers to get inspiration, as suggested by Mikael, a single middle-class dad: "I've always had a rather strained relationship with my dad who always prioritized his job and career over his children, and I said that I don't want to be like that, I want to be the exact opposite."

As we can see in this quote, the relationship vis-à-vis the parental generation in terms of proving a role model for parenting styles is many times characterized by resentment. The current generation of involved fathers are questioning the choices made by their own fathers and are convinced that they want to be something else. Mikael further emphasizes the traditional masculine traits of the old breadwinner father figure, pointing to his proficiency at work: "I hardly ever saw my dad, he was a workaholic, a doctor, and a scientist. He was never at hand when you needed him, not like a caring father. That just wouldn't happen. When I asked my mom if she ever saw my dad changing a diaper she said: 'Forget it.' That just wouldn't happen." The last quote aptly illustrates a turnaround where what used to be coveted signs of masculinity—such as being career oriented, playing a peripheral role in domestic life, and certainly not engaging in such femininely coded activities as changing diapers—all of a sudden have been recoded as liabilities.

The contemporary involved fathers thus have to have to seek inspiration, or identity templates, elsewhere. Apart from state campaigns such as the Swedish Dads project accounted for earlier, various market actors tend to play significant roles in providing the props that are needed to appear as a competent involved father. Earlier research on detraditionalization has shown that this freedom and accompanying identity work are often driven by commercial actors offering the symbolic material needed to bring about a credible new role (McAlexander et al. 2014). On the whole, identity has become an ongoing project where consumption has come to play an increasingly important role (Thompson 2014).

Let us return to the fathers in the vignette having a conversation at the gym, but this time in light of the increasing role that markets are playing today. The fathers' conversation on the one hand revolves around the nurturing activity that includes all sorts of parenting props such as beds, bottles, and baby foods. On other hand, the conversation balances this experience with traditional male identity props, such as gym machinery, rock music, and muscles. We feel how the men are drawn into all the aspects involving child care, while also having to deal with their male identities according to which a fit, strong, and toned body is expected of a progressive Swedish middle-class man of today (Östberg 2019). The identity work that is displayed in the vignette is anything but simple and straightforward, and illustrates how contemporary Swedish fathers have to balance both traditional and progressive views of masculinity. In what follows we will show how individual fathers have struggled with their identity work since parental leave was introduced in 1974. This identity work has included a long range of consumption props such as velour pants, beards, lattes, fancy strollers, and baby carriers.

Soft and Kind, Sure: But not a Velour Daddy!

The Swedish 1970s were characterized by a strong feminist movement influencing the media, popular culture, and politics. One of the concrete political manifestations of this was the launch of the gender-neutral parental leave policy in 1974, which is generally referred to as the "paternity leave reform." To help men navigate the new situation where patriarchy was increasingly questioned, the Swedish Association for Sexuality Education (RFSU) launched so-called man camps. The idea was to break away from a fossilized male role and improve men's contact with both their children and their partners. The overall catchphrase was to get closer to one's feelings. In the summer of 1979, the author and journalist Jan Guillou participated in one of these men camps. A few months later he described his experiences in a well-noticed article where he coined the term "Velour Daddy." He used this expression to claim that the men's movement consisted of "softies dressed in velour who wanted to play women" (Lerner 2007). While the men who took part in the camp wanted to show that masculinity was not a stable and unchangeable phenomenon and that it was possible to be a man in different ways, they were stereotyped as "unmanly" and "feminine." The criticism against these progressive men and the definition of them as unmanly gave rise to a fear of being labeled a Velour Daddy, which in turn may have served to consolidate the norms for who should be regarded as a "real man" (Hill 2007). The symbols related to Velour Daddies of the 1970s, with their velour pants, beards, sandals, and prams or baby carriers, were indeed far from the archaic stereotype of the real man. Rather, these props became antithetical for anyone wanting to be termed a real man. The general sentiment in Sweden was that the men described by Guillou had gone too far, and the message was that a dad should indeed be soft and kind, but not a Velour Daddy (Lerner 2007)!

The anxieties over not being manly enough have not ceased to exist. Rather, the fundamental conundrum that there is nothing more unmanly than to be insecure about one's manliness (Östberg 2010) seems to be even more relevant today as masculinity is in flux. Hans, for example, was the primary caregiver while his wife worked, and admitted that being perceived as a caregiving softy could be challenging at times:

> Well you can't deny that you are perceived [as a softy] by people from the outside, when you're the one who's caring, nurturing and takes on that role in a family … And I can say that it requires some work to maintain your male identity … It takes some work with yourself to maintain it … to understand what you actually give to your children without having to be affirmed by people from the outside.

Thus, rather than seeking affirmation from his surroundings, Hans had to resort to self-affirmation, justifying his choices by asserting that it was in the best interest of the family. This lack of affirmation from the surroundings points to an insecurity about what constitutes a real man in the Swedish context, which was also echoed by Karl, who had lived in many parts of the world over his life and found that navigating Swedish manliness was one of the more challenging endeavors:

> Well, I have to say that it's really confusing. It's associated with big risks to hold up the elevator door for [a woman]. And it is 50/50 if you should pay for the first dinner [when out on a date] or get rapped on your knuckles. There are so many rules. It is just so strange and everyone walks around with this anxiety of doing the wrong thing. … Either you're a male pig or you're a mingy penny-pincher, you just can't win whatever you do.

While Karl mused over the general hardships of being a man in Sweden and finding an adequate balance between conforming to archaic masculinity and being progressive, data from our various studies suggests that these anxieties are further reinforced when fathers assume the position of the prime caretaker for shorter or longer durations.

Being successful in the work force and exhibiting definite signs of masculinity, however, can assist fathers to feel capable and socially acceptable as caregivers (Doucet 2006). A study of single middle-class fathers (Molander forthcoming) confirmed the importance of work life via the busy, juggling lifestyles manifested by the men in the study. Most of them continued to work more or less full time after having become single fathers, even when sharing or having full responsibility for their children. Some also expressed a certain pressure from outside. As an example, Johan, one of the single fathers in the study, said:

> There are very high expectations that I have a high focus on my work. People who call me ask me about how things are going at work. But there is not much about how things are going with [my daughter].

However, the expectations on them as caregivers were lower. Bo, another single father, was surprised by this:

> It seems that the expectations on fathers' caregiving are still so low, something that makes it quite easy to back off, and not take responsibility. I'm a little surprised by this, because I didn't think that was the case [today]. I thought it was obvious [that the expectations would be equally high on both parents].

To be sure, even if the fathers seem to resist it, their work life identity emerges as key, while their involved fatherhood identity is only a bonus.

Commercial Rescue in the Identity Negotiations

When everyday fathers started taking parental leave in larger numbers by the turn of the twenty-first century, Sweden saw a new phenomenon on the streets: Latte Dads, symbolizing gender equality and responsible fathers taking advantage of parental leave while drinking latte with their children in various cafés (Google "latte dads" and "lattepappa" 2018). These young, urban, middle-class dads did not wear velour, but reinstated the beard as they consciously balanced their involved fatherhood identity with that of a progressive man. Like the men described in Ensmenger's (2015) article on bearded programmers in the 1960s and 1970s who constructed a masculine identity that mobilized artistic genius, personal eccentricity, and anti-authoritarianism, the first Swedish Latte Dads were often employed in the creative industries, where these types of attributes are seen as attractive and where a beard at the time was a common aesthetic preference.

Portraits of bearded Swedish fathers have populated both Swedish and international media, but there are also several commercial attempts to reduce the insecurity of the men involved by, in a variety of ways, recoding traditional female activities and making them more male or gender neutral. One example is Bugaboo, a Dutch brand of premium segment prams, that started to gain popularity in Sweden around the beginning of the twenty-first century and subsequently reached a position as the most fashionable pram in the metropolitan areas about a decade later, despite its premium pricing (Sokolow 2009). In an interview, the founder Max Barenbrug said that he consciously created a pram that a man would like and that the chunky design and solid colors owed much to the aesthetics of outdoor gear used for climbing or camping: "It had to be tough, it had to be multifunctional, it had to be used outdoors. Like you want a car, you want this stroller. … The parents who buy this buy it for themselves" (Teather 2009).

The Bugaboo, which is still highly popular (McRobbie 2018) and clearly seeks to attract men, as is evident by the frequent use of male models on the company's homepage (https://www.bugaboo.com), is also available as a jogging stroller. While jogging with a baby in a stroller is an activity potentially catering to both mothers and fathers, the activity has additional connotations for fathers, as it gives them an opportunity to engage directly in identity negotiations that can offset potentially negative connotations of not being manly enough. This balances child rearing with the positive connotations of being athletic and focusing on keeping the body in shape. Men can thereby disavow any (inappropriate) interest in their own appearance, since they are not merely working on and disciplining their bodies, but simultaneously taking care of their children. It is not unusual for men to have their body discipline surrounded by functional rationalizations relating to what the body can do rather than how it looks (Gill et al. 2005; Östberg 2019), be it marathons, triathlons, Ironman, or making a baby fall asleep while running.

The gear stands out as functional rather than cute, and the designs draw associations to adventurous and potentially risky activities such as climbing or camping, rather than drawing associations to over-protection and worry. The latter are typically seen as characteristics of intensive parenting—a child-centered, expert-guided, emotionally absorbing, labor-intensive, and financially expensive type of parenting (Hays 1996, p. 8) that has become the new normal, especially among western middle-class mothers (Vincent 2017), and that many fathers tend to shy away from (Molander forthcoming; Shirani et al. 2012). "You can do a lot of things with this product," Barenbrug explains when elaborating on the Bugaboo's multifunctionality and creative potential. "It is rugged and versatile enough to go into the mountains, to the beach and you can take the seat out, put it on your back, do something different" (Carter 2013). The issue of doing "something different" and being independent from mainstream trends and expert advice are other aspects of men's opposition to intensive parenting. Again, many men hold both progressive and traditional views of fatherhood (Humberd et al. 2015), and consumer society is there to solve this disconnect. The Bugaboo gear clearly does so for fathers who want to balance their masculinity with care and show the world that they know what they are doing, both as fathers and as men. This recoding can also be found in the plethora of changing bags that have been launched in recent years, and that instead of imitating handbags which was the dominant aesthetic in the past now have a more generic design resembling messenger bags in earthy colors.

Another company with a legacy of helping fathers negotiate a suitably masculine role via the marketplace is BabyBjörn, a Swedish company making baby bouncers, baby carriers, and other baby-related paraphernalia. This company embraced and promoted caring fathers early on. As the government started promoting the active involvement of fathers in parenting during the 1980s, the issue became more pronounced in the Swedish political debate, as well as in popular culture more generally. BabyBjörn was quick to include these new masculine identity positions

Fig. 6.4 Advertisement from BabyBjörn (https://www.babybjorn.se/var-historia/). Reprinted with permission

in its marketing communication, as displayed in an advertisement from that time (Fig. 6.4).

Ever since this time, BabyBjörn has adopted the same gender-related political agenda as the Swedish state, namely one of stressing the importance of both parents' closeness to the small child. BabyBjörn's proximity to the Swedish state's gender equality ideology can also be discerned in the company's overall communication today. In 2017, more than 40 of its approximately 50 country-adapted website pages (BabyBjörn 2017) displayed fathers with their children in BabyBjörn baby carriers, surrounded by flowers and pink walls, seemingly embracing their feminine side. The website also introduced a section called "dad stories" displaying images, texts, videos, and hashtags (#dadstories) where fathers shared their fatherhood experiences while posing in BabyBjörn's products. With headlines such as "I just wanted other guys to share that experience" exposing everyday care such as changing diapers, going to the playground, or holding and caressing their babies, these commercial messages imbued the same type of care as the state-sponsored Bävman (Swedish Dads) imagery discussed earlier.

Scandinavian Man: Mythologies of Fatherhood as a Commercial Platform

From an international perspective, the gender equality policies of the Swedish state, and the involved Swedish fathers they have given birth to, are exotic phenomena that provide suitable content for light media articles that garner many likes, shares, and comments both inside and outside of Scandinavia. In these articles, Sweden is sometimes portrayed as a utopia, and sometimes as a dystopia. This type of media attention is something that both Swedish men and Swedish companies seem to enjoy using as a benchmark for the progressiveness of the country, and the articles are often shared and discussed in social media.

In order to capitalize on the international interest in Swedish men and profit from the mythologies about a specific Swedish masculinity, the commercial platform Scandinavian Man (www.scandinavian-man.com) was launched in 2017. This commercial platform consists of an array of activities such as a bi-annual magazine, a website, a radio show, a regular newsletter, an Instagram account, live events, symposiums and a curated pop-up store. It aims to help mainly Swedish, but also other Scandinavian, men's fashion brands to become more successful abroad. The idea behind Scandinavian Man is primarily to sell the idea of the Swedish man as something desirable to an international audience, and then hope that this will generate increased interest in the brands that the prospective audience might imagine that the Swedish man fills his consumption universe with. The example of Scandinavian Man thus shows that the mythology of the particularity of the Swedish father, and Scandinavian men more broadly, has taken on such proportions that is not merely a useful trope for individual companies in their brand-building endeavors, as exemplified by BabyBjörn, but is seen as having a larger potential.

In order to capitalize on the mythologies about Swedish masculinity, Scandinavian Man engages in an unabashed tribute to the idealized image of the Swedish man as gender, feminist, and child minded, but also as someone who is socially competent, professionally successful, and not least style conscious. This mythological creature forms the basis of the platform that Scandinavian Man has launched. Judging by the initial reactions and the commercial success of the project, there are many companies that are interested and see a potential in being associated with these ideas:

> it became clear that there was an inherent need for this. Not just to build a platform for Scandinavian menswear brands ... but to launch the idea of the Scandinavian man to the world. A modern man, style and design conscious, technologically innovative, far ahead on sustainability and equality, and the most present father in the world. (Konrad Olsson, editor's letter, first issue of Scandinavian Man, Autumn/Winter 2017)

Olsson is here talking about an "inherent need" to launch the Scandinavian man to the world. He is evidently making this point to increase the commercial success of his platform, but our interviews with the founders of Scandinavian Man also suggest that it reflects an honest belief that gender relations globally could become better if only more people would realize the benefits of the Swedish model. There is, of course, more than a little smugness involved in this endeavor, suggesting that the rest of the world should mimic Sweden in order to progress. To offset this, Scandinavian Man has seemingly collected "neutral witnesses" that can testify to the greatness of the Swedish model. One such example is Natalia Brzezinski, wife of the former US ambassador to Sweden and CEO of Brilliant Minds, who gets to write about her experiences of the Swedish model in the opening issue of Scandinavian Man:

> This commercial platform consists of an array of activities such as a bi-annual magazine, a website, a radio show, a regular newsletter, an Instagram account, live events, symposiums and a curated pop-up store. America does not prioritize a family in balance. In Sweden, a family in lagom [a Swedish term to connote balance; of having neither too much, nor too little of something] is seen as [sic] important as the sunrise. Living in Sweden for four years brought my family into our own form of beautiful lagom. I'm forever thankful for our time in Stockholm and I'm determined to scale Swedish values to make the world more balanced and fair in work, in life and especially in gender equality. I believe gender equality was born in the Swedish home, and it starts with the Swedish fathers.

By these types of testaments about the merits of the Swedish model of equality, Scandinavian Man is trying to establish a favorable image of Sweden that can subsequently be transferred to the marketing offerings that the platform is trying to sell. When consuming these marketing offerings, some of the positive traits associated with Swedish fathers will rub off on the prospective consumer. The marketplace mythology of the Swedish man hereby functions as a repository for consumers' identity work and hence plays a role in their identity construction (Thompson 2004).

What Scandinavian Man illustrates is yet another example of the linkages between state ideology, individual consumers' lived lives, and commercial activities. The state policies have paved the way for the mythological framework of the Swedish man, and this mythology is now being turned into a marketplace mythology that various brands attempt to capitalize on by attracting individual consumers. However, the Scandinavian Man project does not stop there, but instead proposes that by using the power of the market you can not only sell Swedish fashion abroad, but also help spread a more progressive image of men worldwide. Market actors are thus attributed a role that goes beyond the strictly commercial. The close connection between state and commercial actors is not new to Sweden; the importance of sharing the same type of values was stressed already in 1968, when Gunnar Sträng, the Swedish finance minister, commented on the Swedish car company Volvo and argued: "What is good for Volvo is good for Sweden." The sentiment that arises from this quote is that what Volvo pushed would profit Sweden. When it comes to Swedish fathers, however, there is no doubt that it was the other way around—that what the state pushed would profit various commercial actors.

Discussion

With Swedish fatherhood as our point of departure, the aim of this chapter has been to gain an understanding of how consumer culture evolves at the nexus of the (welfare) state, individual consumers' lived lives, and companies' marketing activities. The point of this has not only been to illustrate the particular idiosyncrasy of Swedish consumer culture and its state-sponsored individual autonomy, but also, and more importantly, to discuss how consumer culture in a welfare state is largely shaped by state ideology. This is something that is typically ignored in research emanating in cultural contexts where the state is not given this role.

By contextualizing today's situation historically, we have shown how the continuing transformation of Swedish fatherhood took off via long-ranging gender ideological work on the state level encouraging fathers to become more involved, while also providing the financial and practical infrastructure to do so. We have also shown how the fathers themselves have both welcomed and shunned this development. On the one hand, our examples have illustrated how fathers have embraced the daily wear and tear, and the intimate contact with the child that brings the nurturing into existence. On the other hand, our examples have also illustrated how this intimate care has challenged their gender identity. Even if involved men have been idealized, they have also been ridiculed as failed men, for example when given the derogatory label "Velour Daddies." Despite these tensions, for progressive Swedish men "it is no longer enough to be rational, goal-means oriented, career oriented, and disciplined. Today, men must also show their readiness to engage in child care, their child orientation, and their willingness to live up to the ideal of gender equality" (Johansson and Klinth 2008, 58).

This development has not been an isolated event between state and citizens, however. Rather, it is embedded in consumer culture, where fathers have handled the necessary adjustments in identity work through consumption. We have shown how companies at the forefront have managed to both encourage and profit from these progressive developments by providing consumption opportunities for men to overcome their existential dilemmas. This has been achieved by recoding traditional female activities and making them more male or gender neutral. It is interesting to note that the market thereby plays a direct role in the Swedish state's political project toward gender equality. To be sure, during the last 20 years the market has increased its role overall in Sweden as various versions of state-sponsored neoliberalism have been embraced. The country's emphasis on individual autonomy, aiming to guarantee that individuals are not bogged down by archaic family ties (Berggren and Trägårdh 2010), has been fertile ground for an ideology that proposes that human well-being can best be advanced by the maximization of entrepreneurial freedoms within an institutional framework characterized by individual liberty and free markets. Still, these same programs also risk counteracting the cherished equal opportunities that the individual autonomy policies were meant to provide. Research shows that the ability to actually exercise freedom of choice varies considerably between citizens, and that children born in under-privileged families have more difficulty profiting from the neoliberal system than those who were not—results that thereby counteract the individual mobility that has been the centerpiece of the Swedish welfare system. As expressed by Harvey (2007, 156), "The redistributive tactics of neoliberalism are wide-ranging, sophisticated, frequently masked by ideological gambits but devastating for the dignity and social well-being of vulnerable populations and territories."

Nevertheless, we have shown that involved fatherhood has become a Swedish national treasure to both state, corporations, and individual citizens. Despite increased inequalities since the 1980s (OECD 2016), Sweden is still seen as one of the most progressive countries in the world and is always ranked amongst the top countries in different international rankings for gender equality. Examples include Y&R's BAV Consulting and the Wharton School at the University of Pennsylvania ranking of the best country in the world for women and for raising kids, where Sweden's gender equal policies and not least its paid parental leave are highlighted (Garcia 2017), and the World Economic Forum's Global Gender Gap Report (World Economic Forum 2017). The question of whether Sweden is also the best place for men to live is not touched on in these studies, but it is interesting to note that the Swedish gender equality ideology builds on the premise that an equal society benefits all, not just women (Jämställdhetsmyndigheten 2018). Swedish corporations have not been slow to profit from the country's reputation. We have already discussed the eagerness with which Scandinavian Man has promoted Sweden's generous parental leave policies and how the baby carrier company BabyBjörn has concretized these policies via its own products since the 1980s. Another company, the music-streaming service Spotify that was recently listed on the New York Stock Exchange, has embraced its Swedish roots by offering its employees across the world six months of full paid parental leave independent of gender (Spotify HR 2017). Clearly, this progressive aspect of Sweden is something that these companies are proud of, want to highlight, and think they can benefit from.

But seeing involvement in child rearing as a treasure is also true for individual fathers. The Swedish Dads project highlighted this aspect in statements from the featured fathers, such as this one from Juan (Bävman 2015): "Because of my long parental leave I believe I am able to connect with my children and get closer to them than fathers that don't stay at home." Research shows that the daily wear and tear and intimate contact with the child are what bring the nurturing into existence (Johansson 2003; Ruddick 1995 [1989]), and based on our empirical material this is also something the fathers seem to highly treasure.

In sum, our work has illustrated the interconnectedness of state ideology and consumer culture in a welfare state. This is most evident in cases where the state assumes the role of changing not only what people do, but also how they think. In Sweden it has been a political project to transform child rearing into shared work among and enjoyed by social equals, but it is also clear that this continuing transformation will not be possible without commercial actors. One of the defining features of consumer culture is that the ever-ongoing staging of one's public persona is furnished with props from the market, whose symbolic content is largely supplied by the dynamics activated by its various actors. The case of Swedish fatherhood illustrates the importance of looking at the nexus of state policies and state ideological work, individual consumers, and company activities if we are to understand how consumer culture and its actors are continuously transformed.

References

Aarseth, H. (2013). De nye barneorienterte fedrene. [The New Child Oriented Fathers]. In B. Brandt & E. Kvande (Eds.), *Fedrekvoten og den farsvennlige velferdsstaten [The Paternal Leave Quota and the Fatherhood Friendly Welfare State]* (pp. 239–250). Oslo, Norway: Universitetsforlaget.

Axelsson, E. (2015, May 30). Mamman och konsten [The Mother and the Art]. *Eskilstuna-Kuriren*. Retrieved July 15, 2018, from https://www.ekuriren.se/kulturnoje/mamman-och-konsten/.

BabyBjörn. (2017). Retrieved from https://www.babybjorn.se/.

Bauman, Z. (2007). *Consuming Life*. Cambridge, UK: Polity Press.

Bävman, J. (2015). *Swedish Dads* (self-published).

Berggren, H., & Trägårdh, L. (2006). *Är Svensken Människa? Gemenskap och Oberoende i det Moderna Sverige [Is the Swede Human? On Community and Independence in the Modern Sweden]*. Stockholm: Norstedt.

Berggren, H., & Trägårdh, L. (2010). Pippi Longstocking: The Autonomous Child and the Moral Logic of the Swedish Welfare State. In H. Mattsson & S.-O. Wallenstein (Eds.), *Swedish Modernism: Architecture, Consumption, and the Welfare State* (pp. 10–23). Black Dog Publishing.

Brandt, B., & Kvande, E. (Eds.). (2013). *Fedrekvoten og den farsvennlige velferdsstaten [The Paternal Leave Quota and the Fatherhood Friendly Welfare State]*. Oslo, Norway: Universitetsforlaget.

Carter, K. (2013, May 23). Bugaboo Designer Max Berenbrug: The Master of Reinvention. *The Guardian*. Retrieved June 6, 2018, from https://www.theguardian.com/lifeandstyle/2013/may/23/bugaboo-designer-max-barenbrug-buggy.

Coskuner-Balli, G., & Thompson, C. J. (2013). The Status Costs of Subordinate Cultural Capital: At-Home Fathers' Collective Pursuit of Cultural Legitimacy Through Capitalizing Consumption Practices. *Journal of Consumer Research, 40*(1), 19–41.

Doucet, A. (2006). *Do Men Mother? Fathering, Care, and Domestic Responsibility*. University of Toronto Press.

Eagleton, T. (1991). *Ideology: An Introduction*. London: Versa.

Ensmenger, N. (2015). "Beards, Sandals, and Other Signs of Rugged Individualism": Masculine Culture Within the Computing Professions. *Osiris, 30*(1), 38–65.

Epp, A. M., & Price, L. L. (2008). Family Identity: A Framework of Identity Interplay in Consumption Practices. *Journal of Consumer Research, 35*(1), 50–70.

Epp, A. M., & Velagaleti, S. R. (2014). Outsourcing Parenthood? How Families Manage Care Assemblages Using Paid Commercial Services. *Journal of Consumer Research, 41*(4), 911–935.

Garcia, P. (2017, March 7). Attention, Ladies: Sweden Is Officially the Best Country in the World for Women. *Vogue*. Retrieved July 15, 2018, from https://www.vogue.com/article/sweden-best-country-for-women.

Gill, R., Henwood, K., & McLean, C. (2005). Body Projects and the Regulation of Normative Masculinity. *Body & Society, 11*(1), 37–62.

Gregory, A., & Milner, S. (2011). What Is 'New' About Fatherhood? The Social Construction of Fatherhood in France and the UK. *Men and Masculinities, 14*(5), 588–606.

Haas, L., & Hwang, C. P. (2009). Is Fatherhood Becoming More Visible at Work? Trends in Corporate Support for Fathers Taking Parental Leave in Sweden. *Fathering, 7*(3), 303–321.

Hagemann, G. (2002). Citizenship and Social Order: Gender Politics in Twentieth-Century Norway and Sweden. *Women's History Review, 11*(3), 417–429.

Harvey, D. (2007). Neoliberalism as Creative Destruction. *The Annals of the American Academy of Political and Social Science, 610*(1), 21–44.

Hays, S. (1996). *The Cultural Contradictions of Motherhood.* New Haven: Yale University Press.

Hein, W., et al. (2016). Gender Justice and the Market: A Transformative Consumer Research Perspective. *Journal of Public Policy & Marketing, 35*(2), 223–236.

Hill, H. (2007). *Befria mannen: idéer om förtryck, frigörelse och förändring hos en svensk mansrörelse under 1970-och tidigt 1980-tal [Free the Man: Ideas of Oppression, Liberation and Change in a Swedish Men's Movement During the 1970s and Early 1980s].* Diss. h: ström-Text & Kultur.

Hobson, B., & Morgan, D. (2002). Introduction. In B. Hobson & D. Morgan (Eds.), *Making Men into Fathers. Men, Masculinities and the Social Politics of Fatherhood* (pp. 1–21). Cambridge: Cambridge University Press.

Humberd, B., Ladge, J. J., & Harrington, B. (2015). The "New" Dad: Navigating Fathering Identity Within Organizational Contexts. *Journal of Business and Psychology, 30*(2), 249–266.

Jämställdhetsmyndigheten. (2018). Retrieved October 2, 2018, from https://www.jamstalldhetsmyndigheten.se/.

Johansson, T. (2003). Pappa på kvartstid, deltid eller heltid. Om pappor och deras barn [Dad on Quarterly, Part Time or Full Time. On Fathers and Their Children]. In M. Bäck-Wiklund & T. Johansson (Eds.), *Nätverksfamiljen [The Network Family]* (pp. 160–171). Stockholm: Natur och kultur.

Johansson, T., & Klinth, R. (2008). Caring Fathers: The Ideology of Gender Equality and Masculine Positions. *Men and Masculinities, 11*(1), 42–62.

Klinth, R. (2002). *Göra pappa med barn: Den svenska pappapolitiken 1960–1995 [Making Daddy Pregnant: The Swedish Fatherhood Politics 1960–1995].* Doctoral Dissertation, Linköping University.

Lerner, T. (2007, May 26). Vi ville lara oss att visa kanslor [We Wanted to Learn How to Show Feelings]. *Dagens Nyheter*. Retrieved May 24, 2018, from https://www.dn.se/arkiv/insidan/vi-ville-lara-oss-att-visa-kanslor/?forceScript=1&variantType=large.

McAlexander, J. H., Dufault, B. L., Martin, D. M., & Schouten, J. W. (2014). The Marketization of Religion: Field, Capital, and Consumer Identity. *Journal of Consumer Research, 41*(3), 858–875.

McRobbie, L. R. (2018, March 20). Perfect Prams for Perfect Parents: The Rise of the Bougie Buggy. *The Guardian*. Retrieved July 15, 2018, from https://www.theguardian.com/news/2018/mar/20/bugaboo-luxury-pram-baby-buggy-stroller-parenting.

Mellström, U. (2006, February). Nytt faderskap i skärningspunkten mellan produktion och reproduktion? [New Fatherhood in the Intersection Between Production and Reproduction], *Socialvetenskaplig tidskrift*.

Moisio, R., Arnould, E. J., & Price, L. L. (2004). Between Mothers and Markets: Constructing Family Identity Through Homemade Food. *Journal of Consumer Culture, 4*(3), 361–384.

Molander, S. (forthcoming). *Swedish Single Fathers*.

OECD. (2016). *OECD Income Inequality Data Update: Sweden* (January 2015). Retrieved July 15, 2018, from http://www.oecd.org/sweden/OECD-Income-Inequality-Sweden.pdf.

Östberg, J. (2010). Thou Shalt Sport a Banana in Thy Pocket: Gendered Body Size Ideals in Advertising and Popular Culture. *Marketing Theory, 10*(1), 45–73.

Östberg, J. (2019). No More Mister Mom: Masculinity and Consumption. In S. Dobscha (Ed.), *Handbook of Research in Gender and Marketing* (pp. 211–228). Cheltenham, UK: Edward Elgar.

Plantin, L. (2003). Faderskap i retorik och praktik. Om "nya" fäder i gamla strukturer [Fatherhood in Rhetoric and Practice. On "New" Fathers in Old Structures]. In M. Bäck-Wiklund & T. Johansson (Eds.), *Nätverksfamiljen [The Network Family]* (pp. 143–159). Stockholm: Natur och kultur.

Plantin, L. (2015). Contemporary Fatherhood in Sweden: Fathering Across Work and Family Life. In J. L. Roopnarine (Ed.), *Fathers Across Cultures. The Importance, Roles and Diverse Practices of Dads* (pp. 91–107). ABC-CLIO.

Ruddick, S. (1989/1995). *Maternal Thinking: Toward a Politics of Peace*. Boston: Beacon Press.

SCB. Statistics Sweden. (2010). *På tal om kvinnor och män. Lathund om jämställdhet 2010 [Speaking of Women and Men. Guide on Gender Equality]*. Retrieved May 23, 2018, from http://www.scb.se/statistik/_publikationer/LE0201_2010A01_BR_X10BR1001.pdf.

SCB. Statistics Sweden. (2014, January). Olika familjer lever på olika sätta—om barns boende och försörjning efter en separation [Different Families Live Differently—On Children's Accommodation and Livelihood After a Separation]. *Demografiska rapporter*. Retrieved November 17, 2014, from http://www.scb.se/Statistik/_Publikationer/BE0701_2013A01_BR_BE51BR1401.pdf.

Shirani, F., Henwood, K., & Coltart, C. (2012). Meeting the Challenges of Intensive Parenting Culture: Gender, Risk Management and the Moral Parent. *Sociology, 46*(1), 25–40.

Sokolow, I. (2009, January, June 1). Bugaboo – en hajpad holländare Svenska [Bugaboo—A Hyped Dutch]. *Svenska Dagbladet*. Retrieved June 6, 2018, from https://www.svd.se/bugaboo%2D%2Den-hajpad-hollandare.

Spotify HR. (2017, January 20). *Thank You Thank You Thank You for Sending Me on Parental Leave*. Retrieved July 15, 2018, from https://hrblog.spotify.com/2017/01/20/thank-you-thank-you-thank-you-for-sending-me-on-parental-leave/.

Teather, D. (2009, September 19). Bugaboo Beyond the Baby Business. *The Guardian*. Retrieved June 6, 2018, from http://www.theguardian.com/business/2009/sep/20/bugaboo-expansion-interview-barenbrug.

Thompson, C. J. (2004). Marketplace Mythology and Discourses of Power. *Journal of Consumer Research, 31*(1), 162–180.

Thompson, C. J. (2014). The Politics of Consumer Identity Work. *Journal of Consumer Research, 40*(5), iii–vii.

Vincent, C. (2017). The Children Have Only Got One Education and You Have to Make Sure It's a Good One': Parenting and Parent–School Relations in a Neoliberal Age. *Gender and Education, 9*(5), 541–557.

Wallendorf, M., & Arnould, E. J. (1991). "We Gather Together": Consumption Rituals of Thanksgiving Day. *Journal of Consumer Research, 18*(1), 13–31.

World Economic Forum. (2017). *The Global Gender Gap Report*. Retrieved October 5, 2018, from http://www3.weforum.org/docs/WEF_GGGR_2017.pdf.

7

Experiencing Nature through Nordic Restrictions and Freedom

Emma Salminen

The constant information overflow is driving consumers into the wild. Nature has a central role in Nordic consumer culture due to the vast forests, numerous lakes, magnificent mountains, long summer nights, and the aurora borealis lighting the sky on a winter night. Consumers in the Nordics are proud of their nature heritage, selling the Nordic nature imaginary through landscapes of wilderness (Hall et al. 2008, p. 130). Nordic consumers enjoy their free time by hiking in the rugged forests of Lapland, heating up a sauna at their summer cottage, or taking a dip in an ice-cold lake in the wintertime. Furthermore, Nordics are often considered forerunners in terms of environmental responsibility (Carlström 2016). Yet, Nordic countries are at times referred to as "nanny states," fueled with constant new regulations and legislation to promote ideologies

This work resulted from the BONUS CHANGE project and was supported by BONUS (Art 185), funded jointly by the EU and Naturvårdsverket (Swedish Environmental Protection Agency) and the Academy of Finland.

E. Salminen (✉)
Aalto University School of Business, Helsinki, Finland
e-mail: emma.m.salminen@aalto.fi

S. Askegaard, J. Östberg (eds.), *Nordic Consumer Culture*,
https://doi.org/10.1007/978-3-030-04933-1_7

and ensure welfare (Østergaard et al. 2014). Therefore, the Nordics serve as an interesting context to study the experience of nature consumption.

This study explores how Nordic consumers' nature experiences are orchestrated through an interplay of Nordic ideologies of nature with Nordic governmental apparatuses. I draw from previous studies focusing on romantic ideals of nature (e.g., Canniford and Shankar 2013), comparing them to contradictory ideologies of nature (see Thompson 2004) to explain how nature experiences are consumed. A specialty in Nordic nature experiences is boundaries, due to the vast regulatory regimes set by the welfare state and freedom brought by everyman's rights (Beery 2013). Thus, this chapter takes a consumer culture perspective to explore local nature identities within Nordic nature experiences. I draw on Nordic sailors' nature consumption experiences by studying both sailing as a nature experience as well as sailboat ownership and maintenance.

Nature Experiences from the Nordic Perspective

Nature is an essential part of consumer culture research. Nature as either a setting of consumption or even an object of consumption has become much discussed in consumer research in relation to, for example, enacting fantasy experiences in a primitive alternative reality of modern mountain man (Belk and Costa 1998), exploring ideological discourses related to technology in a natural health marketplace (Thompson 2004), and developing understanding of technology ideologies contrasting and comparing technology and nature (Kozinets 2007). Nature has been studied in the context, for instance, of extraordinary consumption experiences of river rafting through which consumers gain harmony with nature (Arnould and Price 1993), Burning Man anti-market events where consumers distance themselves from the market in search of "primitive" economies (Kozinets 2002), commercialized climbing expeditions on Everest giving insight into marketplace tensions in relation to community (Tumbat and Belk 2010), and surfing culture giving understanding of purifying practices through which consumers enable romantic experiences of nature (Canniford and Shankar 2013). These studies illustrate how experiences of nature are filled with logical contradictions and contrasts between escaping the modern market and on the other hand using technologies to maintain pure nature experiences (Canniford and Shankar 2013).

Previous research has identified two ideologies of nature: romantic and gnostic ideologies. The romantic nature ideology is described as organic, peaceful, wild, clean, and having a mystical force to heal people from their stress caused by modern life (Thompson 2004). Nature is a mix of mysticism and romance—a maternal power making it easier to relax and get away from hectic life. It is sacred and not taken for granted (Canniford and Shankar 2013) and lived with in cooperation. Nature is pristine and untouched, where no one has entered (Cronon 1996). Therefore, some previous research has sought to distinguish romantic nature from culture, defining romantic nature outside of culture (Canniford and Shankar 2013). However, many studies present how consumers experience nature through modern, urban culture. For example, Arnould and Price's (1993) research exploring commercial river rafting trips found that romantic cultural scripts integrate consumers in harmony with nature. The river rafting guides were enhancing the romantic experience by creating cultural scripts that articulate cultural norms related to the romantic expectations of the customers (Arnould and Price 1993). Similarly, natural health consumers aim for harmony with nature by consuming natural health products (Thompson 2004). Yet, a conflicting ideology of nature, the gnostic ideology, includes survival and preparing for the revenge of nature (Thompson 2004). Following the gnostic ideology, the consumer gains dominance over nature with technology and science. Whereas the romantic ideology of nature often has a passive view of consumers (Scholz 2012), adding the gnostic ideology offers a more dynamic view, seeing consumers as active creators of harmony with nature (Thompson 2004). These two ideologies, romantic and gnostic, bring contradictions in experiencing nature.

Nordic cultural traditions have strong connections to nature (Beery 2013). Nordic consumers seek harmony with romantic nature by going to summerhouses (some of which are intentionally left unmodern), visiting rural areas in Lapland, or setting sail in the Baltic Sea archipelago.

The Nordic nature ideologies have their roots in history in the concept of Nordic freedom (Olwig 1992). The cold northern climates produced a largely ungovernable, freedom-loving populace (Olwig 2005). Most northerners lived in rural areas in the late pre-modern period, spending their time farming, hunting, and fishing (Isberg and Isberg 2007). The Nordic myths reflected the cold and harsh climate, personifying nature's forces as giants made of ice embodying large-scale natural phenomena, and elves and dwarves embodying smaller elements of nature (Andrews 2000, p. 169). The history of freedom originates from the Protestant reformation, forming freedom as a "natural development of Christianity," opposite to the overly civilized Rome and giving rise to a liberal democracy (Olwig 1992, 2005). The cold Nordic countries were seen as so spirited that they could remain comparatively free (Olwig 1992). The history of freedom dates back to the present understandings of the Nordic relationship to nature. For example, the Swedish widely used word *frilutsliv* exemplifies the Swedes' deep connection to nature. The word does not translate well to English, but it "fuses ideas of outdoor recreation, nature experience, philosophy, and lifestyle" that the Swedes have on experiencing nature (Beery 2013, p. 95). Thus, the word does not only refer to specific outdoor activities, but more broadly the connectedness to nature, the joy and harmony of being in nature and learning from it—even to a friendship with nature (Beery 2013).

Yet, at its core the Nordic model relies on principles of strong workers' rights, income redistribution, social safety nets, and the state acting as a check against market externalities, while still embracing markets and entrepreneurship as engines for economic growth (Byrkjeflot 2001). The state has a strong aim of interfering in what people do and think (Østergaard et al. 2014). The Nordic government apparatus leans heavily on a heritage of consensus politics, a high degree of trust across society, and well-functioning markets that are regulated and aided by government bodies with low levels of corruption. The Nordic model remains a product of Nordic culture and ideals such as an "ethos of equality and egalitarianism, a pragmatic political climate which has its roots in the Scandinavian societies' adaptation of Lutheran Protestantism, rural pietism and ideas of the Enlightenment" (Kjeldgaard and Östberg 2007, p. 184). The Nordic countries, which as mentioned are often called "nanny states," are characterized by high taxes and continuous new legislation to formulate wealth redistribution and promote ideologies (Østergaard et al. 2014). The common understanding of the welfare state is to be "equality oriented, but not necessarily aimed at maximum equality; rather, the goal is equal citizenship—enabling everybody to participate in social, political and cultural life as equal citizens despite modest economic inequality" (Andersen 2013, p. 114).

The paradox between strict governmental regulations and free access to nature leads to interesting questions in terms of consumer responsibility in the Nordics. A special characteristic of consuming nature experiences in the Nordics is the concept of everyman's rights. Following the tenets of welfare state ideology, everyman's rights allow everyone equally to experience outdoor pursuits and freely enjoy the vast forests, lakes, and fells. All citizens are equally entitled to walk, ski, cycle, or ride freely in natural areas. These rights do not cover private yards. However, with these rights comes the responsibility to cause no harm or disturbance to the land or other people (Beery 2013). Opportunities like everyman's rights, provided by the welfare state, offer freedom and lean heavily on the high degree of trust across society. Indeed, there are no exact definitions or details of everyman's rights (Beery 2013). An interesting question in terms of creating a responsible consumer from the welfare state point of view is whether or not the welfare state weakens moralistic ties when consumers rely on the welfare state and outsource morality to the welfare state (Byrkjeflot 2001).

Research Methods and Study Context

Sailing on the Baltic Sea provides an interesting and multifaceted context for investigating nature consumption experiences. Sailing is a highly valued activity that enjoys a deep and long cultural heritage in the Nordics. The fact that there are more than three million leisure boats in the Nordics means that almost half of European leisure boats exist in the Nordic countries (Eklund et al. 2013). The roots of sailing in the Nordics are from as early as 500, the first sailors pre-dating the era of the Vikings. Sailors in the Nordics were said to be the most talented shipbuilders in the world

(Hornborg 1965, pp. 108–116). The difficult weather conditions in the Nordics and their distant location from other cultures forced the building of strong boats. The waves were steep and the sea so cold that it would have been impossible to wait for the storm to calm down and the wind was unforeseeable and changeable (Hornborg 1965, pp. 108–116). The practice has thereafter obviously developed a lot, but the harsh weather conditions hold it in place to some extent. Thus, Nordic sailors are not only the luxury-seeking, social status–boosting men who might come to mind, but more nature lovers seeking harmony and peace from their hectic life as well as extreme experiences. The practice of sailing is relatively free, since everyone can start sailing by just buying or renting a boat and setting sail. The secondhand market for sailboats is active and large, thus decreasing the initiation costs for sailors. No formal license for boating is needed in the Nordics. Some boat clubs offer courses, but usually sailing is learnt through practice.

I especially focus on studying not only sailing, but also sailboat ownership and maintenance, which are strongly connected to sailors' nature experiences. Sailboat ownership is full of regulations and interference from the government, giving interesting insight to the study. Sailboats in the Nordics are often owned for a long time, even decades, or passed on in the family. The Nordic sailing season is short, only about maximum of four months from June till the end of September, and boat maintenance needs are significant. The maintenance is often done by the boat owners themselves due to the expensive outsourcing costs.

The research data derives from a larger multidisciplinary research project studying boat maintenance. The ethnographic inquiry studied sailors at Baltic Sea boatyards throughout Finland, Sweden, and Denmark. The analysis included 10 different sites, some of which were visited multiple times. In addition to field notes, observations, and ethnographic interviews, the data includes photography, videos, and secondary data such as boating magazine stories, blogs, multiple sailing forums, and other social media data. The interview data consists of in-depth interviews with 23 sailors and boatyard officials at boatyards and offsite in cafés, as well as 27 shorter ethnographic interviews. The data analysis focused on nature experiences, especially the special characteristic of Nordicness.

Analysis was an iterative, ongoing process throughout the research project that started from analysing the data through open coding coupled with the fieldwork findings (Belk et al. 2012).

Findings

The findings will first cover how Nordic consumers' nature experiences are orchestrated through an interplay of Nordic ideologies of nature. I will then turn to looking into the role of Nordic governmental apparatuses in Nordic nature experiences.

The Search for Freedom through Nordic Nature Experiences

Nordic sailors searched for freedom in their nature experiences. Among sailors, the Nordic nature imaginary is based on pristine nature, scenic landscapes, pure waters, and quiet long nights. Everyman's rights allow Nordic consumers to access nature whenever they want, being seemingly free (Ahlström 2008; Sandell 2006). Similar to, for example, river rafters (Arnould and Price 1993), surfers (Canniford and Shankar 2013), and participants in Burning Man (Kozinets 2002), nature plays an important role in offering freedom from everyday life stress to sailors when they choose to separate themselves from undesired social shaping and feel liberated from society. Following the romantic ideology, sailors step into the world of nature as a benevolent mother far away from modernity (Canniford and Shankar 2013).

The sailors listed reasons to go out to sea as getting away from their hectic lives, being able to feel free, and living in the moment. Every informant had vivid nature experience stories to share. Janne, an entrepreneur, did not own a boat, but only used and was responsible for his scout group's boat. Yet, he explained:

> every time I get to the boat, I just somehow loose myself there, with no disruptions I'm able to relax. I'm not dependent on anything. That's the most important thing in sailing. I just love the sea.

Janne's description follows the common feelings the sailors described when asked what drives them to sailing. Through sailing he experiences freedom from his daily entrepreneurial tasks. Interestingly, he is able to experience independence even though he does not own a sailing boat. Nature and the silence of nature allow "being on a holiday" (Janne). He contrasts the feeling of being out at sea:

> It's very different from sitting in your car during rush hour. Everything is so different. Even people feel different, more friendly and helpful.

Similar to what Moisio and colleagues found (2013) among high cultural capital consumers, the contrast between work and leisure sailing was especially strong when an informant was mainly working indoors (usually with a computer) and experienced sailing and the maintenance duties involved as giving freedom from that. Being one with nature, therefore living in the moment, gives the sailor a feeling of freedom. Therefore, many sailors raised the importance of silence in nature:

> I can remember many times when we have waited close to our home harbour for a wind to blow so we would get home. None of us wants to turn the engine on because we hate the noise it makes. So we rather just go slow. (Emmi)

Emmi explains how the quietness of the ocean gives them enjoyment. It is a silent agreement between the sailors on the boat to wait for the wind to bring them to the shore rather than to turn on the engine.

Following the tenets of the gnostic ideology, many of the informants also described how being at the mercy of the sea gave them freedom from their structured lives. With the help of technology, sailors have to respond to unpredictable weather. Even though romantic summer days where the wind is mellow, like Emmi described, give enjoyment to sailors, the most extensive stories of nature were those about facing stormy nature. Unforeseeable weather conditions such as storms created a magical experience of nature. Tiitta stated:

> If you are afraid of being at the storm you shouldn't leave the shore at all. It is windy at sea sometimes.

Storms are part of the northern sailing experience. The sailors were thus not passively seeking romanticized experiences with nature (Scholz 2012), but rather the changing weather conditions allowed them to have a fulfilling experience of freedom, since they had to constantly respond to changes with the help of technology. One such example of taming nature with technology is using toxic boat hull paints to fight biofouling for increasing speed and maintaining the maneuverability of the boat.

Different practices were important in maintaining the romanticized view of nature. However, similar to what Canniford and Shankar (2013) brought out in their surfing study, various betrayals hinder the experience of romantic nature. Betrayals threaten the pure experience of nature when consumption resources do not meet expectations (Canniford and Shankar 2013). Kaisa's story of a sailing race with a group of women from Denmark to Finland was one of the most vivid:

> Well I went early in the morning to fix the navigation stuff to the boat. At those days there weren't any gps but only a dysfunctional deck navigator with what you could never know whether it was working or not. So I went to take care of it to the boat and I happened to see Expressen [a newspaper] telling that sailors shouldn't go out to sea. That a big storm was coming. I told the news to the girls [with whom she was sailing] when they came to the boat and I was tightening the pontoons with a meter long screwdriver to keep the boat in shape and the girls were laughing at me. I just told them that this is the situation, what should we do? They said we should leave to the sea of course. So we left and the sea was calm once again, there was nothing to worry about, we were smiling and laughing how there was no sign of a storm. But we didn't reach far before the storm so suddenly rose. Reef after reef, when we took one reef off we had to start taking another one and yet a third one and we took the mainsail down. The wind was harsh and it became harder and harder [to sail] and the night came. We had only a small sail a size of a small tissue up with what we were sailing. It was a battle of life and death.

Inherent to sailing is the search for safety, but storms like these act as betrayals of romanticized nature. Even though Kaisa had several similar, even horrifying storm experiences, she still returned to the sea. Kaisa is an 80-year-old sailor who usually sails alone. She said she loves sailing because of the peacefulness it brings. However, the stormy experiences enhanced the nature experiences, making sailing more meaningful to her. This finding, hence, follows Arnould and Price (1993) and Celsi et al. (1993) by exemplifying how the restorative power of nature lies within the fear and survival in nature that further enhance sailors' self-efficacy (Canniford and Shankar 2013). The sea in the Nordics may bring anxiety and is thus a place to test oneself. These experiences enable consumers' perception of self-improvement and help to cope with everyday life. They bring nature closer to the consumer and make them feel "at one" with nature. Nature is constantly testing human survival skills. It can be stressful (Tumbat and Belk 2010).

As mentioned, the search for freedom is not a special Nordic characteristic. Yet, it is essential to understand, as freedom is at the core of experiencing nature from the Nordic perspective (Beery 2013). However, everyman's rights set an interesting framework for the feeling of freedom in nature experiences from the Nordic perspective. A specialty in the Nordic sailing territory is natural harbors. These are free for anyone to enter, and no fees need to be paid. Services at the harbors sometimes include an outhouse and a place to set up a bonfire. Furthermore, a natural harbor can also be just any place on the archipelago where sailors find a place to go to shore. Basically, everyone is entitled to go to any island that is not private land. The state is responsible for the natural harbors. These are thus very different to the so-called guest harbors offering services ranging from minigolf courses to restaurants and saunas. The guest harbors also take a small fee for a berth and they are usually run by a private company. Therefore, whereas guest harbors are similar to any harbor found elsewhere in the world, the natural harbors in the Nordics allow romantic nature to be reached where modern culture is not as evidently present. The interviewees often referred to true sailors as the ones who go to natural harbors. Reasons behind choosing a natural harbor versus a guest harbor for the informants usually included a desire for peace and closeness to nature. Natural harbors allow them to be alone with their sailing companion(s), enable them better to forget the stress of everyday life and get away from the highly governed society for a while.

Yet, the feeling of freedom is to some extent paradoxical since, similarly to the rest of the world, the territorial areas are restricted through seafaring rules and boundaries set by the boat type and nature. Territorial restrictions are also created by the seafaring rules. As sailboats have a deeper draft than, for example, motorboats, sailors are not able to reach all places due to the dense archipelago setting narrow paths for sailing. Even though no formal license for sailing is needed, sailors are expected to know and respect seafaring rules, supervised by the "water police." The social norms around boating are strong too. However, Anni explains how the responsibilities at sea bring freedom and peace of mind:

> That it is nature. That it is not city. That you don't have to think of anything at the city such as school and work and responsibilities. At sailing, you have other responsibilities to think of, such as the ones related to being the skipper at boat. It gives you freedom from your everyday routines.

Adherence to the rules brings social trust to sailing. The responsibilities at sea do not prevent the feeling of freedom for Anni. These responsibilities differ so much from her daily responsibilities at work that they serve as a tool for getting a sense of freedom. The cultural rules and codes in the boating community do not bring anxiety to her, as they allow for a sort of structured freedom and peace of mind. This illustrates well the Nordic tendency to respect rules and egalitarianism (Kjeldgaard and Östberg 2007).

Consuming Nature Experiences through Governmental Apparatuses

I will now turn to looking at nature experiences through the multiple governmental apparatuses. The Nordic consumption of nature experiences is organized through multiple governmental apparatuses. Sailing and boat maintenance are organized through the government, municipalities, and boating communities such as the nearest boat club and environmental organizations. As mentioned, boat ownership is interesting from the perspective of Nordic governmental apparatuses due to the interplay of freedom via everyman's rights on the one hand and strict governmental policies on the other.

Boat maintenance has its specialties in the Nordics due to the short sailing season and cold winter. The Baltic Sea freezes in the winter and the boats are lifted to boatyards to avoid ice damage to hulls and props. In the autumn, around the end of September or October, boats are moved onto land and washed with high-pressure hoses, then covered with protective tarpaulins for the long winter storage at outside boatyards. The boats typically stand in the boatyards from October until the end of April. In the spring, boat owners prepare their boats for the sailing season. Springtime maintenance includes washing the boat, waxing its sides, replacing broken or rusty materials, fixing the engine if needed, and painting the hull with anti-fouling paint to avoid the biological contamination of barnacles and algae.

The Government Sponsoring and Ruling Nature Experiences

From a top-down perspective, in terms of sailing and maintaining sailboats, the highest authority is set by the state. The government sets rules and regulations for seafaring and maintenance to structure nature experiences, whereas everyman's rights give freedom for these experiences. Similarly, boat owners are expected to respect nature within the limits of environmental law and everyman's rights. Everyman's rights give responsibility to consumers by giving them freedom to go to shore in the natural harbors. The government therefore sponsors boating by offering free areas, enabling free access to nature (Beery 2013). Thus, the constitution of everyman's rights sets an infinite consumer imagination for sailors. Furthermore, the government is responsible for ensuring safety at sea by placing sea marks.

Nordic egalitarian politics ensure that everyone has an equal possibility to sail. A Swedish harbor master explained the sociopolitical situation of boating in the Nordics:

> It's a very big difference between boating here in Scandinavia compared to Mediterranean. In the Mediterranean, only the very wealthy people have boats. Here everybody has one. I think Sweden is the country with most boats per capita. Everybody can have a boat here compared to the Mediterranean where only rich people can have a boat. Also, because they don't have sheltered archipelagos to sail in, they have to have big boats. I've seen in Turkey a boat like that [points at a big boat in a harbor], with a rich man with white uniform.

The quote illustrates well how the "commonness" of all social classes is identified as "the middle" (Byrkjeflot 2001). In addition to giving free access to nature, equal opportunity is also ensured with low costs of starting the sailing hobby. No sailing course is needed and a boat spot in a public harbor is relatively inexpensive. The egalitarianism is also visible when visiting the Nordic harbors. All kinds of boats, big and small, new and old, are located even in the most prime locations at the heart of cities.

In terms of environmental responsibility, Nordic sailors were often outsourcing morality to the government (Byrkjeflot 2001) rather than taking responsibility in their own hands. Due to the deteriorating condition of the Baltic Sea and visible problems such as blue sea algae covering the sea on hot summer days, most sailors raised environmental issues when discussing nature experiences. When discussing environmental issues, boat owners often referred to the government not setting enough regulations. The informants thus emphasized the role of governance, exemplifying the law-abiding nature of Nordic consumers. These consumers clearly see themselves as protected citizens rather than environmental stewards (see also Giesler and Veresiu 2014).

One such example of when sailors were pointing at the government was a discussion on the boat hull paints called anti-fouling paints. The more toxic anti-fouling paints containing tributyltin (TBT) were banned by the European Union (EU) in 1989. Yet, due to the copper and zinc in the current anti-fouling paints, they have been proven harmful to the key species in the Baltic Sea and thereafter to its whole ecosystem (Lagerström et al. 2017). The ban brought the problems with anti-fouling issues to boat owners' awareness. Therefore, most sailors do know that boat hull paints are toxic and many boat owners were pondering alternative methods. However, another viewpoint among boat owners was that as long as the paints are not forbidden, their use should be acceptable. Consumers perceived the primary role of authorities to inform them about ecologically hazardous waste that causes pollution and health risks. As long as the paints are allowed by the authorities, they are regarded as safe to use. The boat owners were thus putting the blame on the government.

However, sailors' behavior did not always follow their urge for more legislation. For example, regardless of the ban on more toxic paints in the EU, tests taken at boatyards from boat hulls show that this toxic paint can still be found on boat hulls, indicating usage of the banned paints (Eklund and Eklund 2014). Miikka told us what happened:

> People stored them and bought them in storage. They thought that since the paint will be banned from now on, we should get paint storage that would last for 3 years and hope they'll stay in good shape.

Therefore, outsourcing the responsibility to the state did not have the desired solution to the environmental problem. This example illustrates how consumers do not always follow the state, but aim at finding blind spots to go around the rules.

Municipalities Acting as Intermediaries

The municipalities act as more direct authorities to sailors than the government. Further, the municipalities perform as intermediaries in organizing nature experiences. This is because the state has further transferred the responsibility for the boatyards over to the municipalities owning the land. Some sailors have a direct contract for a boatyard spot with the city. Most boat clubs rent the land from the city they are located in. The contracts prohibit boat clubs from polluting rented land. Even when many boat clubs are located on city-owned land that they rent, the responsibility for the boatyard is placed on the boat club. A city official in Helsinki explains the relatively free system at the boatyards:

> Setting rules and communicating them to members is how the clubs work, they do function a lot better than the general boat owner community. They know each other, they see and control their members. So if you act out something less agreeable, everyone will know you. It works pretty well with the clubs. It is good that the boatclubs exist and they are big parties in the big picture here. … In Helsinki all clubs are located in city owned rental areas so we [the leisure department of the municipality] are their landlords. The city rents the land for the boat owners. 90% [of boat owners] also rent the piers from the city. Our responsibility then is to take care of the technical maintenance. We have the equipment needed and they [the boat owners] don't have to pay to get the working rafts as we already have them. This is communal activity which is pretty widespread here. And of course all the boat related companies are here, as are those who know how to take care of water works needed.

This city official wanted to clarify the responsibilities and explained how the city provides the premises and resources, but does not intervene with setting the rules and monitoring them. That task is left to the sailing community. Also, even though the city sets rules for the boat club to protect the boatyard, the ways to do so have been left to the boat club. A harbor master in a boatyard located in Helsinki even explained how the city officials' visits are usually focused around listening to the demands of the boat club rather than being inspections of the boat club. He also mentioned that they develop and maintain the harbor by themselves.

The boat clubs thus seemed to capitalize (Giesler and Veresiu 2014) the boat owners better than the public boatyards by providing concrete resources supporting individuals' active self-management. For example, in the public marinas in Helsinki, no recycling is provided. Instead, consumers are encouraged to take their hazardous waste to a recycling station located on the outskirts of the city, usually far away from the harbor. The responsibility to recycle is left to the boat owner. This leads to piles of empty paint cans in the public boatyards. In contrast, I was impressed by the recycling provided by all the boat clubs in each country to their members. The boat clubs provided different bins for waste, from oils and paper to hazardous waste. The recycling stations at the boat club–managed harbors were mostly clean, leading to fewer dirty piles of trash in the boatyard area. The boat club thus had capitalized the sailors, whereas the city had not.

The Immediate Community Organizing Nature Experiences Most Directly

Even though the state is strong, some nature experiences are organized by the boating community and the sailors within it. Most boat owners belong to a boat club renting land from the municipality. Therefore, nature experiences are organized most directly by the immediate boating community. Further, the responsibility is given to the boat clubs that engage sailors through formal contracts and informal norms and rules.

The Nordic boating community is built around voluntary work. A common event in boatyards is where boat owners gather in the boatyard after spring maintenance and before autumn maintenance to collect boat stands, piling them up for the summer or placing them back on the boat spots for the boats to be lifted onto them. There is often a penalty if a boat owner does not take part in the work, such as an extra guarding shift. Anna explained how the social pressure to participate in this sort of voluntary work is high:

> We were once sailing together with my father and went to a club owned island. We noticed there was a voluntary work event taking place at the island. We didn't make it to the event since we had to fix some stuff at the boat. So we were treated like "second-class" citizens. We could sense the bad atmosphere.

Anna reported feeling guilty at not taking part of the voluntary event. Anna and her father's act of not participating in voluntary work violated the social trust on which Nordic society is based. The example illustrates well the Northern egalitarian ethos of each and every person participating equally. Consumers value independence and self-sufficiency in life, resulting from the respect of other members in the community. Consumers who need to depend on others are unequal (Berggren and Trägårdh 2010). Even though the Nordic welfare state avoids subjecting individuals to the charity of others, the example of voluntary work in communities illustrates well the dependence on others. This relationship to the community also exemplifies the freedom from personal dependence on the state, representing a constant balance between public collectivism and private individualism (Berggren and Trägårdh 2010). Individuals are authorized (Giesler and Veresiu 2014) to take actions independent of the state.

Another example of authorization of the community is the arrangement of boat inspections. The inspections at the boatyards are organized by the boating communities. Anyone can become an inspector after completing a short training course for it and being assigned by the boat club. The inspections are not necessary, but most boat clubs as well as insurance companies require them. The inspections take place at the boatyard either before or after the boating season. The practicalities of inspections vary a lot. The inspections serve as a great example of a deviation from strict governmental discipline. Miika, an inspector who has his boat at a boatyard, explained the procedures related to inspections:

> While doing it [the inspections] they inspect *visually* that the boat is unbroken and that the safety features are operational, the hoses to gas bottles have been maintained and these fire extinguishers have been maintained and the lights are working—they check that everything *looks* alright.

The inspections are often very informal, with inspectors walking around the boat, maybe checking inside the boat. Thus, even though the responsibility for the boats and safety is placed on the community through the inspections, the ultimate responsibility is placed on the sailors through trusting boat owners enough not to inspect every inch of the boat.

Other communities influencing Nordic nature experiences are different non-profit organizations such as the Swedish Cruising Association, promoting cruising and boating in Sweden, to which nearly all boat owners belong. One of the unofficial environmental authorities in Finland is the Keep the Archipelago Tidy association, which for example takes care of rubbish on the Finnish side of the Baltic Sea area and provides services to the islands such as shelters, wood, and toilets. It also organizes septic tank emptying stations. The organization has established a highly respected position among boat owners due to its good work in improving the quality of service premises as well as keeping the archipelago clean.

Keep the Archipelago Tidy's patch which boat owners display represents belonging to a certain community behaving respectably toward nature and participating in protective work. Anna explained her experience of becoming a member. Anna has a shared boat and considers herself the most environmentally friendly owner of their boat. She recently convinced the other boat owners of the need to become a member of Keep the Archipelago Tidy in order to use the organization's services and support its good work for the environment. She explains the change in their sustainable consumption practices after becoming a member:

> Especially now that we have the Keep the Archipelago Tidy patch on our boat I am constantly reminding the others about that. For example if I see a long stream of washing water full of soap dragging behind our boat, I feel embarrassed. We have the patch so we should represent ecological values.

This serves as an example of personalization, as the association aims to personalize the Baltic Sea's problems to boat owners, making boat owners the central problem-solving agent (Giesler and Veresiu 2014). Anna's experience illustrates the heightened moral responsibility of boat owners through association membership. The patch itself is a symbol of the personalization act of the association. Furthermore, the association enhances the responsibilization of the consumer. In order to use its services, one needs to become a member by paying the membership fee. However, there are no checkups on the islands on who is a member entitled to use the services. In addition, consumers are encouraged to participate in cleaning the premises and taking responsibility for their own as well as others' actions. This can be seen as a way of enforcing the sailors to take authority in setting an example of saving the sea.

Discussion

This chapter has discussed how Nordic consumers' nature experiences are orchestrated through the interplay of Nordic ideologies of nature and Nordic governmental apparatuses. Nature experiences are to a large extent similar to other cultures, but there are specialties in how the Nordic model shapes nature experiences through the interplay of nature ideologies and governmental regimes. As shown through the findings of the study on sailing experiences, Nordic nature experiences are full of paradoxes. Consumers must navigate through the paradoxes of consuming nature experiences seemingly freely, but at the same time being restricted to boundaries and responsibilities within the governmental apparatuses.

On the one hand, the consumers searched for freedom and escaping from routine lives through nature following the romantic nature ideology (Canniford and Shankar 2013). Freedom for sailors comes from the closeness of nature through both romantic summer days with beautiful archipelagos as well as sudden storms that allow one to live in the moment and test one's skills, following the gnostic ideology (Thompson 2004). The extraordinary experience of sailing comes from the feeling of conquering nature with gnostic technology and then transitioning back to a romantic experience. The freedom is especially enhanced by everyman's rights giving access to the sea and natural harbors, where sailors are able to enjoy the silence of nature. Even though the feeling of freedom is to some extent paradoxical due to seafaring rules and social norms, these enhanced the social trust among sailors and brought peace of mind.

On the other hand, these experiences of freedom were constructed by the welfare state through multiple governmental apparatuses. The Nordic model relies heavily on governmental control (Østergaard et al. 2014). The regulations and social norms spanned different governing levels, from the state to the immediate boating community. Also, social norms, for example around voluntary work, restrict nature experiences. Yet, everyman's rights set equal freedom for all citizens to enter nature (Beery 2013) and, for instance, to use the natural harbors. Therefore, Nordic nature experiences are constructed by the paradox of Nordic consumers' feeling of freedom in nature through equally free access and at the same time their need to navigate through numerous regulations.

Even though the Nordics are called nanny states (Østergaard et al. 2014), the findings from the sailing context showed examples of responsibility shifting away from the state where communities took actions. The common ideology in the welfare state is that almost everything comes as given to citizens (Kjeldgaard and Östberg 2007). The state should act on flaws and provide a solution to consumers. However, the egalitarian ethos and social trust enhance voluntary work practices such as communal boat inspections. Thus, the responsibility was not shifted entirely away from consumers.

The findings also revealed interesting insight into Nordic environmental responsibility. Even though the Nordic model relies heavily on governmental regulations and the strong role of the state, there are still examples where control has been given to consumers. For example, Kristensen et al. (2011) describe a new health-care system activating consumers in Denmark. They explain how consumers are regarded as active rather than passive consumers due to a reform introduced in 2007, reorganizing the health-care sector in Denmark between private and public. In the new system in Denmark, consumers are perceived as active health-seeking individuals rather than passive patients. The responsibility of the state is to inform consumers about unhealthy behavior, leaving the responsibility to the consumer (Kristensen et al. 2011). Similarly, the boat owners were seeking ways to influence the environmental situation of the Baltic Sea through communities by adhering to the Nordic egalitarian ethos.

References

Ahlström, I. (2008). *Allt om allemnasrätten: En svenskt kulturarv [Everything About Universal Access: A Swedish Cultural Legacy]*. Solna: Hilmas Förlag.

Andersen, J. G. (2013). Welfare and Solidarity. In B. Brincker (Ed.), *Introduction to Political Sociology* (p. 114). Slovania: Hans Reitzels Forlag.

Andrews, T. (2000). *Dictionary of Nature Myths: Legends of the Earth, Sea, and Sky*. Oxford University Press on Demand.

Arnould, E. J., & Price, L. L. (1993). River Magic: Extraordinary Experience and the Extended Service Encounter. *Journal of Consumer Research, 20*(1), 24–45.
Beery, T. H. (2013). Nordic in Nature: Friluftsliv and Environmental Connectedness. *Environmental Education Research, 19*(1), 94–117.
Belk, R. W., & Costa, J. A. (1998). The Mountain Man Myth: A Contemporary Consuming Fantasy. *Journal of Consumer Research, 25*(3), 218–240.
Belk, R., Fischer, E., & Kozinets, R. V. (2012). *Qualitative Consumer and Marketing Research*. Sage.
Berggren, H., & Trägårdh, L. (2010). The Autonomous Child and the Moral Logic of the Swedish Welfare State. In H. Mattson & S.-O. Wallenstein (Eds.), *Swedish Modernism: Architecture, Consumption and the Welfare State* (pp. 50–65). London: Black Dog Publishing.
Byrkjeflot, H. (2001). The Nordic Model of Democracy and Management. In *The Democratic Challenge to Capitalism: Management and Democracy in the Nordic Countries* (pp. 19–45). Fagbokforlaget.
Canniford, R., & Shankar, A. (2013). Purifying Practices: How Consumers Assemble Romantic Experiences of Nature. *Journal of Consumer Research, 39*(5), 1051–1069.
Carlström V. (2016, July 25). *The Nordics Are Leading the World in Sustainable Development – Here's How They Rank*. Retrieved from http://nordic.businessinsider.com.
Celsi, R. L., Rose, R. L., & Leigh, T. W. (1993). An Exploration of High-Risk Leisure Consumption Through Skydiving. *Journal of Consumer Research, 20*(1), 1–23.
Cronon, W. (1996). *Uncommon Ground: Rethinking the Human Place in Nature*. New York, NY: W.W. Norton & Co.
Eklund, B., & Eklund, D. (2014). Pleasure Boatyard Soils Are Often Highly Contaminated. *Environmental Management, 53*(5), 930–946.
Eklund, B., Haaksi, H., Syversen, F., & Eisted, R. (2013). *Disposals of Plastic End-of-Life Boats*. TemaNord 2013:582, Nordic Council of Ministers 2013. ISBN: 978–92–893-2651-3. https://doi.org/10.6027/TN2013-582.
Giesler, M., & Veresiu, E. (2014). Creating the Responsible Consumer: Moralistic Governance Regimes and Consumer Subjectivity. *Journal of Consumer Research, 41*(3), 840–857.
Hall, C. M., Müller, D. K., & Saarinen, J. (2008). *Nordic Tourism: Issues and Cases*. Channel View Publications.
Hornborg, E. (1965). *Purjehdusmerenkulun historia*. Porvoo: WSOY.
Isberg, R., & Isberg, S. (2007). *Simple Life: Friluftsliv*. Victoria, BC: Trafford.

Kjeldgaard, D., & Östberg, J. (2007). Coffee Grounds and the Global Cup: Glocal Consumer Culture in Scandinavia. *Consumption Markets & Culture, 10*(2), 175–187.
Kozinets, R. V. (2002). Can Consumers Escape the Market? Emancipatory Illuminations from Burning Man. *Journal of Consumer Research, 29*(1), 20–38.
Kozinets, R. V. (2007). Technology/Ideology: How Ideological Fields Influence Consumers' Technology Narratives. *Journal of Consumer Research, 34*(6), 865–881.
Kristensen, D. B., Boye, H., & Askegaard, S. (2011). Leaving the Milky Way! The Formation of a Consumer Counter Mythology. *Journal of Consumer Culture, 11*(2), 195–214.
Lagerström, M., Strand, J., Eklund, B., & Ytreberg, E. (2017). Total Tin and Organotin Speciation in Historic Layers of Antifouling Paint on Leisure Boat Hulls. *Environmental Pollution, 220*, 1333–1341.
Moisio, R., Arnould, E. J., & Gentry, J. W. (2013). Productive Consumption in the Class-Mediated Construction of Domestic Masculinity: Do-It-Yourself (DIY) Home Improvement in Men's Identity Work. *Journal of Consumer Research, 40*(2), 298–316.
Olwig, K. (1992). *The European Nation's Nordic Nature.*
Olwig, K. R. (2005). Introduction: The Nature of Cultural Heritage, and the Culture of Natural Heritage—Northern Perspectives on a Contested Patrimony. *International Journal of Heritage Studies, 11*(1), 3–7.
Østergaard, P., Linnet, J. T., Andersen, L. P., Kjeldgaard, D., Bjerregaard, S., Weijo, H., & Östberg, J. (2014). Nordic Consumer Culture: Context and Concept. In J. W. Schouten, D. M. Martin, & R. Belk (Eds.), *Consumer Culture Theory* (Research in Consumer Behavior) (Vol. 16, pp. 245–257). Emerald Group Publishing Limited.
Sandell, K. (2006). Access Under Stress: The Right of Public Access Tradition in Sweden. In N. McIntyre, D. Williams, & K. McHugh (Eds.), *Multiple Dwelling and Tourism: Negotiating Place, Home and Identity* (p. 278). Oxfordshire: CABI.
Scholz, J. (2012). Myth Busting: Living in Harmony with Nature Is Less Harmonic than It Seems. *Research in Consumer Behavior, 14*, 297–313. Emerald Group Publishing Limited.
Thompson, C. J. (2004). Marketplace Mythology and Discourses of Power. *Journal of Consumer Research, 31*(1), 162–180.
Tumbat, G., & Belk, R. W. (2010). Marketplace Tensions in Extraordinary Experiences. *Journal of Consumer Research, 38*(1), 42–61.

Part II

The Nordic as Market Imagery

8

Danish Welfare Exports as the "New Bacon": Myth and Meaning of the Nordic Welfare Model as Glocal Cultural Commodity

Stine Bjerregaard and Dannie Kjeldgaard

In January 2014, one of the politically leading news media in Denmark published an analysis of the prospects of the so-called *welfare export* under the headline "Welfare may become the new bacon" (Schmidt 2014)—a juxtaposition that quickly gained ground in other Danish news media. The cause for this optimism was a reported interest in the Chinese market for Danish knowhow and competencies in the elder-care sector, and the reference to the commercial success of Denmark's long and solid tradition of bacon exports may be said to mark the culmination of past decades' marketization of Nordic welfare models. Here the process of marketization was no longer mobilizing an internal reorganization of the Danish welfare system and a rationalization of social services alone, but now also took on an outward orientation, where the very notion of welfare was commodified and cast as a commercial entity associated with a significant export potential on global markets.

The scenario illustrated by the news story taps into two simultaneous but somewhat paradoxical tendencies. On one hand, Denmark (along

S. Bjerregaard (✉) • D. Kjeldgaard
University of Southern Denmark, Odense, Denmark
e-mail: dkj@sam.sdu.dk

S. Askegaard, J. Östberg (eds.), *Nordic Consumer Culture*,
https://doi.org/10.1007/978-3-030-04933-1_8

with other Nordic countries) is enjoying international acclaim as an ideal social and political state model that other countries around the world ought to look to as a point of orientation in future political development. Examples of such attention include political economist Francis Fukuyama's (2011, 2014) use of "getting to Denmark" as a metaphor for the development of viable state institutions, with Denmark serving as a symbol for a well-governed, peaceful, prosperous, and uncorrupt place (2011), and *The Economist*'s announcement of Nordic welfare models as "The Next Supermodel" (Wooldridge 2013). On the other hand, however, Danish politics has over the past decades become increasingly preoccupied with domestic debates on the future viability of the universalistic welfare model. With growing globalization, extensive welfare provision is argued to hinder national competitiveness and thus threaten Denmark's position as one of the world's most affluent countries—with the demise of the welfare system altogether being envisioned as the consequence. On this note, both social-democratic and liberal governments have made the Danish welfare system subject to cutbacks, privatization, and a number of more or less neoliberal reforms of public procurement to mimic market conditions, although there is wide agreement on the idea of Denmark being a "welfare society" (Edling et al. 2014). Thus, while the international acclaim of the Danish welfare model is received with pride and self-glorification in the Danish media, the very same model is domestically under critical scrutiny and pressure.

On this backdrop, the present study sets out to explore empirically these dynamics as a cultural commodification process in a domain not commonly associated with market logics, namely public welfare services. While consumer culture theory (CCT) literature has been increasingly concerned with market-level dynamics (e.g., Bjerrisgaard and Kjeldgaard 2013; Giesler 2012; Humphreys 2010; Peñaloza and Venkatesh 2006), few studies go beyond national contexts (one exception is Cayla and Eckhardt 2008) and little research has been done to understand the relationship between state and market in a global social and economic order. This study addresses this gap by exploring how particular public services are articulated as market offerings in an export context, and how the idea of exporting public services illuminates ironic neoliberal relations between ideas of states and global markets.

We do so with a starting point in globalization literature, while theoretically framing cultural commodification as myth marketing (Cayla and Arnould 2008; Cayla and Eckhardt 2008; Holt 2004, 2006; Thompson 2004; Thompson and Tian 2008). We situate our discussion in macro-social explanatory frameworks including not only social and cultural contexts, but also political (Giesler and Veresiu 2014) and institutional contexts (Karababa and Ger 2011).

Glocal Myth Markets

In this section we outline the overall theoretical perspectives that we use to unfold our analysis of the transformation of welfare services into cultural commodities.

Appadurai (1990) describes the process of globalization as a compression of time and space, where geographical space or landscape loses its meaning relative to other structured and structuring "scapes." In other words, a number of social processes related to the economy, politics, and culture become increasingly independent of geographical distances, while such global flows may be argued to be increasingly mediated by the market as a dominant social order (Slater and Tonkiss 2001). However, not only is the idea of a global market an etic category, it also comes to constitute a myth that guides thought and action at the level of practitioners. As Applbaum (2000) has pointed out in the context of international transnational corporations (TNCs), the notion of global markets functions as both "myth and charter" for practitioner action. This perspective becomes an overall thematic guide in our analysis of the discursive articulation of welfare services as global commodities.

On the other hand, the idea of the local, or locality, is part and parcel of globalization processes (Appadurai 1995; Robertson 1995). Local markets are both part of the myth of globalization just discussed as a potential source of sales and success, and something that has a specific sign value for product differentiation. The extensive literatures on country-of-origin meanings and place images testify to this. However, both commonly emphasize the receiving audience/market and do not cater for the process by which the "sender" (here conceptualized as a collective marketer) is making sense and negotiating the value and commercial prospects of its offerings to export markets. For this reason, we turn to the myth marketing literature and the related stream of literature dealing with marketers as cultural producers.

In the myth marketing literature, marketers are considered as cultural producers (Cayla and Eckhardt 2008; Peñaloza 2000; Thompson and Tian 2008); that is, marketing has culturally performative outcomes. Cayla and Eckhardt (2008), for example, demonstrate the role of marketers in creating a transnational sense of Asianness in the process of constructing new markets. In our case, we understand the mythic articulation of welfare services as a marketable offer to be a collective endeavor at national level that ties into popular memory (Thompson and Tian 2008) of the "heroic" establishment and continuation of the welfare state. This addresses contemporary domestic tensions and issues (Holt 2004; Thompson 2004) concerning the future viability of the extensive universal welfare state. The articulation of welfare services as exportable commodities addresses this tension and thus comes to serve national political concerns.

Method

The empirical starting point for the study is a field of actors and activities that assembled around the endeavor of exporting Danish elder care–related products and services to China. Described briefly, the specific focus on the emerging Chinese market for elderly care was introduced to Danish stakeholders in early 2012 with an export promotion program launched by the Danish Trade Council in China. The core of the program was the D'Care (Danish Care) nursing home—a "low-energy state-of-the-art nursing home" (Danish Trade Council 2013) that would integrate as much Danish content as possible. The nursing home was envisioned to serve as a reference for Danish knowhow, services, and products that would assist in "building the image of Denmark in the Chinese eldercare, engineering and design sector" (Danish Trade Council 2013) and was thus part of an entrance strategy paving the way for Danish marketers targeting the emerging Chinese elder-care sector.

Although the D'Care project was abandoned within less than two years and the explicit support from the Danish Trade Council put to an end, the idea of exporting Danish elder care to China had already gained a significant foothold in Danish public debate, and had set in motion a line of other market activities targeted the Chinese elder-care sector. The focus on the Chinese market even found its way into government plans on growth in the health and welfare sector, with special mention of a cooperative agreement between Denmark and China on "care and welfare technologies in the eldercare area" (Danish Government 2013). Although Danish marketers had a hard time carving out business models suitable for the Chinese market, a nursing home with Danish management and Danish care principles did open in a rural Shanghai district in November 2015.

The study presented here is part of a larger ethnographic study of this field with an overall focus on the marketization of Nordic welfare models as it is expressed through the collective public–private endeavor of marketing Danish elder-care solutions on the Chinese market for professional elder care. One of the authors was following this field from 2013 to 2017, mapping out actors and key events, and thus acquired an intimate familiarity with it. In the present study, however, we take a step back from the kaleidoscopic networks of actors and events and focus on the representational level, by exploring the discursive articulation of export activities as it came across in Danish news media at the time.

Taking an analytical starting point in discourse as it is publicly accessible in news media provides an opportunity to assess the general framing of reported events. This gives us important insight into news value or topicality; that is, what a society finds interesting and relevant at a specific point in time. Similarly, the use of tropes and metaphors points to the activation of the popular memory (Thompson and Tian 2008), in terms of what other events or concepts are invoked as sharing some characteristics with the reported event.

Data for the analysis presented here has been retrieved through exploratory searches of the news coverage of the line of activities and discussions set in motion with the D'Care promotion program; that is, the export of elder-care solutions and related products and services to China. Included in this data set are a series of features and letters to the editor authored personally by actors in the Danish elder-care sector. Approximately 60 news stories were the result of this search, of which approximately half were reprints or excerpts from national news media brought to regional news media. While these reprints and excerpts do not add anything at the semantic level, they testify to the local significance attributed to these far-away events.

To contextualize this set of data, a secondary search in a Danish news article database was carried out using the search words "welfare export" (in Danish *velfærdseksport*) and the associated "systems export" (*systemeksport*), providing an overview of the proliferation of the terms over time, their more general use, as well as associated discourses and metaphors since 1990. This data search totaled a number of 1340 news articles.

Findings

The findings section will commence with a largely chronological analysis of the news coverage of elder care–related export activities targeted to the Chinese market, as introduced with the D'Care export promotion program. Interesting in this regard is the unequivocal application of a market logic guiding the collective interpretation of the reported events. Then, the analysis zooms in on the envisioned market offerings, finding articulations in this regard characterized by a curious ambiguity and a lack of delineation. Finally, the analysis turns to the use of tropes and metaphors, arguing that these disclose a second layer of meaning. Despite its outward orientation, the popular rendition of welfare exports as it comes across in the Danish news media seems equally tied to domestic concerns over the Danish elder-care sector and the provision of public welfare services more generally.

Welfare and Profit

As already outlined, the focus on the emerging market for elder care in China was introduced to Danish stakeholders in early 2012 by the Danish Trade Council and its representative in West China, the consul general at the time. The consul general acted as the primary driver of these activities and, while he left his position in August 2013, the D'Care project and the general prospects of exporting Danish elder-care solutions to China had already attracted considerable attention among industry professionals as well as in the broader national press.

The Trade Council's internal documents and presentation material for industry professionals did not initially establish an explicit link to the notion of welfare exports. Welfare exports, however, quickly came to serve as the general frame of reference for most news stories reporting on or referring to Danish activities targeting the Chinese elder-care sector. With a headline reading "Danish welfare is the export commodity of the future" (Elers 2012a), this frame was established right from the very first news story covering elder care–related events in China—an article published in *Børsen*, the leading business-oriented newspaper in Denmark. Accordingly, the large majority of articles reporting on welfare exports to China are placed in business sections rather than international news sections.

As indicated with the collocation of welfare and exports, the overarching logic applied to provide meaning and motive to the events described in the series of news articles analyzed is a market logic emphasizing commercial potential and profit. This is reflected in the headline already mentioned as well as in headlines such as "Experts: Great potential in health- and welfare export" (Lassen 2013), "Chinese elderly boom may reward Linak [Danish manufacturer of lift systems] handsomely" (Rechnagel 2013a), "Danish investors are chasing for profit among China's grey gold" (Rechnagel 2013b), "Welfare may become the new bacon" (Schmidt 2014), and "Elderly Chinese may create new Danish export adventure" (Pedersen 2014).

The prospects of the emerging Chinese market for professional elder care and the business opportunities for Danish organizations are highlighted consistently and frequently. On a spread in *Børsen* on April 3, 2012, a lead paragraph in one article informs the reader that "Investment in billions in the Chinese [senior] care sector may benefit Danish companies. China has little experience in the area and needs foreign competencies" (Elers 2012a), while the adjacent article highlights the D'Care project and sketches a compelling scenario: "Affluent Chinese want

Scandinavian welfare and therefore they are ready to pay the costs for staying in senior housing or nursing homes after the Danish model" (Elers 2012b).

It is noteworthy how the size and prospects of this emerging market are consistently presented with an emphasis on its gigantic scope and magnitude:

> Export of Danish eldercare to China may yield towering returns, says Danish investment advisor behind nursing home project. … I have never seen a business case this good. We are talking about an elderly burden that is the biggest in the world. Moreover the Chinese spending power is exploding at the moment, so the market is enormous, says Jacob Juul-Hansen. (Rechnagel 2013b)

This emphasis on magnitude is also expressed through the common use of figures to attest the need for elder care in China—most often assessed in millions, as in this fact box spelling out the elder-care situation in China (Elers 2012a):

> Facts: A need for more nursing homes:
> - There is a lack of 3.4 million nursing home beds in China
> - 3 percent of the Chinese over the age of 60 yrs. have a need to stay at a nursing home—equaling 5.3 million elderly Chinese—a number that by 2025 will have increased to 8.5 million (estimate of the central government)
> - Chinese nursing home staff counts approx. 1 million of whom only 10 percent are educated or professionally trained
> - The need for personnel is at least 10 million

During the course of the following two years, these figures are frequently repeated—especially the "lack of 3.4 million nursing home beds," while new figures are also sent into circulation, which makes keeping track of numbers almost dizzying:

> in 15 years there will be 100 million more Chinese people over the age of 60 years than today. (Rechnagel 2013a)

> In 20 years it is estimated that there will be more than 400 million Chinese over the age of 60 years. (Strager 2013)

What is interesting as regards the figures reported is how they take on an almost mythic character when compared to the scale of elder-care activities known in Denmark. The CEO of a Danish vocational health-care college comments in a newspaper feature:

> In the metropolis of Chongqing, which is one of the places where we expect to start education in 2014, 60.000 nursing home beds are going to be created according to Hans Halskov. As a comparison, a medium-sized Danish municipality rarely has more than 1.000 nursing home beds. (Strager 2013)

From a Danish perspective, the magnitude of needs assessed in millions appears almost incomprehensible, and as such it is no wonder that the prospects are described with notions such as "goldmine," "business adventure," and "export adventure." In this way, we see the Chinese market for elder care represented through a *frontier myth* echoing past times' fascination for the American West (Holt 2006), with the urgency of the gold rush reflected in the emphasis on "seizing the opportunity before it is too late." Here the Danish consul general in West China is quoted:

> Denmark has a unique chance to become first movers in this area because we, within the eldercare sector, possess the exact competencies that the Chinese are demanding. And now that the Chinese government even urges private investors and foreign companies to help cover the great need, we must be ready to seize the opportunity. (Elers 2012a)

As the Danish news media report on Danish experiences in the Chinese elder-care sector, it is seen how the general Chinese *market potential* is translated into a *demand* for Danish competencies in particular. After the second Danish delegation trip to China in late 2012, *Børsen* describes the situation:

> The demand for Danish competencies in the area of eldercare is so intense that a delegation with 23 companies, municipalities and operators has just

> returned home from China with all of 14 agreements on projects and collaboration. With this, the ground is prepared for a solid Danish export of welfare services. (Elers 2012c)

The Danish consul general explains that "the sole fact that it managed to attract several hundred Chinese participants" he sees as "clear evidence that the Danish knowhow in the domain of eldercare is an exceedingly sought-after offering" (Elers 2012c). Similar experiences are reported from a range of other Danish actors in the field, here the vice president of a Danish university college:

> It is not only the Chinese that are demanding Danish welfare. Also other emerging economies have their eyes on Denmark. … Of course they don't just contact us for the fun of it. We have a product that they would like to have. They need our welfare solutions as their middle class is growing. (Schmidt 2014)

Later in 2014, the same vice president spells out the market logic by referring to welfare export as "sound business logic" (Friese 2014), and by September of the same year the use of market logic reaches a high when the prospects of Danish activities in the Chinese elder-care sector are likened to historic and—at least on a Danish scale—very successful Danish bacon exports:

> Warm Danish welfare hands will now help securing the Chinese elderly a safe old age in beautiful and well-arranged nursing homes, where the nursing staffs are experts in delivering a respectful and obliging care. Thereby the road may be paved for a new business adventure that has the potential to get cold cash rolling into the export account when the sales of welfare solutions turn into the new billion dollar business like the bacon export. (Pedersen 2014)

Summing up, we have in this section seen how articulations related to changing Chinese demographics reveal an implicit translation of demographic facts into a de facto demand, as well as how Danish competencies are articulated as market offerings matching this demand, thereby making the basis for a *market*. That is, we see how a market logic is mobilized to make sense of the state of affairs and the possible implications, rather than, for example, a political logic emphasizing diplomatic relations.

The Market Offering

In this section we turn our attention to the articulation of the actual products and services that Danes are reported to be taking to the market in China and that are envisioned to get the "cold cash rolling into the export account" (Pedersen 2014).

Going through the articles reporting on agreements between Danish and Chinese parties or more loosely envisioned market activities, we see a range of projects and activities described as market offerings. As regards the D'Care project, the market offering is understood to be the nursing home per se. However, in the articles reporting on the project, it is stressed that the nursing home is to be "after Danish model" and that the central idea of the project is to make it a showcase of "Danish welfare technology, knowledge, design, and construction tradition" (Elers 2012b); that is, rather intangible or conceptual notions that seem more akin to product attributes than to actual products or services.

Later, as marketing endeavors mature, the outlines of market offerings become slightly more specific. For instance, a Danish home-care operator is reported to have entered an agreement on the "operation of nursing homes, including recruitment and training" (Pedersen 2012). Yet, it is highlighted that the agreement will also introduce "knowhow on rehabilitation as well as the design of nursing homes" (Pedersen 2012). In other words, the agreement on specific service and consultancy delivery is qualified with a more abstract promise related to some proficiency or special understanding.

However, in almost all news articles that do not report on some specific agreement entered into between Danish and Chinese parties, the market offering subject to export is referred to in rather vague terms, such as "eldercare products," "welfare services," "welfare solutions," "welfare technologies," "welfare competencies or -knowledge," or, as we see in a previous quote, "warm welfare hands" (Pedersen 2014). And in many articles, what is reported as being exported is simply "Danish welfare."

This prevalence of welfare being used as a label for the market offering may be said to echo the proliferation in Danish contemporary society of welfare as a prefix used to describe a host of activities, actors, and concepts that are not commonly delineated in any specific way. The commonality could be argued to be the relationship with a domain, namely the health-care system and social services—a domain that in Denmark is generally known as the *welfare sector*, but the notion of welfare is commonly treated as self-evident and rarely questioned. The so-called welfare sector used to be largely public, but, with a growing emphasis on public–private collaboration and partnerships, private actors are now also referred to as *welfare companies*, thus "welfare" can no longer be equated with "public." As such, the popular renditions of welfare are highly ambiguous and readily associated with anything from a domain of actors and activities related to the provision of specific social and health-related benefits, to a political project or vision for society as a whole.

Turning to the context of exports, the use of welfare in the designation or description of exports and export activities may be argued to blur and conflate the nature of the market offerings targeting foreign markets, where the welfare prefix may not hold similar information and connotations—if any at all. In this sense, it remains unclear whether referring to the notion of welfare means referring to the supplier and its relationship with a specific domain, to the product or service offered, or to the legacy of the Danish welfare state, and thus ultimately to an ideological vision.

The vice president of a Danish university college—one of the most active Danish actors on the Chinese market for elder care—acknowledges this lack of clear delineations in a feature article published in a politically oriented online news medium:

> If we take a look at Denmark's stock of welfare knowledge, it may be difficult to describe the goods that international customers are expecting us to have ready on the shelves. Because this entails that public institutions as ours are capable of thinking as merchants. This is something that we are trying to do and it is present in the government's innovation strategy. But we will not get far if we cannot define the goods. (Friese 2014)

Not only does this public-sector actor quite explicitly refer to the need for adhering to a market logic—"thinking as merchants"—he also readily adopts it when speaking of Denmark's "stock" of welfare knowledge and "customers" expecting "goods ready on the shelves."

The quote illustrates the paradox of the welfare export case. The market logic is readily adopted and put to use, as seen in the obvious way in which ideas, events, and activities are represented in terms of demand, customers, and goods. Yet, when it comes to articulating Danish welfare as more specific, marketable products, matters become more difficult. While the very idea of the market is a myth that resonates globally, being part and parcel of the global ideoscape (Appadurai 1990), the difficulty of commodifying the welfare domain remains in its context-specific nature and its relationship with political expectations, societal development, historical trajectories, and social structures (to name a few)—all pointing to different notions of, for instance, care.

In the following we see how actors draw on imagery related to the national self to more specifically articulate the market offering.

More than Profit: Imagining the Export Market in the Image of (National) Self

In addition to the over-arching market logic applied in the news coverage of activities in China, a series of metaphors and other tropes also appear, with considerable impact. In the earlier quote, "bacon export" is one and "warm hands" is another, while tropes invoked in other news articles include "elderly burden" (Pedersen 2012) and "grey gold" (Rechnagel 2013b).

Interestingly, these tropes seem to reflect domestic issues and concerns more than they address issues on the Chinese market approached. The notions of "warm hands," "elderly burden," and to some extend also "grey gold" are figures of speech that have all been coined in the Danish debate on the domestic situation regarding professional elder care as part of the generally extensive welfare provision in Denmark. As in most other western countries, Denmark is experiencing a general aging of its population due to smaller cohorts following the so-called baby boomer generation and increasing life expectancy. With this scenario, there are simply not enough care professionals, "warm hands" (as opposed to "cold hands"; that is, administrators, robots, and other types of so-called welfare technology), to take care of the allegedly quite demanding baby boomer generation—the "grey gold." "Elderly burden" is thus the somewhat derogatory term for the societal challenge caused by changing demographic patterns.

All this should be seen in light of the negative mentions that the Danish elder-care sector often receives, with common news stories of various disgraceful circumstances at nursing homes as well as among the elderly receiving home care. In other words, Danish elder care is rarely seen as a success story, and this generally negative perception seems to conflict with the sudden international acclaim that Danish elder-care actors are boasting of in relation to welfare exports. In a letter to the editor, two local politicians from a provincial town in Denmark are questioning the spending of public funds by the city councilor in charge of the municipality's elder-care services. This city councilor, Tina, has participated in one of the D'Care delegations to China, and now local politicians are concerned with the benefit of this trip to local citizens, while also bringing attention to objectionable circumstances in the local elder-care sector:

> We would like to know what kind of inspiration Tina and the others brought back to the municipality or if they were only providing inspiration to the Chinese. Tina went over to sell a "gold-plated" project, but China has a different culture, so we doubt that the Chinese are interested in meals brought out from a centralized catering centre, in the lack of cleaning services, and in strictly technology instead of personal nursing and care as we are seeing it in Denmark. (Algren and Beck 2013)

In spite of the irony, the quote clearly illustrates how the attempts to rearticulate Danish elder care globally are contested locally. In the answer from the city councilor, an interesting aspect is brought into the debate, namely the responsibility not only for securing an orderly operation of the municipality's elder-care services, but also for partaking in trade politics for the greater good of Denmark as a nation-state. The key is the "enormous knowledge" that the municipality holds in the domain of welfare, the city councilor explains, "a knowledge that is important to Denmark in many regards, and also a knowledge that may prove important as regards export." The city councilor continues her reply:

> As the city councilor of the sector, I naturally look down at my desk to respond to all the tasks we have internally. But I also look up and away from my desk and out into the world. Because it is there that the opportunity for growth of the Danish export is placed and with that the opportunity to maintain the welfare society we all care about. (Nielsen 2013)

The paradoxical juxtaposition of the troubled character of the Danish elder-care sector and the acclaim received from abroad is also addressed by the president of a Danish vocational health-care college in a feature, here with an emphasis on the implications for the social and health-care profession—a domain that with later years' focus on the importance of higher-level education has become associated with a lower status:

> At a time where being vocationally trained and attending a vocational college does not have a high status, it is certainly interesting to us that both China and Ghana have sent delegations to our school to see how we organize a vocational education program. As a vocational education we have something that is in demand in great parts of the world, and the Danish social- and healthcare assistant may rightly be proud of having a vocational training. The recognition that Danish social and healthcare workers not always think they enjoy in Denmark—this they currently have from a large international society who wants their exact training. ... We have abilities that are in demand: In Denmark we have a high level of professionalism within nursing and care of the elderly. (Strager 2013)

Hence, what we see in the seemingly outward-oriented debate on the prospects for Danish elder-care competencies on foreign markets (here the Chinese) is how it also ties into a domestic debate on the vice and virtues of the Danish elder-care sector. With business opportunities for elder-care solutions opening up on foreign markets, the somewhat troubled Danish elder-care sector is suddenly seen as a central actor in leveraging these opportunities. This brings about a new sense of responsibility, but also new room for maneuver. And as goes for educational institutions more specifically, we see the outline of another motive for engagement in the so-called export adventure, namely the opportunity to raise the level of legitimacy of the respective organizations as regards both student intake and a bolstering against cutbacks in public funding. In other words, this export endeavor may be as much about legitimizing the Danish elder-care sector as it is about the Chinese market for elder care; it is about a largely negative story that is sought to be turned around to a success story, installing pride and hope in a troubled sector.

By projecting Danish elder-care competencies onto a foreign and largely imagined audience through the lens of the market, we see a translation of value, where issues that are found worrying in a domestic context become subject to a positive valorization when viewed in a global perspective, where they are translated into potential market assets. In this light, we may view the public debate in the Danish news media as autocommunicative (Christensen 1997)—a self-referential expression of an identity project at a societal level. It may thus be argued that the notion of a global market or of specific export markets—functioning as "myth and charter" (Applbaum 2000)—comes to act as a catalyst for collective sense-making regarding the legitimacy of the welfare system and thus the future of the nation-state.

Discussion

In this analysis, a core theme is the supremacy of a profit-oriented market logic in a sector that in a Danish context lies close to the core of the welfare state and is characterized by a prevalence of public actors, who are by state regulation restricted in their means of pursuing profit.

Although the sheer pervasiveness of neoliberal sentiments in our present time may challenge the imagination of any alternative rendition of the events reported on, welfare export has a past that is not as explicitly commercial as its present framing suggests. Historically, welfare export is closely associated with the notion of "systems export," which in its heyday in the early 1990s was guided by an altruistic logic, with *helping* or *development* acting as a primary motive for export endeavors. News articles in the 1990s framed as systems export frequently report on agricultural development projects in Africa and democracy projects in Eastern European countries, and do so in a way where the generation of profit (or sometimes merely covering costs) only comes second to the altruistic motive of *doing good.*

However, what is interesting is not only the shift in the guiding logic per se, but also how this market logic is put to use. Tying into the greater narrative of the endangered Danish welfare system, welfare export is not only about generating profit in foreign markets, it is also about the future of Denmark as a welfare society. With the prospects of making a profit in foreign markets based on the competencies accumulated in a largely public sector, the extensive welfare system suddenly acquires a new raison d'être. Welfare export in its new commercial guise can thus be seen as a means to an end that lies beyond profit on its own. In the following, we situate our discussion in macro-social explanatory frameworks, including not only social and cultural contexts but also political and institutional contexts, and unfold the productive capacity of state/market dialectics as regards market creation dynamics.

The Glocal Brand of the Neoliberal Welfare State

Due to the challenges of global economic competition, it has been argued that the role of the nation-state is changing and that social policy is economized as a productive factor in securing economic growth and job creation (Kettunen 2011). Such a tendency is highly present in a Danish context too (Pedersen 2011). However, the popular rendition of welfare export as evidenced in this study also points to another role of the Danish state, namely as a source for the largely immaterial cultural legacy of its welfare system. Projected onto the global market, the notion of Danish welfare comes to function as a signifier that is simultaneously vague in terms of its associated actors and activities and loaded with both a mythologized past and a commercial promise. As the welfare legacy is sought to be commodified, this promise may be argued to spur the mobilization of the Nordic model as a *brand* rather than a conceptually meaningful distinction of a particular welfare state model (Kettunen and Petersen 2011).

Turning to the literature on market creation and markets dynamics more generally, the role of the state is often absent, and when it is considered it is often as a restraining factor. Weijo et al. (2018), for instance, study consumer action targeted at state regulations considered as unduly restrictive. In our study, the role of the state—or the public sector at large—is more ambiguous, as the legacy of the Nordic welfare state and its associated services is mobilized for globally oriented market endeavors to ensure specific actors' political legitimacy locally. As such, we may extend Applbaum's (2000) understanding of "Globalization as Myth and Charter." However, globalization, in the form of success on export markets, may be argued also to serve as a legitimizing myth for practitioner action. More broadly speaking, we can argue that "Globalization as Legitimacy" functions at the level of the idea of the Nordic welfare model as such a legitimizing myth for practitioner action.

On this note, we may point to an irony of neoliberalism as it plays out in this context.

While the pervasiveness of neoliberal ideology has become a "truth" within both scholarship and popular discourse, few scholars have explored neoliberalism as something more than an implicit background explanatory framework (Mudge 2008). In this study we find that the employment of neoliberal principles does not necessarily mark out a one-way road to the diminishment of states in lieu of global markets. Instead, it paves the way for renewed interest in the state, although at a symbolic rather than regulatory level.

Through the glorification of the market as the mediator of exchange between states, the legacy of states' cultural and ideological history is mythologized and provided with commercial value—it becomes a brand. Conversely, this articulation of the cultural ideology of the welfare state in commercial terms is used to renew the legitimacy of such a state.

Neoliberalism is hence mobilized as a resource for a renewed legitimization of the welfare state in a global market order. Neoliberalism provides a discursive resource or framework for social discourse and practice that simultaneously takes neoliberalism to new heights and turns neoliberalism on its head, using neoliberal logics as a means to a non-liberal end; that is, to sustain a large public sector.

Thus, the notions of state and market do not cancel each other out, but rather intertwine in mutually conducive ways, acting as a catalyst for practitioner action.

References

Algren, K., & Beck C. (2013, January 19). Kommunalt betalt Kina-rejse. *Nordjyske Stiftstidende.*

Appadurai, A. (1990). Disjuncture and Difference in the Global Cultural Economy. *Theory, Culture and Society, 7*, 295–310.

Appadurai, A. (1995). The Production of Locality. In R. Fardon (Ed.), *Counterworks* (pp. 204–225). London: Routledge.

Applbaum, K. (2000). Crossing Borders: Globalization as Myth and Charter in American Transnational Consumer Marketing. *American Ethnologist, 27*(2), 257–282.

Bjerrisgaard, S. M., & Kjeldgaard, D. (2013). How Market Research Shapes Market Spatiality: A Global Governmentality Perspective. *Journal of Macromarketing, 33*(1), 29–40.

Cayla, J., & Arnould, E. (2008). A Cultural Approach to Branding in the Global Marketplace. *Journal of International Marketing, 16*(4), 86–112.

Cayla, J., & Eckhardt, G. M. (2008). Asian Brands and the Shaping of a Transnational Imagined Community. *Journal of Consumer Research, 35*(2), 216–230.

Christensen, L. T. (1997). Marketing as Auto-Communication. *Consumption, Markets and Culture, 1*(3), 197–227.

Danish Trade Council. (2013). Danish Care Group Membership Agreement.

Edling, N., Petersen, J. H., & Petersen, K. (2014). Social Policy Language in Denmark and Sweden. In D. Béland & K. Petersen (Eds.), *Analysing Social Policy Concepts and Language: Comparative and Transnational Perspectives* (pp. 13–34). Bristol, UK: Policy Press.

Elers, P. (2012a, April 3). Dansk velfærd er fremtidens eksportvare. *Børsen.*

Elers, P. (2012b, April 3). D'Care – dansk plejehjem i Vestkina. *Børsen.*

Elers, P. (2012c, December 3). Velfærdseksport vækkes til live. *Børsen.*

Friese, P. (2014, May 13). Velfærdseksport er godt købmandsskab. *Altinget.dk.*

Fukuyama, F. (2011). *The Origins of Political Order: From Prehuman Times to the French Revolution*. New York: Farrar, Straus and Giroux.

Fukuyama, F. (2014). *Political Order and Political Decay: From the Industrial Revolution to the Globalization of Democracy*. New York: Farrar, Straus and Giroux.

Giesler, M. (2012). How Doppelgänger Brand Images Influence the Market Creation Process: Longitudinal Insights from the Rise of Botox Cosmetic. *Journal of Marketing, 76*(6), 55–68.

Giesler, M., & Veresiu, E. (2014). Creating the Responsible Consumer: Moralistic Governance Regimes and Consumer Subjectivity. *Journal of Consumer Research, 41*(3), 840–857.

Holt, D. (2004). *How Brands Become Icons: The Principles of Cultural Branding*. Cambridge, MA: Harvard Business School Press.

Holt, D. (2006). Jack Daniel's America: Iconic Brands as Ideological Parasites and Proselytizers. *Journal of Consumer Culture, 6*(3), 355–377.

Humphreys, A. (2010). Megamarketing: The Creation of Markets as a Social Process. *Journal of Marketing, 74*(2), 1–19.

Karababa, E., & Ger, G. (2011). Early Modern Ottoman Coffeehouse Culture and the Formation of the Consumer Subject. *Journal of Consumer Research, 37*(5), 737–760.

Kettunen, P. (2011). The Transnational Construction of National Challenges: The Ambiguous Nordic Model of Welfare and Competitiveness. In P. Kettunen & K. Petersen (Eds.), *Beyond Welfare State Models: Transnational Historical Perspectives on Social Policy*. Cheltenham, UK: Edward Elgar Publishing Limited.

Kettunen, P., & Petersen, K. (Eds.). (2011). *Beyond Welfare State Models: Transnational Historical Perspectives on Social Policy*. Cheltenham, UK: Edward Elgar Publishing Limited.

Lassen, L. H. (2013, April 9). Eksperter: Stort potentiale i sundheds- og velfærdseksport. *Berlingske*.

Mudge, S. L. (2008). What is Neo-Liberalism? *Socio-Economic Review, 6*(4), 703–731.

Nielsen, T. F. (2013, January 24). Eksport af velfærd er vigtig. *Nordjyske Stiftstidende*.

Pedersen, O. K. (2011). *Konkurrencestaten*. Copenhagen: Hans Reitzels Forlag.

Pedersen, F. S. (2012, November 30). Danskere skal drive plejehjem i Kina. *Berlingske*.

Pedersen, F. S. (2014, September 9). Ældre kinesere kan skabe nyt dansk eksporteventyr. *Berlingske*.

Peñaloza, L. (2000). The Commodification of the American West: Marketers' Production of Cultural Meanings at the Trade Show. *Journal of Marketing, 64*(4), 82–109.

Peñaloza, L., & Venkatesh, A. (2006). Further Evolving the New Dominant Logic of Marketing: From Services to the Social Construction of Markets. *Marketing Theory, 6*(3), 299–316.

Rechnagel, U. T. (2013a, April 11). Kinesisk ældreboom kan forgylde Linak. *Børsen*.

Rechnagel, U. T. (2013b, April 30). Danske investorer jagter gevinst i Kinas grå guld. *Børsen*.

Robertson, R. (1995). Glocalization: Time-Space and Homogeneity-Heterogeneity. In M. Featherstone, S. Lash, & R. Robertson (Eds.), *Global Modernities* (pp. 25–44). London: Sage.

Schmidt, J. B. (2014, January 8). Velfærd kan blive det nye bacon. *Ugebrevet A4*.

Slater, D., & Tonkiss, F. (2001). *Market Society: Markets and Modern Social Theory*. Cambridge, UK: Polity Press.

Strager, B. (2013, June 17). Velfærd kan eksporteres. *Kristeligt Dagblad*.

The Danish Government. (2013). *Danmark i arbejde: Vækstplan for sundheds- og velfærdsløsninger*.

Thompson, C. (2004). Marketplace Mythology and Discourses of Power. *Journal of Consumer Research, 31*(1), 162–180.

Thompson, C., & Tian, K. (2008). Reconstructing the South: How Commercial Myths Compete for Identity Value Through the Ideological Shaping of Popular Memories and Countermemories. *Journal of Consumer Research, 34*(5), 595–613.

Weijo, H. A., Martin, D. M., Arnould, E. J., & Ger, G. (2018). Consumer Movements and Collective Creativity: The Case of Restaurant Day. *Journal of Consumer Research, 45*(2), 251–274.

Wooldridge, A. (2013, February 2). The Next Supermodel. *The Economist*.

9

Dark, Difficult, Depressing: Nordic Crime Novels in the Eyes of the Beholder

Pamela Schultz Nybacka

Let us imagine you were to pick up a crime novel by an author from a small and obscure country up in the far north of Europe. Would you imagine the plot set against dark nights and solitary snowy landscapes? Chances are that you would not have to rely much on either genre conventions, or film director Ingmar Bergman's (1918–2007) artful portrayal of Scandinavian guilt-ridden spleen, to envision a certain atmosphere tainted with "Nordic Noir." In fact, this strand of literary hue has become widely popular and played a decisive role in the market for crime literature in Europe since the 1990s. Successful Swedish crime author Viveca Sten claims after meeting her readers abroad that "the Nordic crime novel is now an export product equally famous to Volvo or Swedish steel" (Åkerlund 2018). For example, in Germany across the Baltic Sea, the categories of *Morden im Norden*, *Skandinavienkrimi*, and *Schwedenkrimi* have become parts of a literary brand in themselves.

From a consumer culture theory perspective, brands can be viewed as text that symbolically conveys the manner and modes for reading and partaking in its meaning. Like texts, the meaning of brands is co-created

P. Schultz Nybacka (✉)
Södertörn University, Huddinge, Sweden

S. Askegaard, J. Östberg (eds.), *Nordic Consumer Culture*,
https://doi.org/10.1007/978-3-030-04933-1_9

(co-authored) by a network of stakeholders: the producer (author), popular media, the audience, and others (Holt 2004). The commercial success of the crime genre can only be explained by regarding it as a packaged category on a market, created in an interplay between publishing companies, authors, booksellers, and readers (Berglund 2016). Literary agents have also had a central role in creating the success of Nordic crime literature (Berglund 2014). Like texts, brands cannot be conveyed immediately to an audience, but are always mediated (Lury 2004). Patterns of resonance are part of meaning production and perception of culture (Assman 2012), including brands. Resonance relates not only to cognitive or symbolic functions, but belongs also with emotions and affect: recognition before cognition (ibid.). A cultural perspective on brand resonance involves aesthetic aspects of the brand (Schroeder, Borgerson & Wu 2014).

Like texts, however, brands are also encountered on a threshold, mediated and organized by other texts. Consider, for example, how a text is interpreted by its title, headlines, author's name, and so on. In other words, texts need other texts to even be read as text. This phenomenon is what Gérard Genette (1997) called how text belongs with the *paratext*, namely the internal and external texts that make texts what they are. This concept has become pivotal to the study of marketing within literature and publishing studies (Squires 2009); developing in other media studies (Gray 2010a, b); conceptualized in marketing theory and advertising (Hackley and Rungpaka Hackley 2018); and used in consumer culture theory (Schultz Nybacka 2018). In this chapter, I will use a case of popular genre literature and Nordic Noir to build an argument around how brands are formed and read in both visual and textual terms, as *brand paratext*. Nordic Noir is exemplary in this matter: it has reached unprecedented success on national and international literary markets. In Sweden, the crime novel has become the most popular genre in fiction amongst adults (second after the category of books for children and young people), and it is symbolically framed and communicated by specific takes on the literary genre, book covers, and other paratextual means. Arguably, the brand paratext could be especially important when the literary work is traveling across cultural thresholds.

In order to understand the attraction of Nordic Noir as seen in consumer culture, it will be helpful to regard the brand paratext reflected by its nearest beholders: northern European neighbours in the form of the

German and German-language book markets. This way it becomes possible to discuss the visual mediation and reverberation of the literary brand and discern certain Nordic qualities.

The purpose of the chapter is to explore how Nordic Noir and especially *Schwedenkrimi* resonate as a brand through the brand paratext, related to readers' narratives of meaning outside the text and to visual communication through the book covers and other texts. The main argument is that brands resonate culture and thrive on the paratextual threshold. This argument will be underscored by using illustrative examples: interviews with three German-language crime readers and Swedish publishing professionals (editor, literary agent), illustrations of brand paratext in the form of book cover texts, and descriptions of images that serve to construct the genre as Nordic. Secondary data is used to put the study in historical and contextual perspectives. Taken together, we gain insight into the perceived aspects and qualities of Nordic Noir in the eyes of the beholder.

Theoretical Concepts

The concept of "resonance" carries strong connotations with sound and acoustic phenomena; it is derived from the Latin *resonare*, "to resound," and *resonantia*, which means "echo" (Assman 2012). In cultural mythology, echo or resonance has negative or bleak connotations, because it is dependent on a primary cause. Assman (2012) argues for a positive view of resonance, as it brings a prolongation and recurrence of a sound, either by a "synchronous vibration from a neighbouring object" (ibid., p. 18) or by reflection from a surface. These modes of interplay and mediation have inspired my study to the extent that Germany and the German-language book markets constitute the neighbour, who reverberates the meanings of Nordic Noir. There has to be some sort of impact, such as a clash, for resonance to occur. If there were no response or reverberation, the primary activity would simply vanish into thin air.

Drawing also on the reflection of a surface as mediation, this chapter complements and extends the acoustic view of resonance with a visual view, taking visual consumption and aesthetics into account (Schroeder 2003). In building a theory of media paratext, Gray (2010a) departs from an assumption of consumption as highly speculative, especially when cultural goods are concerned. We cannot know beforehand what entertainment or other value we may have in consuming a book or a film; it all depends on how we view the expectations and prospect of value through various media paratext, typically promos, spoilers, and others.

The book cover is a prime example of how visual paratext and other genre indicators have become privileged as marketing tools, and they develop with the type of product and its form, as well as its links within a broader cultural industry (Matthews and Moody 2007). For example, book covers have developed with the paperback format that is circulated in wider and more popular forms of bookselling (ibid.). Here, geography plays an important part: "books are culturally sensitive things: imagery that might have a subtle resonance in one country can appear meaningless gunk in another; the one-size-fits-all-approach, common in global design, just doesn't seem to wash when it comes to book covers' (Shaughnessy 2004, p. 18, quoted in Phillips 2007, p. 20).

This means that an analysis of paratext as a way to explore how brands resonate cannot be performed by means of simple comparison, surface to surface, of the original cover and its translated version. Instead, I argue we need to frame a visual analysis of surface matters against a complementary analysis of neighbouring reverberations.

Literary Genre and the Phenomenon of Nordic Noir

Literary genre brands like Nordic Noir, *Schwedenkrimi*, and *Skandinavienkrimi* have become part of an overall Nordic brand in Germany (Böker 2018a). A literary genre like crime denotes conventions of content and form, but above all it is a function on the market that enables publishers, booksellers, authors, and readers to communicate their expectations to each other, both visually and textually (Squires 2009; Steiner 2009; Berglund 2016). A crime novel that excels in quality can only do so within the norms of the genre, according to Tzvetan Todorov (2015): to "improve" it would imply that it is a work of "literature" and not a crime novel as such.

How, then, do crime novels relate to Noir? Todorov's classical definition is that crime novels can be categorized into puzzle detective stories and (broadly) thrillers—and the suspense novel as a hybrid. The puzzle detective novel exists on two distinct levels of time, one that belongs with the specific crime and one with its solution at a safe distance. The crime novels that emerged with Noir in the USA after World War II collapsed these narrative planes. They no longer looked back in time, but instead looked to the future. Noir also connected more with the specific environment, its customs and persons. Curiosity and tension are what will engage the readers. Also, the detective became truly vulnerable, everything was put at risk, and anything could happen.

The emergent phenomenon of Nordic Noir has received attention in the leading Swedish business journal *Dagens Industri*, not least because of its exports to Germany: "Darkness, snow, woods, the Nordic mentality and how our societies are organized society, fascinates" (Åkerlund 2018). The allurement amongst German readers belongs with several factors, according to Böker (2018a, b). First, it is important to readers that the books take place in Scandinavia in order to get a fairly simple view of the culture and nature in the region. Moreover, readers expect the narratives to be critical of society, and contain a human and a humane side, creating interplay between idyllic and brutal elements. These are all qualities of bestselling Scandinavian crime fiction.

The crime fiction scene is vivid across the Nordic countries. For present-day authors, the road to international success inevitably leads across the Baltic Sea, through Germany and its German-language neighbours. With reference to high sales in Germany, literary agents can pitch authors to English-language publishers in the UK and across the world. Danish crime novelist Jussi Adler-Olsen explains that the German market allows for translations from many languages, so if you are successful as an author there, it means you are holding up very well to international competition, including from English-speaking bestsellers (Böker 2018a).

Literary sociologist Karl Berglund (2016) has conducted a thorough survey of specifically the Swedish crime novel and its production and circulation during the boom in the 2000s. His analysis includes both the textual and visual aspects of crime novels published in paperback, and it is sensitive to issues of brands and branding in literature. For instance, he points to different paratextual conventions that form the branding of male and female crime novelists and their symbolic meaning and value on the Swedish market. He also observes how paratext no longer seems to cater to the "text," but rather to the author and to the author's brand: "The author is not dead at all—the author is the new text" (ibid., p. 181).

In order to achieve success in Germany, Swedish crime author Viveca Sten says she works hard, engaging in activities outside the text: book tours, talks, and interviews. She explains: "The fun part is that I get to be a part of raising the image of Sweden. Foreign readers find it interesting to get a glimpse of our everyday life. In many cultures the Swedish dads' role in the family, and that children live every second week with divorced parents seems very exotic" (Åkerlund 2018). In this way, crime novels resonate differences across cultural and societal borders.

The Historical Background to the Interest in Nordic Noir

Previous research into the UK reception and experience of Nordic Noir points to the perceived mixture of new exoticism and accessible difference. This has provided fertile ground for so-called Nordientalism, trained on an "imagined elsewhere" with Nordic social values, sustainability, and design—all consumable through Nordic Noir (Stougaard-Nielsen 2016).

The interest in culture that portrays the Nordic countries has a tradition in Germany. There is a longstanding fascination for all things Scandinavian, and it is related to the neoromantic literary Nordic movement at the turn of the twentieth century with dramatists, novelists, and poets: Henrik Ibsen, August Strindberg, Selma Lagerlöf, Knut Hamsun, Hans Christian Andersen, and so on (Böker 2018b).

The first crime authors to gain recognition outside the Nordic countries and a foothold in the German market were the Swedish couple Maj Sjöwall & Per Wahlöö in the 1960s and 1970s. The books in their series were also the first Swedish crime novels to be turned into films, and since then the industry has become more oriented toward brands. They even sold the rights to Beck, their main character (Sjöholm 2011). Today, Sjöwall and Wahlöö are the only Scandinavian crime authors to be selected for a *Zeit Edition* box in the series of the most famous "Kult-Krimis." The use of the word "cult" suggests that they are symbolic objects that are repeatedly worshipped by fans in the know.

The contemporary boom of Scandinavian literature started, according to Böker (2018a, b), not with crime fiction, but with the Norwegian author Jostein Gaarder's all-age novel *Sofies Verden* (1993), followed by Danish Peter Høeg's novel *Frøken Smillas fornemmelse for sne* (1994). Though they were altogether different books, both novels had elements of mystery, intertwined with existential questioning and search for identity, and written in a literary style. The latter was lavishly marketed, with colourful ads where the standard used to be black and white, but there was no mention of Høeg being from Denmark. The brand of Scandinavia was yet to be formed by the bestsellers that soon followed (Böker 2018b).

However, I argue that there are three circumstances that have contributed to the later success of Nordic Noir. The German market for books and print had a longstanding tradition of interest in matters of Noir, both real and fictive, across all media.[1] Even early twentieth-century films by the German Fritz Lang and Friedrich Wilhelm Murnau have also contributed to the specific aesthetics of Noir (Gohlis 2016). The German audience is therefore sensitized to the visual framing of Nordic Noir.

Second, since the 1980s, actors on the German book market had cultivated regional crime to the extent that "the concept of the regional crime novel has become so ubiquitous that it seems as if there is no longer a single town with more than 10,000 inhabitants that does not have its own team of fictional detectives" (ibid.).[2] In other words, when Nordic Noir became popular as a regional marker, the German book market was already primed for it.

[1] Famous examples of German crime literature are Friedrich Schiller's *The Criminal from Lost Honour* (1786) and E.T.A. Hoffmann's *Mademoiselle de Scudéry* (1819). Ever since the nineteenth century, Germans have translated successful French and English literary works, including those from the USA (Gohlis 2016).

[2] Compare for instance the German concept of *Provinzkrimi*. One example could be Rita Falk's humoristic *Weisswurst-Connection* alongside enticing titles such as *Sauerkrautkoma* etc.

Third, regionalization became a force to reckon with in Europe after the end of the Cold War and the breakdown of the Iron Curtain in 1989–1991. Being on the periphery of Europe, the Nordic countries had cultivated inter-relations and a northern identity. The North was to emerge as a progressive third way, distinct from western capitalism and Eastern European socialism. And in contrast to the catholic and conservative South, the North presented itself as democratic, protestant, industrious, and egalitarian. This sense of nordicity is not additional to national identities, but integrated in them all, and pitted against other forms of European identity (Joenniemi and Lehti 2003). When the division between West and East became less emphasized, there were hopes for a new northern region that would bring together the countries on the Baltic Sea. Several initiatives from the Nordic countries at that time aimed at enhancing their role as a blueprint for the northern region, and thereby increasing their own security, economic growth and development, and political strength within the European Union (EU) and Europe as a whole (Smith 2003). This self-serving attitude was to be contrasted and problematized in popular literature.

From Nordic Naivety to Noir and the Emergence of *Schwedenkrimi*

The specific fascination for Swedish crime in Germany could be explained by the striking contrast with the previous image of a particularly naive country. A famous example is the German-produced series of 64 parts (by 2015, and including films) *Inga Lindström*, a pseudonym for the writer Christiane Sadlo (1954–). The series is set in a small, idyllic village somewhere in the Swedish countryside. The portrayal is stereotypical and romantic, with a blonde heroine in focus. Here we are reminded that some part of the neighbourly fascination for the North most probably belongs with a sense of "white nostalgia," whereby UK consumers could easily project their highly problematic desires of a homogeneous ethnicity in a globalized world (Stougaard-Nielsen 2016).

An explanation for the Lindström series' popularity and success is that Sweden, due to its 250 years of lasting peace, appears as an idealized version of Germany, at least one that might have been, if the country had not been at war twice in the twentieth century. The Lindström series is closely associated with the *Bullerbü* phenomenon, with reference to Astrid Lindgren's extremely popular children's books on Bullerby, set in Småland. The German *Bullerbü* concept is an idyllic setting, where only small conflicts arise. This context forms the background to the present-day situation, where the branded understanding of the Nordic countries, and especially Sweden, has shifted thematically from blissful naivety to Noir.

The second wave of Nordic crime novels brought more attention to Swedish authors. After Sjöwall and Wahlöö, the author to gain an international reputation was Henning Mankell (1948–2015), also from Sweden. Mankell's series of Wallander books published in the 1990s portray how global injustices and criminality no longer can be held at bay in Ystad, a small town in the south of Sweden. Where the *Inga Lindström* series showed Sweden under everlasting sunlight, Mankell's portrayal of "Wallander land" in contrast was as dark as a winter's day. His works were critical of society and the media—constantly posing questions about the interplay of world affairs and local everyday life (Sjöholm 2011). Mankell was also a playwright and a poet, and thus he had some literary credibility and cultural capital that were unusual in the category of crime fiction.

German critics usually assess the literary qualities and the extent of societal criticism in crime novels, but they do not explicitly mention whether the novels are from Scandinavia. Instead, this fact is widely marketed and advertised by the publishers (Böker 2018). Mankell's first German book covers resembled paintings, according to Jessica Brogren at the Leopard publishing company, co-started by Mankell and his longtime publisher Dan Israel (interview with the author, May 17, 2018). This artful way of branding symbolically accrued a sort of literary quality on new markets. On the subsequent paperback versions, the endorsements show how women's magazines came to acknowledge Mankell's literary qualities. Even today, the endorsements through critical acclaim on Mankell paperback editions are made by publications like *Journal für die Frau* and *Brigitte*. Hence, it could also be argued that the covers sought to connect with a well-read female audience.

The third wave of Swedish crime specifically spells Stieg Larsson (Böker 2018a). This wave started with the publication of Larsson's Millennium trilogy in 2005 and continues even to this day (Åkerlund 2018). Taken together, Mankell and Larsson have sold 120 million books (ibid.), films notwithstanding. In the course of writing this text, the international film adaptation of Larsson's second book *The Girl in the Spider's Web* has hit cinemas and is expected to renew interest in the series. If anything, the third wave has been widened to include several new authors and been extended by the additional Millennium series of David Lagercrantz.

Literary agencies have been instrumental in the marketing of the genre and its exports. Anna Frankl at Nordin Agency, one of Sweden's most successful literary agencies, describes how they create presentations of their authors for their printed catalogues and website. In terms of building the author's brand, they use book trailers, reviews, interviews, and similar materials in order to present the author from many angles (interview with the author, August 31, 2018). This reflects how brands are both mediated in society and created by means of visual and textual materials: brand paratext.

Larsson's case, however, proved to be a particular challenge. His literary agent at Norstedts, Linda Altrov Berg, explains the circumstances: "His works were sold to a number of countries—and then he *died*. It is not self-evident to sell a dead author" (interview with the author, October 15, 2018). Presumably, it was not just Larsson's critical take on the development of society that caught the world's attention in terms of Noir, but also his untimely death. It may have highlighted the premise of Noir: that the future is uncertain and the hero is vulnerable. Anything bad could happen to anybody, at any time.

Nordic crime is now established as a genre on the world market, Anna Frankl observes, just like American "romance" (Åkerlund 2018). It is captured in the paratext, especially by visual means:

> Typical for a Schwedenkrimi, is according to me, a good puzzle crime novel with a police as a main character, preferably a series which readers can follow, and in Germany it will have a red cottage with white corners on the cover, regardless whether it is cosy crime or hardboiled.

The genre brand of *Schwedenkrimi* then helps to communicate with booksellers and readers. Frankl, however, does not believe the German market makes a clear distinction between the Scandinavian countries:

"Schwedenkrimi is for me simply Swedish or Scandinavian crime novels. It could just as well be Norwegian or Danish, I don't think they make such big difference" (interview with the author, August 31, 2018). Even so, empirical studies show that Swedish crime fiction is by far the most widely accessible and is sold in Germany. More than 70% of Scandinavian bestsellers are Swedish (Böker 2018a). This could suggest that the *Schwedenkrimi* brand does have a certain resonance and impact.

Quality and Ambience

Recently, Scandinavian crime has become established as an upmarket genre, claims Frankl: "this means that one can produce a hardback version and get higher profit-margin" (Åkerlund 2018). In terms of selling Swedish crime novels abroad, Frankl maintains she does not make any special claims specifically to German publishers, compared to other buyers. It all comes down to the unique qualities of the book; generally, though, she will stress that it is "well-written and atmospheric." Hence, it seems the ambiance is an important part of the sale.

There are two authors from Sweden that have helped to establish Nordic crime as more literary than other crime: Håkan Nesser and Arne Dahl, the latter a pseudonym for novelist and poet Jan Arnald. Nesser was the second bestselling Nordic author after Mankell in 1993–2014 (Böker 2018a). Nesser's books are credited with German reviews, even with the critic's name mentioned (*Hamburger Morgenpost*; Jürgen Deppe, *NDR Kultur*). Arnald was one of the first authors in Sweden to switch literary genres specifically in search of a larger audience, and Dahl was a secret identity for some time. Today, his authorship counts as one of the biggest successes abroad. Like Nesser, his style combines crime/thriller elements with literary qualities. The Dahl books have reviewer quotes ranging from local to national media, mostly newspapers in both Sweden (*Smålandsposten*, *Sydsvenskan*, *Dagens Nyheter*, *Expressen*) and Germany (*Spiegel Online*, *Frankfurter Neue Presse*, *Ruhr Nachrichten*, *Westdeutsche Zeitung*, *Münchner Merkur*). One review by Ruhr Nachrichten spoke of Dahl's work *Gier* as the "newest masterpiece of Swedish art of crime" (*schwedischer Krimikunst*).

The Swedish literary agent Anna Frankl explains her perspective on the relationship between crime novels and Noir:

> For me a crime novel is more of a puzzle story, preferably with a police as a main character. The Noir concept is broader; here is everything from psychological suspense to detective mysteries. The main character can be an ordinary person, a detective or a spy. Everything is possible. Both exist within the suspense genre and some crime novels could absolutely fall within the concept of Noir.

Frankl's characterization of Noir shows how the suspenseful narrative is widened and also includes more ordinary aspects of society and life.

This shifting relation between crime and normalcy is reflected in readers' view of Nordic Noir specifically. One woman describes how Håkan Nesser is her all-time favourite crime novelist and she characterizes his books as "difficult … depressive" ("*schwer … depressiv*"). It takes time to get into the books. One of the series is played out in an altogether fictive country/city with a certain atmosphere, peopled by many different types of characters. This could suggest that the ambiance in the texts of Nordic crime is not as tied to geography as one might have expected. In fact, the German publishing house btb Verlag launched the German Nesser editions with stereotypical covers of red wooden cottages (Böker 2018a). There are also other qualities. Especially, the reader describes her fondness for Nesser's characters: "they are not really criminal … just "normal" really, leading their lives like us all, but then something happens." Anti-heroes—she likes that. The characters develop across the books in the series. She explains how the stories are slow: "they are about a person's inside more than anything."

When another woman, from Germany, considers her appreciation of *Skandinavienkrimi*, she too reflects on how they provide understanding of people from the inside. There is also such little difference between criminals and "normal" people, she ponders. This reflection shows how Nordic Noir has extended Todorov's classic premise for Noir and thriller novels. It is not just the detective who is vulnerable and endangered. Ordinary people are also exposed to events that could lead them to criminal behaviour and put them at risk of their lives.

Connecting Outer and Inner Landscapes

Northern nature has a special role in the reader narratives. It helps to explain the links between the outer and inner worlds that are played out in relation to the North and to the crime novels. A German man around 30 years of age speaks Swedish fluently and travels to Sweden around three times a year, since his parents bought a house in Småland back in 1980. His parents had visited a friend, who had defected to Sweden in order to escape German conscription, and they immediately fell in love with Swedish nature: the woods and the lakes. Nowadays they have books by Swedish crime authors, namely Henning Mankell, Håkan Nesser, and Stieg Larsson. In other words, their encounter with Nordic nature was rather romantic and transformative, and in time opened them up to experiences of Sweden through literature.

Conversely, the Nordic Noir novels in turn also inspire readers to reflect on the role of nature and existence. A Swiss woman describes how she is fascinated by Nesser's story of how a man wins the lottery, but does not tell his wife. Instead, he buys himself a house out in the woods: "He wants to go and have another life." She sounds surprised, but emphasizes that she really likes that book.

This woman has also visited the Nordic countries a couple of times:

> I was in Finland with my ex-boyfriend. He now lives there. He was a bit ... introvert. *Verbindung* /a bond/ with the landscape. I think of that landscape. I think of the woods and the seas, and the dark. When I read this book I think of this landscape. No people. Maybe people go mad....

Connecting the existential landscape with the physical may bring a deeper relation between the books, nature, and life at large. In 2017 this woman went travelling in Scandinavia, via Hamburg to Copenhagen, Gothenburg, and Stockholm, all by herself: "I needed some time for me." The North has become associated with withdrawal and establishing a new relationship to oneself.

This existential theme is recurring in the narrative of a German woman, approaching 50 years old. She loves Nordic *Krimis*, just like she loves reading. She enjoys Ost-Friesland *Krimis* too, because they reflect that way of living. The only thing she says she avoids is American books and films; she is just not interested. This statement points less to the state of affairs than to a form of cultural positioning.

She has also travelled North, visiting friends who live in Stockholm and Uppsala. But when it comes to Scandinavian *Krimis*, she says she would not recognize their local flavour of course. Sadly, this woman was just recently diagnosed with cancer, and the prognosis for her survival looks dark. On this bad news she decided to go on a trip for herself over the weekend. She went straightaway to buy a pair of expensive binoculars for birdwatching, and a ticket to Sürt, an island in the northwestern part of Germany. This way she figures she can then come back strengthened and face her doctor. She is bringing a tent so she can stay on a camping site, close to nature. Perhaps her reading of regional crime novels and especially Scandinavian *Krimis* has nurtured a sense that nature is a place to withdraw and find oneself at a time of existential crisis.

Illustrative Examples of Brand Paratext

In order to discuss how paratext is used to construct books as Nordic, I have chosen a number of illustrative examples of authors and their books. Most examples are Swedish in reflection of the dominance of *Schwedenkrimi* on the German market, and one example is from Iceland.

One instance of paratext is words and texts printed on the cover. The example of Ninni Schulman's (2018) book, translated as *Stets Sollst Du Schweigen*, is explicitly categorized as *Schwedenkrimi* on the front cover. This book is the fourth in a series called "Värmland Krimi," or the "Hagfors series". The first two books in the series by Heine were categorized as "crime novel" only.

Another instance of paratext is the back-cover text. Here, the publisher has a chance to attract consumers with a description of the story. In Schulman's title, the back-cover text first gives a quote from the novel, then introduces directly the setting of the rural small-town context: "Hagfors, Värmland." This location conveys a dark and solitary sense of the provincial setting. There is no ridicule about the narrative's provinciality; rather, it is expected that the story will reach the bare existentiality of the human predicament. This meaning is also emphasized by the book cover image. Here, nature is ever-present, covering the entire image from the dark woods in the background and the cold, quiet lake in the foreground. Red is the only colour, highlighting an empty rowboat and the title in capital letters against the black and white background. The design is aligned with the third book in the series (*Still Ruht der Wald*), where the cover shows a colorized red cottage in the midst of a black-and-white forest and the label of *Schwedenkrimi* is introduced. Here the publishers have changed their paratext tactics, possibly because her name could be interpreted as German and does not disclose her Swedish citizenship.

In contrast to Schulman, Håkan Nesser's books are tagged as "novels" on the cover, and most of them revolve around a brutal death regardless of whether they belong in his crime novel series or not. They have a more literary aesthetic than most other Nordic crime novels: the images are less dramatic and the colours are brighter. As noted by Böker (2018a), the German covers of Nesser's crime series about Van Veeteren have traditional *Schwedenkrimi* attributes: solitary red cottages, lakes, and rowboats—even though the stories belong in a fictitious setting. One Nesser book, *Elf Tage in Berlin*, reverberates with the German understanding of Swedish innocence: "The Swede Arne Murberg is young and naive, but he has a strange gift: believing in humankind" (my translation). Here the Swedish naivety is striking and is used as a selling point to the book's German audience.

The Swedish author Jonas Moström's "Nathalie Svensson" series is translated by Nora Pröfrock and is a relative newcomer to the market. The aesthetics are reminiscent of Nesser's novels: bright backgrounds with serene, yet dark, country scenery—an attempt at branding Moström as Nesser's literary heir. Parts one and three feature snowy landscapes with red cottages, and the second part, *Dominotod* (Domino death, 2017), a red house on the edge of a lake. Arne Dahl endorses this book in a quote with large capital letters in matching red, explaining how the intensity of Moström's literary style does not slacken. Several books by other authors (Arne Dahl, Ingrid Hedström, Alexander Söderberg, and many more) have variations of the same motif: a solitary house close to the water, on the point of danger, and a single rowboat. The intertwining of typography, image, aesthetics, and ambiance builds the identity of the book and connects it with literary forerunners in the previous waves of crime literature.

The regional and countryside perspectives have become especially dominant when it comes to the design of book covers. Böker (2018a) describes how Icelandic author Arnaldur Indriðason's crime series is set in the capital of Reykjavik and still is presented with countryside images on the covers. Ragnar Jónasson's (2013) *Todes Nacht* (translated into German by Tina Fleck) is categorized on the cover as an "Iceland thriller" (*Island thriller*). The back-cover text says the book is the second part of the "Dark Iceland" series. The author's name and other text are printed in yellow, instead of the red which is used on the covers of Swedish crime novels. The cover image foregrounds a set of white and scruffy stone buildings, ripe with neglect. The buildings are set against a dark and foreboding mountain covered with trees and silhouettes of further mountains in the far distance. The image continues on the back cover and gives a dramatic sky as background to the book's description. Small print next to the EAN code discloses that the design bureau is German and the photograph was taken by Jim Smithson and bought via Getty Images, an international agency. The landscape, however, does not look at all like Iceland, but rather resembles the contours of Swedish (or possibly Norwegian) woodlands. Presumably, even though there are minor adjustments, the *Schwedenkrimi* aesthetics and nature have become the primary lens through which Nordic crime novels are viewed. This could be quite problematic in terms of the internal power structure amongst the countries in the Nordic region.

Concluding Discussion

The reasons for the remarkable success of Scandinavian crime in Germany are quite straightforward, according to Böker (2018a). Readers want to get an easy view of (especially) Swedish nature and society, and engage in societal critique. The interviewed readers add to this picture by emphasizing the perspectives of people's inside struggles, and accepting that criminals are not so different from "normal" people. There is a deeper existential mode of relating to the narratives, one where the ambience allows for greater reflection, perhaps greater awe or empathy toward people and their choices. Not least with regard to the German experience during World War II, the Nordic crime novels may bring a more complex and nuanced understanding of human nature, operating under pressure. Indirectly, they resonate with specific cultural memories.

From the consumers' perspective, the three interviewed readers had all been traveling in the Nordic countries, gleaning insights into how human nature is reflected in the natural environment, and especially in a dark and empty landscape. Even a German woman who was not directly captivated by the Nordic landscape in her journey expresses a sense of relation to nature, seeking solace from sickness and an existential crisis in a remote northern corner of her country. Nature in the North is thus regarded as both the cause of madness and pain—and their remedy. These reader narratives may be regarded as isolated anecdotes, but reflect a long tradition stemming from Swedish seventeenth-century propaganda, by which northern nature is rendered with transcendental qualities: "the duality of eternal light and eternal darkness being employed to underline its divine characteristics" (Joenniemi and Lehti 2003). This duality remains underscored in the cover images of Nordic crime novels. Nevertheless, with knowledge of Noir genre conventions, we can expect of Nordic Noir that nothing is sacred; anything is possible, and everything is at risk—even inner life.

The textual and visual paratext of books constitutes a communicative threshold on the market. It helps to construct identity markers in terms of literary genre, which functions as a way to communicate expectations among publishers, authors, booksellers, and readers. Taking into account that consumption of cultural goods is speculative (Gray2010a), paratext could be even more important when selling books across cultural borders. It is well known that other intermediaries (or co-authors) such as literary agents are partly responsible for the successful selling of Nordic crime. They rely on an array of secondary visual and textual paratext to present the authorship from different angles and build the author's brand. Berglund (2016) observed how the author increasingly replaces the primary "text." The agents' author-centred paratext, however, is not adapted specifically to the German market. It could still be expected that Nordic and especially Swedish paratext resonates well with German publishers and is reverberated in their further mediations. Here, the success of *Schwedenkrimi* has probably foregrounded presentations of other Nordic novels. When nature is portrayed in "Iceland *krimi*" it is presented with a cover image of deep woods reminiscent of Swedish nature. Brand paratext can thus reflect and reproduce certain power structures, which can be quite problematic.

It is also important to acknowledge that while Germany has had a keen eye on all things Nordic for a long time, that fact alone cannot explain the development and success of Nordic Noir or *Schwedenkrimi*. The German market was already inclined toward Noir and has been innovative in Noir aesthetics throughout history (Gohlis 2016). Second, the German literary market was already primed by regionalization. Nordic Noir presented itself at a time when European politics opened up to a new geopolitical organization beyond the Cold War division of West and East. The Nordic countries presented themselves as a progressive alternative, ready to take the lead into the future (Joenniemi and Lehti 2003). When these promises fell through, there was a growing audience who were curious about the contrast between the ideal and the more, dark, depressive, and difficult sides of Nordic societies, especially in terms of everyday, local life.

According to Böker's study, critics in Germany do not usually single out which works are Scandinavian or not; instead, this is communicated by publishers. Investigating the paratext shows the way that publishers quite often use Nordic critics' reviews from both regional and national media. The various endorsements on the back covers of books show how quotes from local Swedish media, commenting on the quality of a book title in relation to other (national) authors, have become transported to a German-language context. Considering that the Noir narratives also foreground countryside scenes and settings, the local perspective is, somewhat paradoxically, integrated and pervasive in the communication of national and super-national identity.

To conclude, the case of crime novels and Nordic Noir highlights how paratext can bring out symbolic qualities of a text in a way that resonates and reverberates a brand, and especially across cultural borders. The concept of "brand paratext" serves to capture how identity markers in the form of text and images not only pertain to the single product or author, but manage to create an interplay of local and symbolic qualities that helps to establish and extend a brand as a composite whole. If it were not for successful brand paratext, Nordic Noir could not have got away with more literary approaches to the genre and still call it crime. Indeed, it is with the careful use of brand paratext that reflects the quality of authors' works that Nordic Noir is now considered an "upmarket genre" compared with other crime. The waves of Nordic Noir are still crashing onto the shores of Germany, though their impact may not be as striking today as it once was. Yet, as agent Altrov Berg observes, there is still space left for more.

References

Assman, A. (2012). *Impact and Resonance: Towards a Theory of Emotions in Cultural Memory*. Södertörn Lectures 6, Huddinge: Södertörn University.

Berglund, K. (2014). A Turn to the Rights. In J. H. S. Kärrholm & A. Steiner (Eds.), *Hype. Bestsellers and Literary Culture* (pp. 67–87). Nordic Academic Press.

Berglund, K. (2016). *Mordförpackningar. Omslag, titlar och kringmaterial till svenska pocketdeckare 1998–2011*. Uppsala: Avd. För litteratursociologi, Uppsala University.

Böker, E. (2018a). *The Incredible Success Story of Scandinavian Bestsellers on the German Book Market*. Unpublished Manuscript. [Forthcoming in *The Scandinavian German Literary Relationship*].

Böker, E. (2018b). *Skandinaviska bästsäljare på den tyska bokmarknaden – en analys av den nuvarande litteraturboomen*. Unpublished Manuscript. [Forthcoming].

Genette, G. (1997). *Paratexts. Thresholds of Interpretation* (Jane E. Lewin, English Trans.). Literature, Culture, Theory 20. Cambridge: Cambridge University Press.

Gohlis, T. (2016, December). *German Crime Fiction. Considerable Quantity, Increasing Quality*. Goethe Institut.

Gray, J. (2010a). *Show Sold Separately. Promos, Spoliers, and Other Media Paratexts*. New York: New York University Press.

Joenniemi, P., & Lehti, M. (2003). The Encounter Between the Nordic and the Northern: Torn Apart But Meeting Again? In M. Lehti & D. J. Smith (Eds.), *Post-Cold War Identity Politics. Northern and Baltic Experiences* (pp. 128–156). London and Portland: Frank Cass.

Jónasson, R. (2013). *Todes Nacht* (Tina Flecken, German Trans.). Fischer Verlag.

Matthews, N., & Moody, N. (Eds.). (2007). *Judging a Book by Its Cover. Fans, Publishers, Designers, and the Marketing of Fiction*. London and New York: Routledge.

Moström, J. (2017). *Dominotod* (Nora Pröfrock, German Trans.). Ullstein.

Schroeder, J. E. (2003). *Visual Consumption. Routledge Interpretive Marketing Research*. London and New York: Routledge.

Schulman, N. (2018). *Stets sollst du schweigen* (Susanne Dahman, German Trans.). Bastei Lubbe.

Sjöholm, C. (2011). *Litterära resor. Turism i spåren efter böcker, filmer och författare*. Göteborg and Stockholm: Makadam bok.

Smith, D. J. (2003). Nordic Near Abroad or New Northern Europe? Perspectives on Post-Cold War Regional Co-operation in the Baltic Sea Area. In M. Lehti & D. J. Smith (Eds.), *Post-Cold War Identity Politics. Northern and Baltic Experiences* (pp. 50–77). London and Portland: Frank Cass.

Squires, C. (2009). *Marketing in Literature. The Marketing of Contemporary Writing in Britain*. London: Palgrave Macmillan.

Stougaard-Nielsen, J. (2016). Nordic Noir in the UK: The Allure of Accessible Difference. *Journal of Aesthetics and Culture, 8*(1), 1–11.

Todorov, T. (2015). Kriminalromanens typologi. In D. Hedman & J. Määttä (Eds.), *Brott, Kärlek, Främmande Världar. Texter om Populärlitteratur* (pp. 245–256). Lund: Studentlitteratur.

Åkerlund, C. (2018). Brott lönar sig. *Dagens Industri Sektion, 2*(35), 36–42.

10

Nordic Branding: An Odyssey into the Nordic Myth Market

Lars Pynt Andersen, Dannie Kjeldgaard, Frank Lindberg, and Jacob Östberg

The Nordic region has captured the attention of global audiences and become a rich resource for branding ideas, products, places, and experiences (Waade and Jensen 2016; Leer 2016; Byrkeflot et al. 2013). The regional construct of "Nordic" (e.g., as New Nordic) is a recent appropriation of a mythology building on the previous ideas of Scandinavia, the Nordic countries, and their national mythologies (Hermansen 2012).

L. P. Andersen (✉)
Aalborg University, Aalborg, Denmark
e-mail: pynt@hum.aau.dk

D. Kjeldgaard
University of Southern Denmark, Odense, Denmark
e-mail: dkj@sam.sdu.dk

F. Lindberg
Nord University Business School, Bodø, Norway
e-mail: frank.lindberg@nord.no

J. Östberg
Stockholm Business School, Stockholm University, Stockholm, Sweden
e-mail: jacob.ostberg@sbs.su.se

S. Askegaard, J. Östberg (eds.), *Nordic Consumer Culture*,
https://doi.org/10.1007/978-3-030-04933-1_10

Brand actors are tapping into these symbolic resources in very diverse ways and sectors. In this chapter, we are interested in mapping and analysing the existing variation of branding strategies in the Nordic myth market.

We consider a brand to be a socially constructed "commercial sign (or set of signs) that is referring to the value universe of a commodity" (Askegaard 2006, p. 91), and from this perspective we will embark on a journey into the Nordic value universe and the mythology that structures it. Our focus is on the branding process: the agency of brand managers and other central stakeholders that strategically select symbols, tell stories, and invoke myths, in their ongoing efforts to produce a sense of Nordicness (Östberg 2011). We suggest that the "Nordic" is a complex brandscape, just like a film franchise (e.g., James Bond in O'Reilly and Kerrigan 2013) or a café (Starbucks in Thompson and Arsel 2004). The Nordic' offers a very diverse sign economy and values universe, which constructs "a cultural space where brand meanings are developed and circulated within an ideological setting" (O'Reilly and Kerrigan 2013). A department store such as the Danish Magasin du Nord boasts a Nordic Living section with Nordic interior and fashion design, and books on Nordic living and cuisine often circulate globally (e.g., in the Great Northern Food Hall at Grand Central Station in New York). A more spurious example is the (personal) brand universe created by Danish celebrity Jim Lyngvild that has created Nordic fur fashion, beer, cosmetics, and generated renewed interest in the Norse religious community in recent Danish history. All these are cultural spaces of the Nordic, a very diverse pool of symbolic resources, signs, practices, and myths for consumers and brand actors to appropriate for commercial and identity value. We wonder, however, how brand actors construct compromises so that Nordic values as expressed in brands and products are amenable to the market, utilising a mode of sanitised Nordic mythology.

What Is Nordic Branding?

Nordic branding has at least two inter-related meanings or modes: the branding of the Nordic region as a geographical place of Nordicness (place branding); and branding strategically invoking Nordicness in the hope of becoming a more distinct and meaningful product or service—regardless of whether this has any "real" relation to the Nordic region as "produced in" or "designed in" (Östberg 2011). Both benefit from leveraging Nordic symbolic resources and narratives (Gyimóthy 2017). The place branding of the Nordic region by destination marketing organisations (e.g., Visit Denmark) or the Nordic Council works strategically to support the pool of symbolic resources and maintain these myths, but in a process of conjoint efforts with entrepreneurs and small to medium enterprises (SMEs; Gyimóthy 2017; Larsen and Österlund-Pötzsch 2015; Byrkeflot et al. 2013). Despite this interdependence, we will focus on the latter rather than the place branding efforts by actors such as destination marketing or public organisations.

Östberg (2011) maps out four categories of Swedish branding, utilising various strategies of Swedishness: as intended for national or international markets, and as based on national or international place branding. In this chapter, we are not interested in branding strategies that use international or pseudo-international strategies; that is, brands that originate in the Nordic region but make no reference to this, or even try to hide this origin, posing as American or Italian brands (see also Kjeldgaard et al. 2015). We include the concept of Swedishness/Danishness and so on as more regionally specific representations of Nordic branding and consumer culture. The recent interest in the Nordic has established a strong narrative that invites consumers and marketers to think and position Nordic product and place brands as local expressions of the "Nordic," "New Nordic," or "Nordic living," drawing on similar symbolic resources. Paradoxically, this development may end up threatening the distinctiveness of local and regional product and place brands, as they appropriate similar rhetorical strategies of Nordic myth and symbolism—in order to be distinctive (Gyimóthy 2017).

As a strategy of country of origin (COO) branding, the Nordic country brands—such as Danish butter, Norwegian salmon, and Swedish cars—have a long history (Askegaard and Ger 1998; Hermansen 2012). However, recently national COO branding strategies have been increasingly reframed and reinvigorated as Nordic or Scandinavian. The global attention for the concept of New Nordic Food (also known as New Nordic Cuisine) invokes symbolic resources such as purity, freshness, simplicity, and ethics associated with the region's produce of Nordic climates, landscapes, and waters (New Nordic Food 2004). The success of the Danish restaurant Noma—since its launch in 2003 the restaurant has repeatedly been voted one of the world's top restaurants and it currently has two Michelin stars—has inspired many local food entrepreneurs to appropriate the New Nordic label and concepts (Byrkeflot et al. 2013; Gyimóthy 2017; Larsen and Österlund-Pötzsch 2015). New Nordic Cuisine also inspired brand actors across many other sectors to use the regional construct of New Nordic and Nordicness as a symbolic resource in branding (Thorsøe et al. 2016). One of the most important cross-sectoral appropriations of Nordicness has been interior design and fashion (Roncha 2008), for example the brand Muuto, a celebrated Danish furniture company aiming to represent "the best of Scandinavian design today" (https://muuto.com), which reconstructs a Nordicness of purity, simplicity, craftsmanship, and honest expression in its interior design. Magazines and cookbooks have nurtured Nordicness with a distinct visual aesthetics that blends seamlessly with Nordic living as art, fashion, architecture, design, life, leisure, career advice, and "hygge." Signifying successful informal socialising, hygge is an important thriving mythology of its own, packaged and circulated in products, services, books, and blogs on Nordic living (e.g., Brits 2017; Wiking 2016) within and beyond the Nordic region. Hygge may be a complex social concept, the "structuring principle of a fundamental moral order for everyday Scandinavian life" (Linnet 2011, 2015), but it is also the name of a scented candle from the brand Skandinavisk, designed to create "intimacy, fellowship and cosiness in the smallest everyday moments. With echoes of tea and baked strawberry cake, rose petals and wild mint" (Skandinavisk brand website, Hygge Candle n.d.). The Hygge candles are designed by a British person and made in France (tea lights and candles preferred by native Nordics are rarely scented). It may seem that the most extreme essentialism and daring clichés are invoked by non-Nordic brand actors (Östberg 2011), but for our purpose they still represent Nordic branding.

Nordic Mythmaking

In order to understand the Nordic brandscape and its perpetuation in branding strategies, we rely on myth market theory. Regional and national mythmaking is a highly contested, political, and ideological field (Thompson and Tian 2008; Leer 2016). Stern (1995), as one of the first to study marketplace mythology, argues that four myths—tragedy, comedy, romance, and irony—structure holiday branding. Thompson (2004), studying the natural health marketplace, extends the early analyses drawing on Slotkin's conceptualisation of national mythologies depicting how "cultural myths are leveraged to create distinctive marketplace mythologies that, in turn, serve diverse, and often competing, ideological interests" (p. 163). Relevant for our explorations is the theorising of the romantic and gnostic myths, which can reveal how a marketplace might face tension due to different versions of well-being, such as that between nature ("romantic") and technology ("gnostic"). Whereas the romantic myth is based on the idea of nature as an organic, dynamic, and mystical force in which "veneration of creativity; authentic self-expression; the cultivation of imagination" take place, the gnostic myth resembles science and technology as "divine tools that enable mankind to attain his rightful dominion over nature and to overcome the constraints and limitations posed by embodiment" (Thompson 2004, pp. 164–165).

Drawing inspiration from this research, we note that Nordic brands rely on contextually based narratives and myths that manifest as reconstructions between multiple ideological agendas. The "Nordic" offers a rather extreme example of this, as the Nordic countries are suggested as both resources of a utopian mythology of inclusive, egalitarian welfare state ideology (Andersson 2009; Østergaard et al. 2014) and as a worst-case scenario of unsustainable leftist welfare and multicultural collapse (recently manifested by President Trump's use of "#lastnightinsweden" in February 2017, or Fox Business Network host Trish Regan's attack on

"Socialist Denmark" in August 2018). Non-Nordics invoke these utopian/dystopian myths of the Nordic countries to serve seemingly local or personal agendas. But native Nordics can play this game too: examples of "internal Nordic self-othering" are legion, typically when the subject is immigration or gender politics (Andersson and Hilson 2009; Østergaard et al. 2014). Retaining Thompson's (2004) theorising, reconstructions of Nordic branding might vary, depending on different ideological agendas, between romantic "authentic Nordic nature" and "high-tech Nordic" mythology, for example varying promises on how brands may provide simplicity, purity, mystique, and Nordic well-being. It has been suggested that the New Nordic branding in the cuisine sector, as exemplified by the success of both the restaurant Noma and the New Nordic Food Manifesto more broadly, was a powerful strategy exactly because it allowed urban, cosmopolitan consumers a mode to circumscribe nationalist longings into a more politically palatable mythology (Hermansen 2012). At the same time, New Nordic Cuisine has been appropriated and cast in gnostic terms by other actors, for instance by the Nordic Council of Ministers to improve diets and ultimately the health of Nordic citizens, or mobilised for welfare export (see Bjerregaard and Kjeldgaard, Chap. 8 in this volume).

Empirical Approach

The findings in this chapter are based on a collaborative project that invited brand actors to reflect on and explore their ideas of Nordicness, their basis in Nordic values, and how these were reflected in their branding strategies. The participants were mainly young chefs and restaurant owners (Norway), key persons in fashion organisations (Sweden), and branding agencies working with introduction of Nordic brands (Denmark). The mode of investigation was qualitative and explorative, based on interviews with founders, managers, and key personnel (mainly considered as "expert informants"), combined with observations and analysis of related communication material and commercial spaces (brand communications, visiting head offices, production, showrooms, restaurants, cafés, shops). All informants accepted to be quoted and have previously been part of a podcast series (Andersen 2017) on the topic.

Our aim was to gain insight into the marketplace mythology of the regional Nordic brandscape. Our focus was on the dissemination, translation, and appropriation of ideas of "Nordicness" and "Nordic values" across sectors in the aftermath of the New Nordic Cuisine movement. Several of the previous studies on market mythology are based on analysis of advertising articulations (Stern 1995; Thompson 2004; Pietilä et al., Chap. 11 in this book). In designing the study, we were particularly inspired by Thompson and Tian's (2008) discourse analyses of mythmakers related to myths of the American South, since they focus on active reconstructions rather than mere marketplace articulations.

The selected commercial actors were selected by purposeful sampling based on the criteria of geographical and brand variation to enable exploration into myth heterogeneity rather than homogeneity. The total sample consists of 9 contexts/organisations (some with multiple brands) and interviews with 17 informants, lasting 1–2 hours (see Table 10.1). We conducted observations of packaging, store design, advertising, and online brand communications (including multimodal texts such as webpages with images and brand videos). In addition, we observed and participated in the brandscapes: we dined New Nordic and Viking style, tried Scandinavian sneakers, sampled artisanal bread and *mjød*.

The actual journey through the geographical landscapes from southern Denmark, via Stockholm, to northern Norway (and back to Denmark) was performed through the winter of 2016/17. For practical reasons, we were not able to include Finland in this journey (see, however, Pietilä and her coauthors' exploration of the mythology of Finnishness in Chap. 11).

Findings

In the following we present our findings as a metaphorical journey through a Nordic myth market brandscape. We found that the commercial actors mobilised a quite diverse mythical and symbolic scenery: from grimy roaring Vikings to sustainable sneakers and the Happiest Place in the World. Overall, two distinct symbolic universes were evoked: one

Table 10.1 Project data across countries

Country	Context/organisation/ SME/brands	Interviews	Observations/ interviews
Denmark	WODEN—Scandinavian sneakers	Founder/CEO	Main office, showroom, shops
	RedInk Frejdahl Ragnsborg (Lyngvild)	Owner/branding consultant	Main office
	BRØD	Founder/CEO	Café visits Visit to workshop
	OAK—The Nordic Journal	Founder	Main office
Sweden	Sandqvist Bags	Founder/head of marketing	Main office, showroom, shops
	Aifur		Restaurant, dining Informal talk with staff and guests
	Swedish Fashion Council	CEO	Kungliga Tekniska Högskolan
	Association of Swedish Fashion Brands	Secretary general	Main office
	Beckmanns College of Design	Director of external relations Director design communication courses	Visit to college premises
Norway	Restaurant Nyt, Bodø	Founder/manager Founder/owner/head chef Chef/apprentices	Restaurant, dining, visit to kitchen
	Radisson Blu, Bodø	Head chef/manager Chef	Interviews in restaurant Nyt

which draw on the imagined past in the form of Viking and Norse legacy; and the other referring to more contemporary ideas of the Nordic natural and social utopia. We found that within each of these a set of compromises of the romantic and gnostic mythos were made in the effort to construct brand expressions that would resonate commercially and culturally.

The Myth of the Vikings

What better place to look for the grimy side of the Nordic myth market than a basement in the old part of Stockholm? On a Monday evening, we descend into the restaurant Aifur through a wooden portal adorned with Norse-style ornaments. This Viking-themed restaurant is devised and owned by the musician E-type, who is famous for the electro-pop hits he had in the 1990s (spurious trivia: his debut album was called *Made in Sweden*). An employee dressed in themed attire meets us. He blows a fanfare on a cow horn and announces us (in English) to the room of fellow diners with our names and tribe (nationality). Despite the time of the week, the place is packed and diners are sitting rather close together at the long communal tables and benches. As we are led to a place to sit, we discover that we seem to be the only Nordic natives present this evening. The cuisine offered on the menu is named after famous Viking heroes—from history as well as fiction—for example "Tore Hjort's Venison" and "Toke's Tripod." The menu describes both the food and the merits of the heroes. Toke is a fictional character from the Viking novel *Röde Orm* by F.G. Bengtsson, but Tore Hjort is a historical person:

> Our venison is inspired by Tore Hjort who was a Norwegian chieftain from Vågen in Hålogaland. He fought in a terrible hailstorm on Jarl Håkons side at the battle of Hjörungavåg in the year 986, only to die by another King's hand, Olav Tryggvasons, in the year 999. (From the Aifur menu)

The level of intricate historical detail offered in this justification of a menu item is a narrative device, underlining the mythological significance of Tore Hjort as a romantic hero. It could be intended as a strategy of legitimisation, of constructing authenticity through a historical narrative with information on names, dates, places. Another interpretation is that the dissonance in the form of "too much detail for the context" is a clue to rhetorical irony—an irony that stipulates a contract of meeting minds (Booth 1974): we understand each other; we know this is just playing with signs, playing with Viking myths (Stern 1990). It could be criticised as messy branding or praised as polysemic branding that allows the brand to engage several consumer segments (Puntoni et al. 2010).

Either way, Aifur is very directly sourcing a Norse myth market in its branding.

The Finnish producers of a range of spirit brands, Koskenkorva, market the brand Valhalla as "The Herb Shot for True Warriors." The landing page of the brand's website is dominated by a large image of three grimy Viking hands bumping their fists together in a toast of Valhalla liqueur; below this image, we find the following description:

> Valhalla liqueur was inspired by the rough conditions of the Nordics. Valhalla is made from plants that have had to withstand rough conditions to survive and grow. This evolutionary process is what makes Nordic plants unique, resulting in a distinctive and powerful taste. (Valhalla (the drink) n.d.)

Again, we find warrior archetypes, anthropomorphically extended to "warrior herbs" that are victorious survivors of the "rough" Nordic nature. Apparently, Mother Nature in this part of the Nordic myth market is one that deals in "tough love."

Aifur and Valhalla represent an extreme in the Nordic brandscape. The romantic mythology and heroic plots are all over the branding and the servicescape. Aifur uses iconic historical details and actual Norse symbols, mythology, and imagery (e.g., Harald Blåtand, the Midgaard snake—see Fig. 10.1). However, the Norse symbols and narratives are presented as stereotypes. Maybe consumers indulge in the experiences with nationalistic nostalgia, playful irony, suspension of disbelief, or a mode of cultural reflexivity; we do not know (this was not the focus of the study). Aifur and Valhalla can be seen as a mode of Norse mythology simulation—as popular culture recirculating symbols and signs of "Viking mythology" referring only to itself (Baudrillard 1994). As such, these playful appropriations of the Norse myth market depoliticise their ideological potential by the mode of simulation: the cultural tensions of nationalist romanticism and warrior pathos become opaque, bracketed, and thus more acceptable to the indigenous social values of inclusiveness and moderate nationalism.

Going deeper into the Norse myth market, we find the entrepreneur Jim Lyngvild. He is living in a wooden Viking "castle" called Ravnsborg on the island of Fyn, in Southern Denmark. He has launched a series of brands based on Norse mythology: a range of micro-brewed beer under

Fig. 10.1 Aifur interior. Notice the depiction of the worm of Midgaard snaking its way above the entrance portal (photo by first author)

the brewery name Frejdahl, cosmetics under the brand Raunsborg, and fur fashion under his own designer label. These differ from the more "folklore" stereotyped examples above, in that they very explicitly try to harness the full religious and ideological potential of Norse mythology. Lyngvild has nurtured a controversial media persona through participation in several reality TV shows—for instance *Expedition Robinson* (*Survivor* as it was called internationally) and competing in chocolate eating on *Britain's Got Talent*—and through frequent media commentary. Lyngvild has also been involved in building a Norse temple and founding a Norse congregation (Augustinus 2016).

The polytheistic Norse mythology has a wide gallery of narratives, gods, and mythical characters that are not common knowledge to most Nordic people. The Lyngvild brands and products all have names and narratives that borrow from the deeper layers of Norse mythology, not as common in popular culture. Most people have rudimentary knowledge of the "thunder god" Thor and Valhalla, the place where those who have gloriously died in combat end up waiting for Ragnarök, the end of the world. Fewer would know that "Nidhug" beer is named after a dragon that gnaws at the root of the tree of life, Yggdrasil, or that the beer "Fulla" is named after the golden-haired fertility goddess who is a counsellor to Frigg (the wife of Odin). The beer "Skolder—Viking Voyage" is co-branded with Highland Park whisky (sold as a box set), and the storytelling on the packaging details the romantic mythology of Viking conquest and looting the Orkney Islands (site of the Highland Park distillery) for silver—hence the silver design of the box (the silver patterns are inspired by a historical silver box from the Orkney Islands, brought back by the Vikings, now owned by Jim Lyngvild, see weblink for design: Frejdahl n.d.). Interestingly, Highland Park whisky also relies heavily on Viking mythology in its branding, stating the heritage of Viking settlers as the "Viking soul" of the brand, making full use of symbolic resources in the storytelling and design of bottles, and packaging with Norse ornaments in silver (Highland Park n.d.).

The power of nature is a pivotal metaphor in the romantic mythos (Thompson 2004): the magical maternal powers sanctify nature and allow agentic metaphorical constructions of herbs and landscapes, which stretch far in the horizons of Nordic myth markets. It is just as important in the Norse myth market as it is in the New Nordic Cuisine blending of romantic myths in the form of the Nordic terroir (Gyimóthy 2017; Hermansen 2012) with the gnostic myths of scientific production (e.g., the molecular gastronomy and "food lab" of Noma).

The cosmetics brand Raunsborg is a departure from Frejdahl's reliance on the romantic mythos. Raunsborg's branding blends romantic Norse mythology with gnostic elements of scientific harnessing of the power of nature: under the headline "Nature Meets Science," it is claimed that "the key is hidden in the Nordic nature … but nature does not do it alone … [Raunsborg products offer] a new scientific and innovative standard of skincare technology" (Raunsborg n.d.). The different products in the Raunsborg portfolio have different balances of romantic and gnostic themes, and Norse ideology is still quite present, for example in the Raunsborg "Hávamál" perfume for men, which is described as "a masculine perfume, identical to the original scent used a thousand years ago by our forefathers." Hávamál means "The Speech of the High One," and is the name of a complex ninth-century poem, where Odin tells of his wisdom for life.

The Nordic brandscape of Lyngvild is a rather significant blending of the full ideological agenda in romantic Norse with the gnostic mythos of "state-of-the-art science." According to Thompson (2004, p. 168), the apparent ideological conflict of innovative science and Norse mysticism is not a problem of (self-)contradiction or conflict, but rather offers consumers a "miraculous blending" of mythological promises, making brands and products "a divine tool … for personal transformation." It does indeed seem to work for the Nordic cosmetics of Raunsborg, and perhaps this strategic mix of romantic and gnostic themes is even palatable today in wider consumer segments than the "cultural creative" class that Thompson (2004) based his study on—particularly if carefully balanced branding strategies were used to "sanitise" the symbolic resources.

Another instance of sanitising symbolic resources is the sneaker brand WODEN. In a warehouse on the docks of Århus harbour, we find its head offices. WODEN is declared the condensation of "WOrk of DENmark," thus inscribing the country of origin in the actual brand name, but further underlining Nordicness with the tag line "The Scandinavian Sneaker" (Fig. 10.2). The brand was conceived by the founder and owner Carsten Holm, who had previous marketing experience at the Danish brand ECCO, a classic functional shoe brand that uses "clean" and modern aesthetics of light, Nordic design with wooden surfaces in store design, though without overtly branding ECCO with "Nordicness" in advertising and online communications. Holm realised

WODEN

scandinavian sneakers

Fig. 10.2 WODEN logo (http://woden.dk/). Reprinted with permission

that the region of origin meant something important to global consumers; being a Nordic brand offered "something mysterious and exciting."

According to the founder, WODEN is a brand that is based on Scandinavian values of sustainability, product quality, and respect for nature. Instead of synthetic materials, the sneaker sole is made of natural cork. The North Sea Collection was recently introduced under the slogan "Inspired by Nature." These sneakers are made of waste products from the Icelandic fishing industry: fish leather (instead of animal leather or polyester). The fish leather is produced in Iceland with a sustainable process using the country's natural geothermal hot spring water. Even the marketing of WODEN is claimed to be a form of "non-marketing," an approach of not touting product superiority through advertising, but humbly performing good business practice and acumen. That eventually attracts the right retailers, customers, and word of mouth.

When Holm was designing his own brand, he did extensive research on how to design the new sneaker brand in a way that could tap into Nordic/Scandinavian symbolic resources:

Holm: …the official story is that it means Work of Denmark, but the unofficial is that I was digging into Norse mythology, because when you are looking for something Scandinavian or Nordic, then that is a relevant factor. So I was looking for names like Odin and North and after some time came upon Wodens day, Wednesday is actually named after Odin in English. Woden means Odin, and I thought, damn, that sounds cool, that has power and some good story behind it. But I didn't want it to be a Norse mythology brand … because … well … it is Scandinavian, but … it could give the wrong impression…

Interviewer: Well, what's wrong about that?

Holm: You should not talk religion or something when you talk about the brand, no opinions on something I don't have … that should not be…

Interviewer: Okay, you should not be religious…

Holm: No, exactly … if you looked up Woden you could find a lot of stuff related to that, and I do not want that.

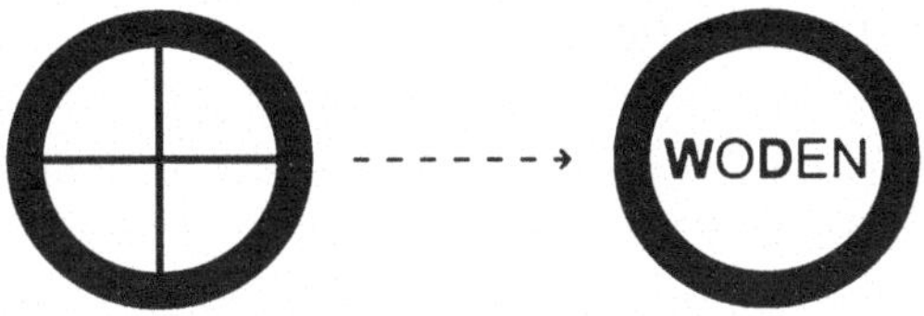

Fig. 10.3 From the Sun Cross to the WODEN logo (http://woden.dk/about-woden/). Reprinted with permission

The fact that WODEN's founding history has official and unofficial versions clearly shows how the branding is trying to carefully walk "on the edge" of the ideological potential of the mythology. It wants to harness the "power" and "good story"—but without being tied to uncontrollable ideological agendas of Norse mythology. The CEO may well be aware that there is "stuff" to be found in the mythological basement. On the WODEN brand website, the genealogy of the brand logo is explained without any reference to Odin/Woden or Norse mythology. The account explains how the fat circle around the brand name is inspired by the Bronze Age symbol of the Sun Cross (see Fig. 10.3), thus connecting WODEN brand identity to the ancient deification of nature and cults of the sun (WODEN mentions examples from China, Babylon, Shamash cult, and astrology; WODEN n.d.).

However, this particular section of Norse symbolism has had more recent appropriations by nationalist extreme right movements and the Nazi ideology: the Sun Cross was used by regional Nordic Nazi movements (e.g., Quisling's party, Nasjonal Samling of Norway); the Norse Sól rune (a jagged "S") was used by Hitler's SS on their uniforms. The swastika is a symbol with widespread use from India to Crete, in Roman culture and also Norse mythology as the symbol of Odin/Woden, and the Sun Cross was before Nazism appropriated as an "encircled" swastika (Koch 2013). Indeed, it was a Pandora's box, and certainly a place of strong cultural tensions.

The Myth of the Nordic Utopia

Using a branding strategy of being sustainable, artisanal, fair trade, or organic is not in itself distinct, and neither is it specifically "Nordic." However, it may be a more distinct brand identity if these elements are inscribed in the mythology of the "unique" Nordic terroir (Gyimóthy 2017; Larsen and Österlund-Potzsch 2015), and the New Nordic Food Manifesto is essentially a very direct stipulation of the Nordic utopia mythology. The cultural production and successful export of Nordic TV drama as Nordic Noir or Scandi-drama is a myth market of the Nordic utopia, regardless of the tragic themes in the crime fiction of *The Killing* or the pragmatic politics of *Borgen* (Østergaard et al. 2014; Waade and Jensen 2016; see also Chap. 9 in this volume, where Schultz Nybacka discusses Nordic crime fiction).

The myth market of the Nordic social utopia is a mythology of the inclusive, egalitarian, gender-reflexive, well-balanced welfare state (and hygge). It is a metaphor of the Nordic "socio-economic terroir," making real the modern promises of individual freedom and security (Berggren and Trädgårdh 2015) and fostering "the happiest people in the world" (Brits 2017; Booth 2014; Brown 2008). These myths blend and support each other as they align with romantic and gnostic metaphors. The romantic stance worships the Nordic landscape, the gnostic sings scientific praise of the socio-economic miracle of the Nordic model (e.g., Fukuyama 2011) and *homo reciprocans* ("the altruistic tax-payer," Bowles and Gintis 2000). Historically the Nordic landscape is both tough and generous, it both nurtures and disciplines the Nordic people, but in the contemporary utopian myth market it is mostly a source of harmony, hygge, and healing. This connection and continuity of landscape and people foster a sense of coming together, of community and sharing (Hermansen 2012 with reference to Löfgren 1992). It is built on a mode of non-aggressive nationalism, of harmony and balance (Hermansen 2012). This "myth of balance" is pervasive in ideas of nature/culture, social security and free markets (sometimes referred to as "flexicurity"), work/life balance, gender equality, and the Scandinavian idea of "individual freedom through communal institutions and welfare"—for example in "The Swedish/Nordic Theory of Love" (Berggren and Trägårdh 2015; Partanen 2017).

The coffee table book-sized periodical *Oak, the Nordic Journal* is a catalogue of Nordic utopian mythology. The more than 160 beautiful pages chronicle the creative "Echoes of the Nordic Way of Life" that is performed by people in the Nordic region, or bring the "Nordic way of life" to the world. For example, a cover story about Olafur Eliasson sets off like this:

> Oak stopped by to talk to Eliasson himself about avoiding the mythologizing that comes with running the world's most famous studio and how he's built the unlikeliest of things, a deeply pragmatic utopia. (*Oak* vol. 9, 2018, p. 106)

Just like the many other myths (e.g., flexicurity), this mythology of the Nordic hero has internal paradoxical tensions: the "myth avoiding mythologising" while creating a "pragmatic utopia." Amongst other questions, Eliasson is asked: "How did the landscape influence your work?" Fortunately, it did: his sense of light is influenced, apparently, by his childhood experiences of the special blue, Icelandic twilight. The mythological landscape is widely used as a romantic metaphor that can give narrative context and magic to the utopian myths.

Further south, in Stockholm, we find the company Sandqvist, which is branding "sustainable bags" with the slogan "From the Nordic Landscape":

> Sandqvist was founded in Stockholm, Sweden in 2004 by Anton Sandqvist. Together, with his brother Daniel and their friend Sebastian, they are the soul behind the brand. The Nordic landscape with its forests, rivers and vast unpopulated areas as well as an urban city lifestyle have always been our main inspiration. Accordingly, the Sandqvist designs are uncomplicated, functional and beautiful, with clear Swedish heritage. (Sandqvist Bags n.d.)

The brand video portrays the three friends canoeing, hiking, and camping in the Nordic landscape. The video is narrated by Anton

Sandqvist himself: "the love of the Scandinavian nature literally came with the breast milk, and partly made us who we are today" (Sandqvist Bags n.d., brand video 1:27). The Nordic landscape is presented in very beautiful, intimate closeups and almost sensuous detail (water, snow, friends around the camp fire). Here, nature is more the "fourth friend" than the awe-inspiring deity. The brand video tells a story of how the friends join the Nordic landscape for relaxed, intimate communality (hygge), not survivalist individualism.

In the interview, head of marketing (and co-founder) Sebastian Westin explains the brand's proposition as a simple and sturdy everyday bag for everyday urban living. But it should also remind you of your connection with the Nordic landscape: "you would like to be the outdoor person, but perhaps you just don't get around to it very often." The design is inspired by "classic" and functional design, such as vintage Volvo cars. Sebastian wouldn't really recommend the Sandqvist bags for serious hiking in Nordic nature, and points to the many brands that offer more appropriate, "technical" outdoor bags and equipment. Thus, Sandqvist bags strategically position the brand away from the (crowded) gnostic myth market, harnessing the symbolic resources of the Nordic landscape, with utopian themes that romanticise both the geographical and social "terroir" of Sweden/the Nordic countries (and the ideal connection of these).

Leaping north of the Arctic Circle, to the Norwegian city of Bodø, we find a very different and more dramatic Nordic landscape of steep mountains, deep fjords, and icy waters. This is the region of Nordland, and an important locus of the Norwegian national identity. Here, we also find the restaurant Nyt (meaning "enjoy"). It is a New Nordic Food–inspired restaurant founded by two young cuisine-entrepreneurs that has recently been awarded a prize for the "best restaurant in Norway"—not by Michelin, but by the patrons, a clear indication that Nyt is more about the relation to the patrons than fine dining elitism. The decor clearly appropriates the Bodø landscape, which is portrayed on numerous large photos on the walls. Books on Nordic produce and New Nordic Cuisine decorate the lounge. Regionalism is part of Nyt's cuisine and branding, but also is a communal effort, reaching out to the locals of Bodø:

> Our cuisine is anchored in history. The Nordic to us means looking back in Nordland regional culinary traditions. What did people do before the fridge and the freezer? … So, we invited the regional media to ask for traditional local recipes and ingredients including the stories and why we should retain them. (Bjørnar Bakklund, founder and manager, Nyt)

Unfortunately, the attempt did not prove very fruitful: the local knowledge of culinary traditions had seemingly been lost. The mythical resources of regional culinary specificity seemed as scarce as the market for fresh Bodø vegetables in March. But the project of Nyt is of an existential nature to the founders and staff. They feel a strong connection to the landscape and the community. They have created Nyt in Bodø, because they want to live and do high-quality cuisine *in Bodø*, as this “”just feels right.” As a workplace, Nyt is defying the traditional social hierarchy of fine cuisine: it is an equal and communal effort of the team, and even the apprentice is invited to be creative and to go into the restaurant to present his work to the guests. Nyt is intended as a magical place of the Nordic utopia: an informal meeting around the best food the landscape can offer, enjoyed with “relaxed happiness” (they only use the word “hygge” cautiously, but the mythology clearly resonates).

Switch to Swedish fashion, where we find a different formulation of the Nordic utopian myth. This industry is a major business sector of the Swedish economy (Kreativ Sektor 2015). It has several sector organisations, such as the Association of Swedish Fashion Brands and Swedish Fashion Council. Head of the Association of Swedish Fashion Brands, Emma Ohlson, struggles with the question when asked how Swedish fashion taps into “Nordic values” or “Nordic living” branding. She believes that overtly signalling “Nordic” or “Swedish” in the branding would be too nationalistic and inappropriate. In addition, the idea of invoking Norse mythology or symbols would be completely inappropriate and lead to accusations of nationalism, racism, or even Nazism. Instead, she suggests the use of Swedish immigrant designers, such as when the Swedish hip-hop label RMH Sweden, representing artists like Silvana Imam and Michel Dida, was invited to collaborate with Stockholm Fashion Week. What we see here is that these types of diverse cultural expressions are turned into an appropriate way of constructing Swedishness: through Sweden as a multiethnic, inclusive place.

Elin Frendberg of the Swedish Fashion Council also rejects the overt use of "Nordic" branding. She adds to the description of the current use of "Swedish" values in branding that feminist and transgender perspectives are a "new normal" in leading Swedish fashion branding and photography. There is a strong trend by designers not to distinguish between fashion for "men" and "women," just to make fashion. When producing fashion branding, it is equally important to avoid any gender stereotypes and heteronormative imagery. It would be "gender-washing" and half-heartedly playing with "progressive gendering" if a brand is using a transgender model in ways that seem like a "token transgender" (all the crew must be transgender).

These examples of the ideological tenets of good fashion branding are operating in the myth market of the "Swedish social utopia." These complex tensions of identity politics make it important to negate any overt themes of Nordicness or Swedishness when constructing the "non-nationalistic" inclusive Nordic utopia. This is indeed a hard course to plot, as the Scylla of non-distinction threatens on the one side and the Charybdis of stereotypes and taboo threatens on the other (Östberg 2011). The social utopia also denies cultural tensions and class and power struggles: we are just all one big happy family having a "hyggelig" time. But there are cracks in the façade of this nicely polished branding universe: the staff of Nyt are really enjoying working hard around the clock to get the local produce and to prepare it perfectly. They are probably very happy, but what if they are not? The Sandqvist bags from the Swedish landscape are sustainably produced—in India.

Conclusion

This chapter has ventured into the myth market of the Nordic brandscape and plotted a few directions and articulations of the mythological resources that are used by brand actors to construct Nordicness. Our brandscape odyssey found two pervasive forms of mythologising Nordicness, by drawing either on Norse mythology or on Nordic utopia.

Ultimately these commercialised renditions of cultural imagination of the Nordic will have placemaking outcomes in the form of reproducing and rearticulating a sense of regionality and shared history and ideology; a sort of regional imagined community (Anderson 2006; Cayla and Eckhardt 2008).

Building on Thompson's (2004) formulation of the all-pervasive cultural mythology of the "Romantic and Gnostic mythos," we have tried to unravel and map how these blend into the Nordic myth market. On the one hand, we have explored the myth market of Norse mythology, and found a rich and ideologically charged symbolic resource, which is strategically sanitised to be palatable to broader segments of both Nordic and international markets. On the other hand, we have explored the broad and diverse myth market of the Nordic utopia, which blends the mythology of the Nordic landscape with the Nordic "socio-economic terroir" into compelling narratives of perfect harmony and happiness. Embedded in these mythical formulations are also countervailing concepts that can be seen as paradoxically meaningful, or magically balanced tensions. The tensions revolve around balancing modern Nordic aesthetics with Viking imagery and Norse mythology; egalitarian inclusiveness with fine dining/haute cuisine culture; traditional gendered fashion with post-gendered/LBTQ fashion; and ethnocentrism with multiculturalism. In analysing, how the different brands construct compromises of these tensions so that Nordic values are expressed in brands and products, we note that many times a sense of balance is achieved by utilising a mode of sanitised Nordic mythology. Apparently, it requires a careful cultural compass to manoeuvre through the Nordic branding waters and stay clear of the dead waters and high cliffs of pathetic clichés and political taboos.

Perhaps the Swedish notion of *lagom* adequately summarises many of the branding balancing acts that we have witnessed during this Nordic branding odyssey. *Lagom* is a term that can be roughly translated as "in moderation" or "neither too much, nor too little." This might not sound particularly distinctive, but it is often put forth as the one defining characteristic of Swedish society (see Dunne 2017 for a particularly vivid perpetuation of this myth). While many in the other Nordic countries would probably protest wildly, stressing that they are by no means plagued by the numbing blandness of the Swedish *lagom*, we nevertheless find that the careful mix of different branding elements to construct something seemingly very spicy but actually rather palatable is predicated on this type of balance. For the concoction to be spicy enough, however, a pressure release valve is necessary, and this exists in the rhetorical form of irony and sarcasm, which are both common in the Nordic countries (Andersen 2004). It has even been suggested that the Vikings were the ones who originally brought a sarcastic sense of humour to Britain (Carter 2014). The pressure release valve of irony and sarcasm works by dismantling most charges that drawing on the Nordic mythologies is over the top: "No, we're not really serious about this Viking stuff, of course, did you really think so? Oh, that's cute!" The one place that was distinctly over the top, E-Type's Viking-themed restaurant Aifur in central Stockholm, was catering only to foreign visitors. The orchestration of Viking history taking place there would probably be quite hard to digest—and we are not talking about the food, it was surprisingly edible!—for most with a somewhat more comprehensive understanding of the local conditions. Not even a heavy dose of sarcasm and irony could completely shelter you from the fact that you are being served by a six foot four man, completely covered in tribal tattoos, and wearing his long blond hair in Pippi Longstocking pigtails… We would like to reiterate Östberg's (2011) point here that branding initiatives drawing on local mythologies but catering to an international audience typically are much blunter than those catering to the local market, as the intended audience lacks the competencies to critically reflect on the viability of the symbolic materials being used.

The nature of branding dynamics is always to strategically enhance the perceptions of "the value universe" of the brand (Askegaard 2006). Unsurprisingly, the myth market of Nordic branding is also a translation of Nordic exceptionalism: the superior values of the Nordic region (land, culture, people, and traditions). This may raise serious issues of charging the already growing regionalism and nationalism, and the "Swedish" formulation of the Nordic social utopia mythology that is "non-nationalistic" and inclusive is equally politically charged. While acknowledging that this is by no means a complete road map for future Nordic branding ventures, but a sketch, maybe with too much detail in some regions and far too little in others, we nevertheless hope that these explorations into the Nordic myth markets may be relevant for further theorising of regional consumer culture. Perhaps an appropriate start would be to look into the cultural specificity of the Nordic that is not quite as steeply predicated on Nordic exceptionalism—but perhaps we should let this last point be a challenge to non-Nordic scholars whose minds are not tainted by centuries of over-consumption of *mjød*....

References

Andersen, L. P. (2004). *The Rhetorical Strategies of Danish TV Advertising: A Study of the First Fifteen Years with Special Emphasis on Genre and Irony*. Ph.D. Dissertation, Samfundslitteratur.

Andersen, L. P. (2017). Nordic Branding Podcast 1–5. *Brandbase*. Retrieved from https://soundcloud.com/user-419653229.

Anderson, B. (2006). *Imagined Communities: Reflections on the Origin and Spread of Nationalism*. Verso Books.

Andersson, J. (2009). Nordic Nostalgia and Nordic Light: The Swedish Model as Utopia 1930–2007. *Scandinavian Journal of History, 34*(3), 229–245. https://doi.org/10.1080/03468750903134699.

Andersson, J., & Hilson, M. (2009), Images of Sweden and the Nordic Countries. *Scandinavian Journal of History*, *34*(3), 219–228. ISSN: 0346-8755 print/ISSN 1502-7716.

Askegaard, S. (2006). Brands as a Global Ideoscape. In J. Schroder & M. S. Morling (Eds.), *Brand Culture* (pp. 96–106). Routledge.

Askegaard, S., & Ger, G. (1998). Product-Country Images: Towards a Contextualized Approach. In B. G. Englis & A. Olofsson (Eds.), *ACR European Advances in Consumer Research* (pp. 50–58). Provo, UT: Association for Consumer Research.

Augustinus, M. S. (2016). Jim Lyngvild: Gudetemplet i Korith står færdigt. *Fyens Stiftstidende*, 31. marts. Retrieved from https://www.fyens.dk/faaborg-midtfyn/Jim-Lyngvild-Gudetemplet-i-Korinth-staar-faerdigt/artikel/2969369.

Baudrillard, J. (1994). *Simulacra and Simulation*. University of Michigan Press. *The Nordic Journal*, vol. 1–9. Oak Publishing, Copenhagen. Retrieved from http://oakthenordicjournal.com/. (Includes Free Audio Podcasts).

Berggren, H., & Trägårdh, L. (2015). *Är svensken människa? Gemenskap och oberoende i det moderna Sverige*. Norstedts.

Booth, M. (2014). *The Almost Nearly Perfect People – The Truth About the Nordic Miracle*. London: Jonathan Cape.
Booth, W. C. (1974). *A Rhetoric of Irony*. Chicago: University of Chicago Press.
Bowles, S., & Gintis, H. (2000). Reciprocity, Self-Interest, and the Welfare State. *Nordic Journal of Political Economy, 26*(1), 33–53.
Brits, L. T. (2017). *The Book of Hygge: The Danish Art of Contentment, Comfort, and Connection*. New York: Penguin.
Brown, A. (2008). *Fishing in Utopia: Sweden and the Future That Disappeared*. Granta Books.
Byrkeflot, H., Pedersen, J. S., & Svejenova, S. (2013). From Label to Practice: The Process of Creating New Nordic Cuisine. *Journal of Culinary Science & Technology, 11*(1), 36–55.
Carter, C. (2014). Vikings 'Brought Sarcastic Sense of Humour to Britain'. *The Telegraph*. Retrieved October 8, 2018, from https://www.telegraph.co.uk/history/10677904/Vikings-brought-sarcastic-sense-of-humour-to-Britain.html. Published Online 5 March 2014.
Cayla, J., & Eckhardt, G. M. (2008). Asian Brands and the Shaping of a Transnational Imagined Community. *Journal of Consumer Research, 35*(2), 216–230.
Dunne, L. (2017). *Lagom: The Swedish Art of Balanced Living*. London, UK: Gaia Books Ltd.
Frejdahl. (n.d.). Retrieved November 5, 2018, from https://bryggeriet-vestfyen.dk/brands/skolder-limited-edition/?lang=en. [The Product Webpage of Frejdahl Skolder Beer, Depicting Also the Silver Box Design].
Fukuyama, F. (2011). *The Origins of Political Order: From Prehuman Times to the French Revolution*. Farrar, Straus and Giroux.
Gyimóthy, S. (2017). The Reinvention of Terroir in Danish Food Place Promotion. *European Planning Studies, 25*(7), 1200–1216.
Hermansen, M. E. T. (2012). Creating Terroir: An Anthropological Perspective on New Nordic Cuisine as an Expression of Nordic Identity. *Anthropology of Food, S7*, 7249. Retrieved from http://aof.revues.org/7249.
Highland Park. (n.d.). Retrieved from https://www.highlandparkwhisky.com/our-story/.
Kjeldgaard, D., Askegaard, S., & Eckhardt, G. (2015). Glocal Brand Relationships. In S. Fournier, M. Breazeale, & J. Avery (Eds.), *Strong Brands, Strong Relationships* (pp. 48–59). London: Routledge.
Koch, R. (2013). *The Book of Signs*. Courier Corporation.
Kreativ Sektor. (2015). *Innehållsinnovation och internationell tillväxt i kreativa näringar*. En rapport från Kreativ Sektor.

Larsen, H. P., & Österlund-Potzsch, S. (2015). Islands in the Sun: Storytelling, Place & Terroir in Food Production on Nordic Islands. *Ethnologia Scandinavica, 45*, 29–52.

Leer, J. (2016). The Rise and Fall of the New Nordic Cuisine. *Journal of Aesthetics & Culture, 8*(1), 33494. https://doi.org/10.3402/jac.v8.33494.

Linnet, J. T. (2011). Money Can't Buy Me Hygge: Danish Middle-Class Consumption, Egalitarianism, and the Sanctity of Inner Space. *Social Analysis, 55*(2), 21–44.

Linnet, J. T (2015). Cozy Interiority – The Interplay of Materiality and Sociality in the Constitution of Cozy 3rd Place Atmosphere. *Ambiances, Perception – In situ – Ecologie Sociale*, Retrieved June, from http://ambiances.revues.org/543.

Löfgren, O. (1992). Landskabet i: Den nordiske verden 1. København: Kirsten Hastrup (red.), 109–190.

New Nordic Food. (2004). *The New Nordic Kitchen Manifesto*. Retrieved August 10, 2018, from http://newnordicfood.org; Direct Link to Archived Version of Original Manifesto. Retrieved August 10, 2018, from http://en.arkiv.nynordiskmad.org/about-nnf-ii/new-nordic-kitchen-manifesto/.

O'Reilly, D., & Kerrigan, F. (2013). A View to a Brand: Introducing the Film Brandscape. *European Journal of Marketing, 47*(5/6), 769–789.

Östberg, J. (2011). The Mythological Aspects of Country-of-Origin: The Case of the Swedishness of Swedish Fashion. *Journal of Global Fashion Marketing, 2*(4), 223–234.

Østergaard, P., Linnet, J. T., Andersen, L. P., Kjeldgaard, D., Bjerregaard, S., Weijo, H., et al. (2014). Nordic Consumer Culture: Context and Concept. In J. W. Schouten, D. M. Martin, & R. Belk (Eds.), *Consumer Culture Theory* (Research in Consumer Behavior) (Vol. 16, pp. 245–257). Emerald Group Publishing Limited.

Partanen, A. (2017). *The Nordic Theory of Everything: In Search of a Better Life*. Gerald Duckworth & Co.

Puntoni, S., Schroeder, J., & Ritson, M. (2010). Meaning Matters: Polysemy in Advertising. *Journal of Advertising, 39*(2), 51–64.

Raunsborg. (n.d.). Retrieved August 10, 2018, from https://raunsborg.dk/om-os/.

Roncha, A. (2008). Nordic Brands Towards a Design-Oriented Concept. *Journal of Brand Management, 16*(1–2), 21–29.

Sandqvist Bags. (n.d.). Retrieved August 10, 2018, from https://www.sandqvist.com/en/about. [Brand Video and Storytelling of the Brand].

Skandinavisk. (n.d.). Retrieved August 10, 2018, from https://skandinavisk.com/product/hygge-190gr-scented-candle/.
Stern, B. B. (1990). Pleasure and Persuasion in Advertising: Rhetorical Irony as a Humor Technique. *Current Issues and Research in Advertising, 12*(1–2), 25–42.
Stern, B. B. (1995). Consumer Myths: Frye's Taxonomy and the Structural Analysis of Consumption Text. *Journal of Consumer Research, 22*(September), 165–185.
Thompson, C., & Tian, K. (2008). Reconstructing the South: How Commercial Myths Compete for Identity Value Through the Ideological Shaping of Popular Memories and Countermemories. *Journal of Consumer Research, 34*(5), 595–613.
Thompson, C. J. (2004). Marketplace Mythology and Discourses of Power. *Journal of Consumer Research, 31*(1), 162–180.
Thompson, C. J., & Arsel, Z. (2004). The Starbucks Brandscape and Consumers' (Anticorporate) Experiences of Glocalization. *Journal of Consumer Research, 31*(3), 631–642.
Thorsøe, M. H., Kjeldsen, C., & Noe, E. (2016). It's Never Too Late to Join the Revolution! Enabling New Modes of Production in the Contemporary Danish Food System. *European Planning Studies, 25*(7), 1166–1183. https://doi.org/10.1080/09654313.2016.1267112.
Valhalla (the drink). (n.d.). Retrieved August 10, 2018, from http://www.valhallaspirit.com/the-drink/.
Waade, A. M., & Jensen, P. M. (2016). Nordic Noir Production Values: The Killing and the Bridge. *Academic Quarter, 7*, 189–201.
Wiking, M. (2016). *The Little Book of Hygge: The Danish Way to Live Well.* UK: Penguin.
WODEN. (n.d.). Retrieved August 10, 2018, from http://woden.dk/about-woden/.

11

Mythologies of Finnishness in Advertising

Juulia Pietilä, Jack S. Tillotson, and Søren Askegaard

Introduction: A Regional Framing

Regions have only recently begun to serve as a means of theorizing culturally-based marketing and consumer research (Arnould and Thompson 2015). In the past, geographical frontiers were used only to delineate and contextualize marketing and consumer research, and not to advance theoretical development (Arnould et al. 2006). To further the discussion of geographical boundaries, the concept of glocalization has been used to describe local interpretations of transnational mythologies like the global youth segment (Kjeldgaard and Askegaard 2006). From examinations of the anonymity and shared aspects of transnational Asian brands, we now know biopolitical national boundaries to be mythological

J. Pietilä • S. Askegaard
University of Southern Denmark, Odense, Denmark
e-mail: aske@sam.sdu.dk

J. S. Tillotson (✉)
Liverpool Business School, Liverpool John Moores University, Liverpool, UK
e-mail: j.s.tillotson@ljmu.ac.uk

S. Askegaard, J. Östberg (eds.), *Nordic Consumer Culture*,
https://doi.org/10.1007/978-3-030-04933-1_11

(Cayla and Eckhardt 2008). Recent research has offered regionality as a new way of understanding social organization to "help researchers grasp phenomena that span over areas larger than a single locality" (Chelekis and Figueiredo 2015, p. 321).

We enter the conversation on regions as a means of theorizing culturally-based marketing research by examining the regionality–marketer nexus. We pose the question: How does myth narrate the imaginaries of the Nordic socio-cultural region through advertisements? Through a study of advertisements found in Finnish magazines, with discursive roots that span both intranational and international audiences (Östberg 2011), we find that mythic narratives, archetypes, and plotlines speak to contradictions or paradoxes that are immanent in the natural and social experience of consumers living in Finland, or as travelers confronted with advertisement-based narratives of Finnishness. Despite the fact that some of the mythological imagery that we visit in this chapter is definitively and specifically Finnish, we allow ourselves to speak in terms of "regions," because we find that some of the imagery pertaining to Finnish national mythology is inscribed in a broader framework of Nordic and Arctic references; further, it is not always obvious exactly where the line is drawn.

The chapter is structured as follows. We first discuss current literature that is addressing myth in the world of marketing, building on consumer culture theory and marketing scholarship. We then describe our research design and subsequently present our analysis of the mythic portrayals of Finnishness in print advertisements. Finally, we present our findings and state a brief conclusion.

Mythology in the World of Marketing

Our examination responds to the call for more research that reflects "greater sensitivity to place and history" in operationalizing regionally based marketing and consumer research by mobilizing theory on myth (Chelekis and Figueiredo 2015, p. 321). The continuity of mythic symbols, motifs, and narratives reveals the *longue durée* of mythologies that correspond to structures that have an extreme longevity (Frog et al. 2012). Adhering to Barthes (1957), we take myths to be a representational mode of signification, comprising a system of signs and signifiers that encode cultural meanings into an object, subject, image, text, or practice. Myths are a type of narrative, archetype, or plotline that social groups rely on to explain the nature of the world and the rationale for social conduct in a given culture (Tillotson and Martin 2014). Also, myths "provide a logical model capable of overcoming contradictions or paradoxes in natural and social experience" (Levy 1981, p. 51). Updated to suit contemporary conditions, mythic narratives, archetypes, and plotlines grounded in the most fundamental concerns of human experience draw from a vast historical supply of cultural meanings that supersede historical particularities (Martin et al. 2014). Myths are "as old as humanity, yet [are] constantly renewed to fit contemporary life" (Stern 1995, p. 183). Throughout various historical and cultural contexts, mythologies are purposefully created and used to propagate ideologies and serve different social, political, and commercial goals (for specific Nordic examples, see Kristensen et al. 2011; Tillotson and Martin 2015). On their creation, myths channel powerful, ideologically steeped meanings that consumer groups experience in advertising messages (Parker 1998). Much like myths, ideologies are frameworks for understanding the world that is "shared by members of social groups" and "constituted by relevant selections of sociocultural values" (Van Dijk 1995, p. 248). Myths naturalize ideologies and "individuals become immersed in a shared understanding whereby the culturally contingent aspects of social life (such as common cultural associations, social practices, or power relationships) are seen as being the natural order of things" (Thompson and Haytko 1997, p. 20).

In this chapter, we shed light on how advertising coupled with mythological systems of Finnishness constitutes a specific way of receiving and interpreting global consumer culture that reproduces the regionally based Nordic socio-cultural model (Østergaard 1997, 2006). Advertising takes on points of ideological instability common to the Nordic milieu and, through myth, transforms cultural conflict and contradiction into something with value and marketability, even for international audiences. The concept of a nation can be seen as a myth that is produced in a certain historical context, but taken as the natural order of things. To those in the community, a nation is a mythic phenomenon in itself, but it is also a mythological narrative construct to those outside of that community.

Nations become part of a signification process regarding "foreign–domestic" and "country X–country Y" (Anderson 1983; Askegaard and Ger 1998; Cayla and Eckhardt 2008; Ger 1999). National myths shape individual, social, economic, and political life:

> At the individual level, myths are key source material for stitching people to national identities, imbuing personal identity with the solidity, status, and camaraderie that comes from the felt participation in collective ideals and achievements. At a societal and political level, myths serve a conservative political function, smoothing over contradictions and challenges to ideology. (Holt 2006, pp. 359–360)

Regional cultural contradictions become fodder for national mythologies. Cultural contradictions function as points of ideological instability. Mythic narratives or plotlines serve to smooth over these points as they resonate within a cultural group (Thompson 2004; Slotkin 1992).

Research on commercial mythology offers insights into the application of regionality in advertisements, revealing that commercial mediated mythology "[harnesses] myth for commercial purposes through the marketplace" (Cayla and Arnould 2008, p. 101). Advertising operates not in product markets but rather in myth markets, where "the topic of the conversation is the national ideology, and it is taken up by many contenders" (Holt 2003, p. 44). Importantly, mythologies can serve multiple ideological agendas that pull consumer identities and lifestyles in particular directions (Thompson 2004). Myths "permeate consumer culture" and play a significant role in the media and advertising texts as creators of an appealing brand and product images (Thompson 2004, p. 162). Commercial mythmaking refers to the efforts of marketers to associate their brands, products, and services with culturally resonant stories. Consumers use those mythic stories to help resolve acute tensions in their lives, and thus myths contribute to various consumer and communal identity projects (Thompson 2004).

An emphasis on the purposeful creation of myths in the commercial setting is useful to marketers. Narratives, archetypes, and plotlines can serve as implements of cultural codes—compelling cultural content that allows consumers to easily understand and experience intended advertising meanings (Holt and Cameron 2010). A bias toward seeing advertising as competing for cultural share heightens awareness of myths' effectiveness in shaping behaviors at the individual and community levels (Holt 2004). The perspective of commercial mythologies as an ideological process produced by marketers emphasizes myths' framing power more than their playfulness. We believe this may facilitate understanding of the commodifying of cultural identities in the Nordics. Finally, in a study of iconic brands, Holt (2006, p. 359) calls attention to a promising potential of myth, namely that of "narrating the imagined nation." Our study takes one step in the direction of realizing that potential in the realm of the Nordic socio-cultural region.

Research Design

The broad aim of this chapter is to produce an account of the complex interplay of visual, verbal, and narrative symbols in advertisements (Phillips and McQuarrie 2010). Advertising remains a relevant and exciting focus of research exploring the flow of cultural meanings, particularly since companies spend billions of dollars annually on advertising as a communications channel. There are at least three main grounds for focusing on advertisements. First, advertising brings together consumer goods and the culturally constituted world, so that consumers make associations between the attributes of a particular good and a certain desirable concept within the culturally constituted world (McCracken 1986). Second, myths work through advertisements, as encoded symbols of meaning, engaging the receiver's imagination to spark an affective response through contradiction with conventional understandings of the world (Hackley and Hackley 2016; Holt 2004; Stern 1995). Mythologies animate advertisements; they become a "kind of knowing" and, thereby, construct ideological meaningfulness in our experiences with the world (Doty 2000, p. 55; Barthes 1957; Levy 1981). Third, advertisements are polysemic and ambiguous, carriers of multiple meanings as mythic symbols become a medium for different ideologies (Brown et al. 2013; Luedicke et al. 2010). Through mythology, advertisements can become instruments of power and rhetorical force in society (Thompson 2004).

In the rest of this section, we turn to specific techniques and procedures concerning data collection and analysis. A presentation of our findings will follow before drawing some brief conclusions.

Data Collection

The primary sources of data for this study were 30 print advertisements that appeared in either of two Finnish magazines: *Eeva* and *Blue Wings*. We selected these advertisements on the basis of their relevance to the research question: How does myth narrate the imaginaries of the Nordic socio-cultural region through advertisements? Each advertisement seemingly expresses Nordic regional elements by appealing to the idea of Finnishness, which can be deciphered with the chosen methods. We make no claims about the commonness of cultural, mythic elements in advertising in general, but rather gauge the use and application of regional–cultural mythology in advertising where such mythology has recently been discoverable. We chose advertisements appearing in 2014 to allow a focus on contemporary brands and their respective marketing methods.

The common denominator for advertising texts selected for analysis includes those that invoke the use of Finnishness for consumer appeals. According to Media Audit Finland, *Eeva* is among the most widely read women's magazines in Finland (379,000 readers), and has the target demographic of "discerning women, who value themselves and a good quality of life" (Finnish Periodical Publishers' Association [FPPA] 2015). *Blue Wings*, the Finnair in-flight magazine, has as its main target group business travelers (FPPA 2015). It was chosen as one of the sources to include the international aspect of marketing through national cultural mythic elements in the empirical part of the study. It features many Finnish brands and its readers are of diverse nationalities.

Data Analysis

Recognizing that Finnishness is discussed from mythic points of view, our attention focused on salient themes tied to narratives, archetypes, and plotlines linked to the Nordic region. Data analysis occurred as a continuous act throughout the research project. Visual communication is exceedingly culture-specific: different cultures may interpret given visual cues in very different ways. We identified cultural codes and references that connected the ads to the larger realm of collective cultural imagery. In the early phase of analysis, we identified three themes in print advertisements that revolved around the regional symbolism of Finnishness: (1) cultural stereotypes, (2) romantic nostalgia, and (3) social politics. These themes were continuously refined, collapsed, reworked, and discarded as we sought to make sense of our findings in a conceptually coherent way (Belk et al. 2012). In acknowledgment of the importance of connecting images to the cultural context of the marketplace, we individually reanalyzed the advertisement material and generated analytical codes that explored how images "embody and express cultural values and contradictions" within consumer culture (Schroeder 2006, p. 303). We then analyzed each of the themes to evaluate in more detail how advertisements functioned concerning the marketplace and leveraged mythology to narrate imaginaries of the Nordic socio-cultural region. We began another iteration of coding our data. As we moved between theory and data, we were able to find distinct yet interconnected dimensions of marketplace myths foregrounding (1) mythic symbols of Finnishness, (2) the propagating of localist, protectionist, and regionalist narratives, and (3) romantic nostalgia. In the coming section, we outline these dimensions in more detail.

Findings

Mythic Symbols of Finnishness

Mythic portrayals of Finnishness in advertising appeal to and strengthen and extend a collective sense of national and cultural identity. The advertisement in Fig. 11.1 relies on a blue and white font and background coloring theme that matches the Finnish national flag, invoking the idea that Nordea Bank understands Finns and therefore must be adept at managing their finances. While the bank is based in Helsinki, Finland, the name Nordea comes from a Swedish company, but as the name

Fig. 11.1 Nordea advertisement. Reproduced with permission from Nordea Bank OYJ. Reprinted from *Blue Wings*, 11/2014, p. 25

underlies it has a clear strategic vision about being "Nordic." While blue has been found to be the most commonly used color, particularly in finance advertising (Gorn et al. 1997), there are instances where cultural disposition resonates new meanings through the ambiguous character of mythic symbols (Brown et al. 2013). Furthermore, as we know from reader-response theory (e.g., Scott 1994), while their colors were also blue and white prior to the spread to other Nordic countries, this fact does not prevent Finns from identifying the blue and white colors as resonant with Finnish national symbolism.

The Nordea advertisement shows a piggy-bank pig sustaining the weight of a set of coins on its nose. The text below asserts: "Keep your finances in top shape. Do not let your assets degenerate or your condition for results deteriorate. *Sisu* puts your money in a systematic training." Here, Nordea Bank draws on *sisu*, the mythic quality of Finnish perseverance under extremely harsh conditions. An illustrative example is the Winter War miracle myth of outnumbered but persistent Finnish troops, who in 1939–1940 managed to fight back against the Russians in extremely adverse circumstances using *sisu*. Like Finnish men in the Winter War, Nordea bankers are perseverant fighters who will overcome any obstacle imposed by the complicated world of finances to make your money work for you. The connotation of *sisu*, as used to describe the Finnish character, is that life is hard work and your money should work hard for you too (with the help of Nordea, of course). *Sisu* associates the Nordea brand with a favorably viewed cultural trait that represents "us," and reinforces these agreeable components of a national identity. Later, *sisu* is intentionally given a double meaning: *sinun suunnitelmasi*, which means "your plan" or your financial plan.

Localist, Protectionist, and Regionalist Narratives

National symbolism and implied domestic product origins are leveraged to propagate localist, protectionist, and regionalist narratives with moralistic undertones. An example of national symbolism tied to localist narratives is the "land of engineers" myth. *Suomalainen insinööritaito* (Finnish engineering skills/competence) and Finland as a "land of technology" are related ideas that perpetuate the belief that Finns have a unique way of looking at the world, making them exceptionally adept in technological and engineering pursuits. Despite post-Nokia industry-wide struggles relating to technological innovation, the popular memory of the "Nokia Miracle" lives on and contributes to this notion. One exceptional company, Nokia, saved Finland from a severe economic downturn during the early 1990s. A central figure in the Finnish national epic, *Kalevala*, is Ilmarinen, a blacksmith and inventor who can be seen as the origin of this mythic idea of Finnishness. For example, in a situation where the enchantress and wicked queen request a magical object in return for a rite of passage, Ilmarinen turns out to be the only one capable of forging such a magical object—the *Sampo*—a kind of mill capable of producing flour, salt, and money out of nothing. The object is—for obvious reasons—believed to bring good fortune to its holder. The idea of a "technological fix" is therefore deeply inscribed in Finnish mythology.

While there may be little difference in the actual policies in terms of the political focus on the Arctic areas between the three Nordic countries of Norway, Sweden, and Finland (e.g., Suorsa 2007), it may be possible to state that the northernmost parts of these countries play different roles in the national imaginaries of the respective countries. While the self-imagery of Sweden, backed by a not too distant past as the regional superpower, as a global player and moral model of modernity (Trägårdh 2018) leaves little room for a central role for the remote and undeveloped "north," the imagery in Norway and Finland is different. In spite of the fact that, in particular, the northern Finnmark region in Norway has been subject to a degree of both marginalization and exoticization due to its Sami population, there is a long tendency in Norway for stressing and supporting local development in the peripheries (e.g., Amdam 2002), not least sustained by the oil income. The Norwegian state has implemented an "Arctic identity" policy (relatively unthinkable in Sweden), albeit with results that are far from unambiguous so far (Medby 2014). Likewise, Finland has since long promoted the northern region of Lapland as a high-profile tourist destination, including a fully grown Santa Claus industry (Pretes 1995). A relatively forgotten inter-Nordic conflict, which we will also not unpack here, between Finland and Greenland (and even a few small towns in Norway) is who can claim to have the authentic home of Santa Claus. Finland is in the lead not least due to the significant resources invested in one of the world's strongest brands (Hall 2008). Owing to the presence of this industry, the Arctic plays a more central role in the Finnish national self-understanding compared to Sweden.

Beyond—or rather in addition to—the local traditionalist and Arctic references, we also find references to the insertion of Finland in the Nordic region. For example, in an investor- and citizen-oriented campaign, the city of Oulu appropriates a regionalist narrative that aims to create associations between Oulu and "Scandinavia." The official slogan of the city, "the Capital of Northern Scandinavia," is highlighted, portraying Oulu as a "first-rate operating environment for companies." The myth of the land of engineers is evoked throughout the text and makes references to constructing a smart city that utilizes "ICT technologies." By introducing Oulu as a business-friendly environment and the capital of northern Scandinavia, the local political and business scenes hope to attract more capital and innovation. Arcticness is referred to explicitly through narratives that highlight it as the "Arctic Smart City" and in the body text: "The goal is to focus on the development of sustainable and energy-efficient city planning and construction that answer the challenges imposed by the extreme conditions of the Arctic." We interpret the convergence of "Scandinavianness" with "Arcticness" and "Nordicness" as the imagination of an identity that places all the emphasis on the collective (Kjeldgaard and Östberg 2007), at once establishing consensus and conformity to a regional brand while also establishing its exceptionalism amongst the international audience (Browning 2007). As can happen in cases of American exceptionalism tied to mythic narratives (Luedicke et al. 2010), the advertisement harnesses the land-of-engineers myth to position the city as ecologically and socially responsible, playing off the theme of sustainability and its moral implications.

The Finnish "key flag symbol," found in the bottom right corner of the Isku advertisement (Fig. 11.2), assumes at least two narratives. For local audiences, as well as informed foreigners (people who know the Finnish flag), it represents the myth of the nation (Askegaard 1988) as a classical country-of-origin or, as we prefer to say, product-country-imagery narrative (Askegaard and Ger 1998). What such a narrative contains is not easy to isolate or explicate. The late semiotician and novelist Umberto Eco wrote in his *Foucault's Pendulum*: "To each memorable image you attach a thought, a label, a category, a piece of the cosmic furniture, syllogisms, an enormous sorites, chains of apothegms, strings of hypallages, rosters of zeugmas, dances of hysteron proteron, apophantic logoi, hier-

Fig. 11.2 Isku advertisement. Reproduced with permission from Isku Interior Oy. Reprinted from *Eeva*, 8/2014, p. 47

archic stoichea, processions of equinoxes and parallaxes, herbaria, genealogies of gymnosophists—and so on to infinity" (Eco, cited in Papadopoulos 1993, p. 3). What this eloquent list of features signals is the complex web of knowledge and belief, hierarchizations of elements, cultural categories, analogies, and connotations that each (relatively) complex image engenders. The reference to a country (like Finland) through its flag definitely falls into this category. The intended message may very well be a kind of localist narrative, demarcating the local (and consequently favorable) origin of products and brands. At least potentially, it ideologically motivates consumers' moralistic identity work.

Such a campaign may also be interpreted as "protectionist," a highly contested qualifier in this day of global trade wars between groups often characterized as "liberal globalists" and "populist nationalists." As an explicit reference to the Finnish origin of the product, the Finnish key flag symbol was found on many product advertisements, ranging from health products like lactase pills, melatonin, and skin creams to grocery chains and furniture companies. In this context, most of these flag symbols represent a campaign that urges consumers to "favor the Finnish" (*suosi suomalaista*).

Finnish origin represents a responsible and moral choice for consumers, as they care about the success of their countryfolk and gladly ignore the more attractive foreign deals brought to them by globalization. Consumption of foreign brands is implied as a less moral choice, triggering guilt. If this strategy proves successful, systematic consumer "solidarity" toward Finnish origin undoubtedly benefits domestic brands that negotiate global competition. Further, this converges with findings of previous studies that suggest Nordic countries are built on export economies (Tillotson and Martin 2015), and the Finnish origin allows companies like Isku to become distinctive in their home market, while also spreading Finnish/Nordic know-how, quality, and industrial innovation abroad.

Romantic Nostalgia

Mythic portrayals of a rustic lifestyle of the past enable Finnish consumers to regain a material connection with a "paradise lost" of traditional Finnishness. Idyllic imagery from the countryside and Finnish nature represents an "exotic other" for appeals to international consumer segments (Ger 1999). For example, place branding and tourism companies draw on the dream-like imagery of a "winter wonderland" with Santa Claus or a land of a thousand lakes with the "beauty" and "purity" of Finnish nature. In Fig. 11.3, the town of Raseborg (Raasepori) appeals to intranational readers with place branding through the idyllic and rustic,

Fig. 11.3 The town of Raseborg advertisement. Reproduced with permission from visit Raseborg/Raseborg tourist information. Reprinted from *Blue Wings*, 12/2014, p. 79

and to international consumers with the exotic. We see the "ideal" in the upper part of the picture: a rural red wooden cottage, a child enjoying playing out in the snow, and traditional Finnish Christmas decorations. The "real" in the lower part of the picture explains the nature of the city. Raseborg is portrayed as being close to Helsinki, and thus a convenient place to live and do business. However, the advertisement suggests that Raseborg is "different" in addition to being close to the city. Both the text below and the pictorial motifs of the advert explain exactly how we are supposed to think Raseborg is different: it is an idyllic little town that has maintained an endearing rustic lifestyle. The innuendo is intended to remind Finns of the good old times in the countryside, as opposed to the dull and dusty urban life they most probably currently lead. The advert also provides prospective tourists with appealing exotic imagery of a "true, traditional Christmas" in a "fascinating maritime idyll and old towns filled with old-fashioned wooden houses."

Serving to bridge community-specific displaced meanings (McCracken 1986), Nordic-based global brands harness pastoral and bucolic motifs to associate themselves with mythic imagery of high nostalgic value. In the Finnish context, such displaced meaning often lies in romanticized narratives and popular memories of a pastoral lifestyle and a sense of togetherness of the past. Connecting with these displaced meanings is supposed to alleviate consumer anxieties in ever-changing societal circumstances.

Transnational brands, like Arla in Fig. 11.4, harness regional myths of Finnishness by attempting to tap into a previous narrative by the iconic brand Valio, which was traditionally the leading dairy brand in Finland (Tillotson and Martin 2015). The Arla advertisement features two photographs. On the left we see "Pentti," a Finnish male baby boomer, surrounded by rustic countryside imagery. In the upper right corner is a smaller image of the Arla milk packaging and a glass of milk in a rural setting. The text on the right says: "If you do not have time to listen, do not ask Pentti why he loves milk so much. Milk that has its home in Finland." The Arla slogan urges the consumer to "enjoy the good." Arla Foods is a company and brand that span the Nordic socio-cultural region by way of Finnish, Swedish, and Danish borders. It has a long history in Finland, with roots deep in Finnish culture and the dairy business since

Fig. 11.4 Arla advertisement. Reproduced with permission from Arla Oy. Reprinted from *Eeva*, 7/2014, p. 13

1929. In the advertisement, Arla has taken to the market the myth of the local with its numerous Finnish references. While one could argue that similar rustic imagery may also be part of Danish or Swedish mythology, every attempt is made to portray Arla as Finnish and to dispel any foreign "cultural odor" (Iwabuchi 2002), employing a character with the name of

Pentti, a traditional and uniquely Finnish male given name, and the slogan of "milk that has its home in Finland." We interpret this to mean that the milk that Arla sells in groceries comes from Finnish farmers. The image of Pentti, a Finnish farmer, is a mythic symbol that solicits the audience to become emotionally invested with the Arla brand through its links to the Finnish way of life. Apparently, this strategic approach has proved effective, as Arla has recently surpassed Valio in daily milk production by a significant margin (Mainio 2015).

The dairy industry and its connections to the countryside link narratives of Finnishness to a mythologized, bucolic way of life. Despite the concentration of the Finnish population in three larger urban centers, romantic elements of the "simple life" emerge from Finland's heritage as an agriculturally-based community. These mythic symbols work to assuage the stresses associated with the hustle and bustle of urban living common in contemporary times (Tillotson and Martin 2015). Further, "The connection between a healthy countryside lifestyle and the consumption of fresh milk" inscribes feelings of "social pride and strength" in Nordic food culture (Kristensen et al. 2011, p. 200). Idyllic, harmonious, and communal notions of the countryside ground Finns' idea of a united nation, language, and culture, which has established itself as a significant part of the Finnish collective imagery (Korkiakangas 2005). This bucolic rural imagery is among the essential constituents of not only the Finnish national identity, but also the Nordic socio-cultural region, and as such serves as an intertextual symbol established by reference to one's previous intranational experience (Östberg 2011). Interpreting the mythic symbol gains one membership to an exclusive club, where each act of interpretation serves to revitalize the feelings of belonging to that cultural group (Barthes 1977).

Advertising texts frame their products and brands as solutions to unique problems experienced by the regional cultural group. The goal of such solutions is to alleviate difficulties like living in rough Arctic conditions with harsh weather and no daylight.

For instance, a juice producer, Marli Vital, provides vitality and light to the dark Arctic conditions (Fig. 11.5). Its advertisement points out that Finland has little daylight during certain months of fall and winter. The text in the advertisement reads "when the sun is on vacation," and

Fig. 11.5 Marli Vital advertisement. Reproduced with permission from Eckes-Granini Finland Oy Ab as a Marli Vital brand owner, and Folk Finland as an advertising agency. Reprinted from *Eeva*, 11/2014, p. 79

includes several photographs lined up next to one another depicting a dark silhouette of a house over a 24-hour period. The repeated image emphasizes the darkness, as it occurs around the clock in the middle of the Arctic winter, and the harsh living conditions without daylight. Depression and fatigue are rampant during this particular season; therefore, it is a good idea to enjoy some juice that will make the consumer more healthy and vital. After all, the brand name suggests giving "vitality from nature" (the tagline below the logo).

A well-known French-based probiotic yogurt brand, which we will refer to under the pseudonym Digest Well, developed a campaign designed to engage Finnish consumers in a similar way, where advertising texts frame the products and brands as solutions to unique problems experienced by the Nordic socio-cultural group. The text in its advertisement asserts: "the Finnish winter is easy to digest." In Finnish, the verb *sulattaa* has various meanings (to digest; to melt, to defrost), which allow the ad to play on words. First, as Nordic people, Finns can easily "digest" the winter (as in tolerate it), but especially if they use this yogurt brand to promote better functioning of the digestive organs. The second meaning, to melt, evokes an idea of the melting of the snow shown in the image. In the lower part of the advertisement, the text reads: "The [Digest Well] flavor of this winter is the forest berry. It has such softness full of light that every winter stomach dreams of. If food digestion troubles you, [Digest Well] helps." Digest Well is a brand that can alleviate the harm and physical ailments that incur from those rough and perpetual Arctic natural conditions.

Discussion

We propose that mythology and its premises represent a means to capture and explain regional imaginaries through advertising. In addressing our research question, we have identified three interconnected dimensions of marketplace myths that become inscribed in a broader framework of Nordic, Scandinavian, and Arctic references: (1) mythic symbols of Finnishness, (2) propagating localist, protectionist, and regionalist narratives, and (3) romantic and historical nostalgia.

Over the course of this chapter, we have made selective comparisons with other culturally oriented consumer and marketing research that have touched on the premise that mythology plays an important role in delineating regional phenomena like nations, imaginary transnational brand communities, or global consumer culture (Cayla and Eckhardt 2008; Chelekis and Figueiredo 2015; Holt 2004; Kjeldgaard and Askegaard 2006; Thompson and Tian 2008). We propose that mythologies are a kind of episteme and therefore a mutually constitutive process, whereby the meaningfulness of experiences cannot be determined outside the stories told of them; in turn, the meanings of those stories cannot be resolved without any reference to the world in which they originate (Widdershoven 1993). Here, mythology can be considered a system of signs or a web of practical significance provided by the socio-historical and material context that helps constitute knowledge about the world.

Our findings are suggestive of the importance of mythology to marketers and advertisers and of their efforts to build an affective link between cultural contradictions and the therapeutic benefits afforded by mythic symbols (Humphreys and Thompson 2014; Holt 2004). The mythic symbol of Sisu, like that of the American frontier (Slotkin 1992), the man-of-action hero (Holt and Thompson 2004), the American South (Thompson and Tian 2008), the mountain man (Belk and Costa 1998), the American West (Peñaloza 2001), Chinese political myths (Zhao and Belk 2008), as well as indie consumers (Arsel and Thompson 2010), emplots a strong heroic performance in the face of overwhelming forces. Through the lens of what "other people" believe, myths engage the imagination and ignite an emotional response through contrast and disjunction from ideological opposition, while at the same time defining and identifying oneself in relation to those "others" (Arsel and Thompson 2010; Kozinets 2001; McAlexander et al. 2014).

Through mythology, Finnishness converges with the Nordic, Arctic, and Scandinavian identity, revealing Nordic regionality through advertising. Marketing scholars interested in regional theory development may wish to pay attention to commercial mythology in advertisements for many reasons. Perhaps the most important is that commercial mythology helps see how brands can create an imagined regional identity—in this case, a regional "Scandinavian myth" or "Nordic myth"—for commercial purposes via the marketplace. In advertising or marketing, harnessing place and country of origin is "always contingent on the various mythologies that are always already available regarding a place" (Östberg 2011, p. 232). We propose that intertextuality and ambiguity of mythic symbols provide the condition of possibility for interpreting Finnishness as a Nordic, Scandinavian, or Arctic regional phenomenon. A brand can borrow successful mythic notions of the context of another place if the extension of the place to its context is narratively acceptable and believable (Ricoeur 1980). The city of Oulu, which seems to be aspiring to Scandinavianness with its marketing communication, takes this approach. By attempting to create an associative link between the city of Oulu and Scandinavia, the marketers evoke positive regional imagery. Ultimately, the brand value of Scandinavianness would translate itself into more capital and innovation in the city.

Our analysis has implications for research on cultural strategy. Much like the case of Swedishness (Östberg 2011, p. 233), companies might "oscillate between a provincial position" in their local market and a Finnish position in the international market. In the case of Isku, we suggest that the key flag symbol offers a dual narrative. The product–country–imagery narrative speaks to the quality of the product and brand for international audiences who are "in the know" (Askegaard and Ger 1998). Protectionist narratives encourage local audiences linked to the origin of the brand to "buy local" to support national interests (Luedicke et al. 2010). Cultural strategy is said to guide managers to leverage ideological opportunities to repurpose cultural content and become a salient brand (Holt and Cameron 2010). Ideologies refer to a normative system of ideas, beliefs, and ideals of a group or culture (Crockett and Wallendorf 2004). Following the cultural strategy logic, we have particular advertisements that leverage normative ideologies calling for social and ecological responsibility. By presenting the brand as socially or ecologically responsible, the official story goes, marketers can attract consumers who are increasingly willing to consume for a better conscience. This of course feeds a larger mythology and ideology of Nordic supremacy and leadership in terms of reconciling capitalism and social responsibility. Likewise, the regionalist myth conveys an endearing brand image with a "personality," better equipped to "out-local" large global brands (Ger 1999).

Finally, pointing consumer attention to regions also propagates a protectionist, moralistic ideology of consuming the local for the common good of one's compatriots. However, a reference to regionality does not mean that a brand is a small local producer. A big international corporation, like Arla, may use the story of a small regional producer, which is wrapped up in the conglomerate, to advertise for local appeal (Östberg 2011).

To conclude, our analysis of Finnishness in advertisements is an attempt to cast light on how myth narrates the imaginaries of the Nordic socio-cultural region. Advertising is a marketing communication and branding event that is particularly appropriate for mythic portrayals of national and cultural identity (Holt 2004). The recognition that advertisements using myths of Finnishness do so through localist, protectionist, and regionalist narratives with moralistic and nostalgic undertones adds new layers to consumers' conception of self. The analysis of mythic narratives of Finnishness, seen as a point of passage between global consumer culture and national identity, can help us think beyond geopolitical frontiers as natural boundaries of market and consumer contexts—making these findings relevant for theoretical development relating to the role of regions for marketing and consumption-oriented social science.

References

Amdam, R. (2002). Sectoral Versus Territorial Regional Planning and Development in Norway. *European Planning Studies, 10*(1), 99–111.

Anderson, B. (1983). *Imaginary Communities: Reflections on the Origin and Spread of Nationalism*. London: Verso Books.

Arnould, E. J., Price, L., & Moisio, R. (2006). Making Contexts Matter: Selecting Research Contexts for Theoretical Insights. In R. Belk (Ed.), *Handbook of Qualitative Research Methods in Marketing* (pp. 106–125). Edward Elgar Publishing Limited.

Arnould, E. J., & Thompson, C. J. (2015). Introduction: Consumer Culture Theory: Ten Years Gone (and Beyond). In A. E. Thyroff, J. B. Murray, & R. W. Belk (Eds.), *Consumer Culture Theory (Research in Consumer Behavior)* (Vol. 17, pp. 1–21). Emerald Group Publishing Limited.

Arsel, Z., & Thompson, C. J. (2010). Demythologizing Consumption Practices: How Consumers Protect Their Field-Dependent Identity Investments from Devaluing Marketplace Myths. *Journal of Consumer Research, 37*(5), 791–806.
Askegaard, S. (1988). The National Flag and the Myth of the Nation. *The Flag Bulletin, 27*(1), 16–22.
Askegaard, S., & Ger, G. (1998). Product-Country Images: Towards a Contextualized Approach. In B. Englis & A. Olofsson (Eds.), *European Advances in Consumer Research* (Vol. III, pp. 50–58). Provo, UT: Association for Consumer Research.
Barthes, R. (1957). *Mythologies* (A. Lavers, Trans.). New York: Hill and Wang.
Barthes, R. (1977). Rhetoric of the Image. In S. Heath (Ed.), *Image, Music, Text* (pp. 32–51). New York: Hill and Wang.
Belk, R. W., & Costa, J. A. (1998). The Mountain Man Myth: A Contemporary Consuming Fantasy. *Journal of Consumer Research, 25*(3), 218–240.
Belk, R., Fischer, E., & Kozinets, R. V. (2012). *Qualitative Consumer and Marketing Research*. London: Sage.
Brown, S., McDonagh, P., & Shultz, C. J., II. (2013). Titanic: Consuming the Myths and Meanings of an Ambiguous Brand. *Journal of Consumer Research, 40*(4), 595–614.
Browning, C. S. (2007). Branding Nordicity: Models, Identity and the Decline of Exceptionalism. *Cooperation and Conflict, 42*(1), 27–51.
Cayla, J., & Arnould, E. J. (2008). A Cultural Approach to Branding in the Global Marketplace. *Journal of International Marketing, 16*(4), 86–112.
Cayla, J., & Eckhardt, G. M. (2008). Asian Brands and the Shaping of a Transnational Imagined Community. *Journal of Consumer Research, 35*(2), 216–230.
Chelekis, J. A., & Figueiredo, B. (2015). Regions and Archipelagos of Consumer Culture: A Reflexive Approach to Analytical Scales and Boundaries. *Marketing Theory, 15*(3), 321–345.
Crockett, D., & Wallendorf, M. (2004). The Role of Normative Political Ideology in Consumer Behavior. *Journal of Consumer Research, 31*(3), 511–528.
Doty, W. G. (2000). *Mythography: The Study of Myths and Rituals* (pp. 1–552). University of Alabama Press.
Finnish Periodical Publishers' Association (FPPA). (2015). Retrieved from www.aikakausmedia.fi.
Frog, M., Siikala, A. L., & Stepanova, E. (2012). *Mythic Discourses: Studies in Uralic Traditions* (Vol. 20, pp. 1–320). Helsinki: Finnish Literature Society.

Ger, G. (1999). Localizing in the Global Village: Local Firms Competing in Global Markets. *California Management Review, 41*(4), 64–83.

Gorn, G. J., Chattopadhyay, A., Yi, T., & Dahl, D. W. (1997). Effects of Color as an Executional Cue in Advertising: They're in the Shade. *Management Science, 43*(10), 1387–1400.

Hackley, C., & Hackley, R. A. (2016). The Iconicity of Celebrity and the Spiritual Impulse. *Consumption Markets and Culture, 19*(3), 269–274.

Hall, C. M. (2008). Servicescapes, Designscapes, Branding, and the Creation of Place-Identity: South of Litchfield, Christchurch. *Journal of Travel and Tourism Marketing, 25*(3–4), 233–250.

Holt, D. B. (2003). What Becomes an Icon Most? *Harvard Business Review, 81*(3), 43–49.

Holt, D. B. (2004). *How Brands Become Icons: The Principles of Cultural Branding*. Cambridge, MA: Harvard Business Press.

Holt, D. B. (2006). Jack Daniel's America: Iconic Brands as Ideological Parasites and Proselytizers. *Journal of Consumer Culture, 6*(3), 355–377.

Holt, D. B., & Cameron, D. (2010). *Cultural Strategy: Using Innovative Ideologies to Build Breakthrough Brands*. Oxford: Oxford University Press.

Holt, D. B., & Thompson, C. J. (2004). Man-of-Action Heroes: The Pursuit of Heroic Masculinity in Everyday Consumption. *Journal of Consumer Research, 31*(2), 425–440.

Humphreys, A., & Thompson, C. J. (2014). Branding Disaster: Reestablishing Trust Through the Ideological Containment of Systemic Risk Anxieties. *Journal of Consumer Research, 41*(4), 877–910.

Iwabuchi, K. (2002). *Recentering Globalization: Popular Culture and Japanese Transnationalism*. Durham, NC: Duke University Press.

Kjeldgaard, D., & Askegaard, S. (2006). The Glocalization of Youth Culture: The Global Youth Segment as Structures of Common Difference. *Journal of Consumer Research, 33*(2), 231–247.

Kjeldgaard, D., & Östberg, J. (2007). Coffee Grounds and the Global Cup: Glocal Consumer Culture in Scandinavia. *Consumption Markets and Culture, 10*(2), 175–187.

Korkiakangas, M. (2005). Perheen voimavaroja etsimässä: tapaustutkimus asiakaslähtöisistä työorientaatioista lastensuojelunpperhetyössä. *Nuorten ystävät.*

Kozinets, R. V. (2001). Utopian Enterprise: Articulating the Meanings of Star Trek's Culture of Consumption. *Journal of Consumer Research, 28*(1), 67–88.

Kristensen, D. B., Boye, H., & Askegaard, S. (2011). Leaving the Milky Way! The Formation of a Consumer Counter Mythology. *Journal of Consumer Culture, 11*(2), 195–214.

Levy, S. J. (1981). Interpreting Consumer Mythology: A Structural Approach to Consumer Behavior. *The Journal of Marketing, 45*(3), 49–61.

Luedicke, M. K., Thompson, C. J., & Giesler, M. (2010). Consumer Identity Work as Moral Protagonism: How Myth and Ideology Animate a Brand-Mediated Moral Conflict. *Journal of Consumer Research, 36*(6), 1016–1032.

Mainio, T. (2015). Valion ote maitomarkkinoista lipeää – Arla on mennyt ohi. In *Helsingin Sanomat*. Retrieved April 9, from http://www.hs.fi/talous/art-2000002849958.html.

Martin, D. M., Bullis, C., Tillotson, J. S., & Schouten, J. W. (2014). Only You Can Prevent Brand Burnout. In S. Brown & S. Ponsonby-McCabe (Eds.), *Brand Mascots: And Other Marketing Animals* (pp. 191–203). London: Routledge.

McAlexander, J. H., Dufault, B. L., Martin, D. M., & Schouten, J. W. (2014). The Marketization of Religion: Field, Capital, and Consumer Identity. *Journal of Consumer Research, 41*(3), 858–875.

McCracken, G. (1986). Culture and Consumption: A Theoretical Account of the Structure and Movement of the Cultural Meaning of Consumer Goods. *Journal of Consumer Research, 13*(1), 71–84.

Medby, I. A. (2014). Arctic State, Arctic Nation? Arctic National Identity Among the Post-Cold War Generation in Norway. *Polar Geography, 37*(3), 252–269.

Östberg, J. (2011). The Mythological Aspects of Country-of-Origin: The Case of the Swedishness of Swedish Fashion. *Journal of Global Fashion Marketing, 2*(4), 223–234.

Østergaard, U. (1997). The Geopolitics of Nordic identity: From Composite States to Nation-States. In Ø. Sørensen & B. Straath (Eds.), *The Cultural Construction of Norden* (pp. 25–71). Oslo: Scandinavian University Press.

Østergaard, U. (2006). The History of Europe Seen from the North. *European Review, 14*(2), 281–297.

Papadopoulos, N. (1993). What Product-Country Images Are and Are Not. In N. Papadopoulos & L. Heslop (Eds.), *Product-Country Images: Impact and Role in International Marketing* (pp. 3–38). New York: International Business Press.

Parker, B. J. (1998). Exploring Life Themes and Myths in Alcohol Advertisements Through a Meaning-Based Model of Advertising Experiences. *Journal of Advertising, 27*(1), 97–112.
Peñaloza, L. (2001). Consuming the American West: Animating Cultural Meaning and Memory at a Stock Show and Rodeo. *Journal of Consumer Research, 28*(3), 369–398.
Phillips, B. J., & McQuarrie, E. F. (2010). Narrative and Persuasion in Fashion Advertising. *Journal of Consumer Research, 37*(3), 368–392.
Pretes, M. (1995). Postmodern Tourism: The Santa Claus Industry. *Annals of Tourism Research, 22*(1), 1–15.
Ricoeur, P. (1980). Narrative Time. *Critical Inquiry, 7*(1), 169–190.
Schroeder, J. E. (2006). Critical Visual Analysis. In R. Belk (Ed.), *Handbook of Qualitative Research Methods in Marketing* (pp. 303–321). London: Edward Elgar.
Scott, L. M. (1994). The Bridge from Text to Mind: Adapting Reader-Response Theory to Consumer Research. *Journal of Consumer Research, 21*(3), 461–480.
Slotkin, R. (1992). *Gunfighter Nation: The Myth of the Frontier in Twentieth-Century America*. University of Oklahoma Press.
Stern, B. B. (1995). Consumer Myths: Frye's Taxonomy and the Structural Analysis of Consumption Text. *Journal of Consumer Research, 22*(2), 165–185.
Suorsa, K. (2007). Regionality, Innovation Policy and Peripheral Regions in Finland, Sweden and Norway. *Fennia – International Journal of Geography, 185*(1), 15–29.
Thompson, C. J. (2004). Marketplace Mythology and Discourses of Power. *Journal of Consumer Research, 31*(1), 162–180.
Thompson, C. J., & Haytko, D. L. (1997). Speaking of Fashion: Consumers' Uses of Fashion Discourses and the Appropriation of Countervailing Cultural Meanings. *Journal of Consumer Research, 24*(1), 15–42.
Thompson, C. J., & Tian, K. (2008). Reconstructing the South: How Commercial Myths Compete for Identity Value Through the Ideological Shaping of Popular Memories and Countermemories. *Journal of Consumer Research, 34*(5), 595–613.
Tillotson, J. S., & Martin, D. M. (2014). Understanding Myth in Consumer Culture Theory. In N. Campbell, J. Desmond, J. Fitchett, D. Kavanagh, P. McDonagh, & A. Prothero (Eds.), *Myth and the Market* (pp. 184–198). Ireland: University College Dublin.
Tillotson, J. S., & Martin, D. M. (2015). Myth-Mediated Branding. In A. E. Thyroff, J. B. Murray, & R. W. Belk (Eds.), *Consumer Culture Theory (Research*

in Consumer Behavior) (Vol. 17, pp. 189–221). Emerald Group Publishing Limited.

Trägårdh, L. (2018). Scaling up Solidarity from the National to the Global. In N. Witoszek & A. Midttun (Eds.), *Sustainable Modernity* (pp. 79–101). London: Routledge.

Van Dijk, T. A. (1995). Discourse Semantics and Ideology. *Discourse and Society, 6*(2), 243–289.

Widdershoven, G. A. (1993). The Story of Life: Hermeneutic Perspectives on the Relationship Between Narrative and Life History. *The Narrative Study of Lives, 1*, 1–20.

Zhao, X., & Belk, R. W. (2008). Politicizing Consumer Culture: Advertising's Appropriation of Political Ideology in China's Social Transition. *Journal of Consumer Research, 35*(2), 231–244.

12

Perspectives on Hygge: The Kolonihave Discourse

Jeppe Linnet and Jonathan Bean

In preparation for this book, two scholars who have both spent considerable time and energy delving into the concept of hygge came together to have a conversation about this supposedly unique Danish concept that has recently caught the global public's imagination. Lounging in one chair was Jeppe Linnet, a Danish anthropologist with a PhD in the area of consumer culture theory, specifically focusing on hygge. In the other chair was Jonathan Bean, an American who also focused his doctoral work on hygge and whose recent work connects taste, design and consumption.

Jeppe: So, here we are … talking about hygge in a place that should somehow suit the topic. I mean … I know that in this international attention to Danish manifestations of hygge, the *kolonihave* [allotment

---

J. Linnet (✉)
Linnet Research, Copenhagen, Denmark
e-mail: jeppe@linnetresearch.dk

J. Bean
University of Arizona, Tucson, AZ, USA
e-mail: j.bean@arizona.edu

S. Askegaard, J. Östberg (eds.), *Nordic Consumer Culture*,
https://doi.org/10.1007/978-3-030-04933-1_12

garden] has also been singled out as sort of a … you know, like an icon of Danish hygge.

Jonathan: Yeah, when I was doing my research, everyone said, "Oh, you have to go see a kolonihave because that's really what hygge is."

Jeppe: Yeah, so and here we are at my kolonihave and I am Jeppe Linnet and you are Jonathan Bean. And so, can you feel the hygge?

Jonathan: That's a very personal question for this early in the conversation, isn't it?

Jeppe: Ha! I'm sorry.

Jonathan: Already? You are already asking me that question? Okay. The kolonihave is like a super concentrated semiotic resource of hygge, all of this. The resources associated with hygge are all plainly visible here. We are sitting outside in a very pleasant afternoon in the sun, sitting in the shade, looking over a garden with plants that are blowing around in a very gentle breeze and there is a hammock that we are not sitting in but we … but it is inviting, and there is a chaise lounge over in the corner of the yard also beckoning us out, and behind where we are sitting is this kolonihave, which is a small … how can I describe this. It's a … probably about 20 … it's the size of an American double garage. Actually a little bit smaller, not as deep as a double garage but just as wide, and inside there is a very small room, a bedroom that holds probably a double-size bed and then a living room with the couch and a table and a small kitchen and in terms of standards for domestic space it is not … it's small and cozy but by Danish standards this is not tiny. Is it, Jeppe? It's small.

Jeppe: It's small, yeah. I guess it's not tiny. Yeah, I guess you are right about that. Anyway, it is sort of … I mean, you expect a kolonihave to be small, tiny, so it's kind of … you know, an oxymoron. Is it? To say a 'small' kolonihave because of course it's small. I mean, it's a problem if it gets big. A lot of people here are worried about houses getting too big or tall.

Jonathan: Right, and so that's been sort of visually managed from a design perspective. You have a little annex that's a separate building and another separate storage shed that we can see. So rather than one large building, there is sort of three buildings, each looking like a funny smaller version of the other in a sort of fairy-tale way (Fig. 12.1).

Jeppe: Like Russian dolls.

Fig. 12.1 The kolonihave. Photo: Jeppe Linnet

Jonathan: Yeah, they are all painted the same color. A sort of dark sky blue, which helps, and I can't miss it, but there is this very Danish sort of spatial configuration over it. Something that runs through everything that is visible. Like from the window in the house where you can see the table with the pendant light overhead. Did it just come like that, or did you set it up?

Jeppe: No, I put that up. Yeah, actually for the purpose of being able to work, and you know, sit with papers. Otherwise it is not … I mean, in terms of lighting in there, you would rather have ten candles burning in the room in various places. That's what we usually do. It's supposed to really make you wind down, and that's obviously what all this dispersed lighting does, right? And also, I guess, the fact that we are sort of sheltered from the surrounding world. But we are not completely shielded off, right? It is, I think, one of the keys to hygge; to have the right balance between being invisible yet still slightly visible. Or, being able to see what's around you and yet not being visible. We also see that in cafés, for example. When people refer to a place as hyggelig, they rarely … it's rarely a place with panoramic windows where people who pass by can see them very clearly. On the other hand, it is also not a place that is completely blinded, cause that would be a bit suspicious. Why would someone want to do that? So it seems that in public space, in third places, hygge relies on a balance between how much you are being seen and how much you see.

Jonathan: So we are not … it's not a fishbowl. Fishbowls are not hyggelig.

Jeppe: No, no, that's true.

Jonathan: In the 1960s one of the articles that was written for the Danish daily newspaper *Politiken* in a series they published about hygge talked about how *uhyggeligt*—so not just not-hygge, but borderline creepy—it was to be in one of these new all-glass buildings. It was floor-to-ceiling glass exposure, and that makes me think of a couple of things. I mean, looking around here at your kolonihave, it is hard not to think of Grant McCracken's article on homeyness because we are surrounded by all of these multiple layers of enclosure. There is a nice green hedge surrounding the entire property, so there is a very clearly delineated boundary, but then the hedge is clipped and I don't know whether this is on purpose or by design or what? But it is clipped so you can see just the ridge of the house next door, right, so you are aware that you are not completely alone but you are also reminded that that person … those people can't see you. Ha ha.

Jeppe: Yes.

Jonathan: I think the other thing that it reminds me of is something we talk about in architecture a lot and it is often ascribed to Frank Lloyd Wright. Although I don't think that he really deserves the ownership of the term, but it is this idea of prospect and refuge. You are able to look out and kind of have your back to a solid surface.

Jeppe: Yes.

Jonathan: Which then gets us into the dangerous realm of environmental psychology. Maybe not dangerous but…

Jeppe: Out of fashion for many years at least, right?

Jonathan: Yeah, yeah.

Jeppe: But I think that would actually be one angle on hygge that should be explored. I mean, the feeling of hygge—if that it is not, you know, an instinctual sign that you are in a safe space sort of, socially as well as materially, and simply connected to the fundamental need to recharge your batteries and being able to sleep or whatever … not that this is necessarily the central question at all, but if you want to take the conversation a step outside all the culturalist and interpretative approaches and just ask 'why would we have this … be able to have this sense at all?'. I mean, I don't think that question counters all the clearly important interesting cultural questions that can be asked, but still I think, you know, the emotional reward of pleasurable hygge is probably connected to some intuition that, in the perspective of flight and refuge, which, for example, Hildebrand applies to architecture, a given spot is a good and safe place in which to spend some time.

Jonathan: I was just at the public policy in marketing conference and there was somebody there giving a presentation about biophilic design, so that is environments where things are patterned after nature, and designers use natural colors and fractal patterns that represent supposedly how the leaves on trees look. They are doing experimental research to show that people prefer these kinds of environments and they feel more at ease, and they are more productive in them. They were talking about different kinds of states of sensory arousal where you can be in a state of having your senses engaged and feeling curious and aware while also feeling secure—and that's actually a fairly unusual place to be in. And it struck me at that moment that this is part of what is going on—with the allure of hygge, if not the actual experience of it. It's a place where you are both engaged and relaxed. In contemporary life that's a place that's hard to get to.

Jeppe: It's interesting because in all of the many sessions of meditation that I have been in, this is very often what is described as the goal of meditating. To enter that state of, you know, being at once "*vågen og venlig*" [awake and kind] or something like that. It sounds a bit cheesy but it's kinda, you know, being alert to the experience of living but definitely still of course grounded and friendly and not intense in, like, in any sort of dominating way. But also not sedated or like, you know, you're not just tripping on what is happening inside you without any contact, I mean…

Jonathan: Did you say "vågen og venlig"?

Jeppe: "Vågen og venlig" I think I might have heard that. That sounds a bit cheesy I think.

Jonathan: What does it even mean? I don't know.

Jeppe: Awake and kind.

Jonathan: Oh, "vågen"! Like "woke". Huh.

Jeppe: "Vågen", yeah. The phrase sounds like something they might have taken from kindergarten, or I don't know. But anyhow, yeah, I mean I thought about the parallels between mindfulness and hygge. In terms of how they are both very popular, and I think people seek, in hygge, some of the same qualities that they seek in meditation … but on a social scene, in a social domain, whereas meditation happens on the individual level. Still, you could say that whether you meditate or whether you're having hygge with other people, in both cases you are oriented to the "here and now". And both of them are sort of satisfying people's longing for the ability to be present and *be*, not just become all the time. And both of them are described as antidotes to a competitive society that propels everyone forward all the time and creates stress. Also there is this new hygge movie coming out [*Finding Hygge*] that, if it hasn't premiered yet, then it will very soon, made by somebody called Rocky Walls. I saw an early screening of it recently and he said that it was going to be featured at a Buddhist film festival, I think. Or maybe it was a festival of spiritual movies in general. I'm not sure. But like a festival of movies with a spiritual angle in Asia, I think South Korea, where Buddhism has played a large role, even if society is today secular. So it's interesting how, in all the different ways that the world has picked up on hygge, it is apparently because it is a state of mind, a state of experience that is slow, and not associated with consuming a lot of resources, but very much with this aspect of being in the here and now. Apparently in the case of that Asian film festival, hygge resonates with a sort of spiritual orientation.

Jonathan: That's interesting to me and got me thinking. I'm looking over your shoulder—there is a pretty ordinary-looking dresser I guess or sideboard. What would you call that? I would describe it as just sort of Danish design. It looks like it's probably made of teak and it is elevated above the floor about 8–10 inches on legs that are slightly tapered and—in comparison to most of the modern Danish furniture that people in the US are familiar with—it is quite small. That is one of the distinguishing things between Danish modern furniture in Denmark and Danish modern furniture in the US. It all got scaled up and that was an intentional thing that happened, but the last time I was here a couple of years ago there was an exhibit at the Kunstindustri Museum on the origins of Danish modern design and the connections to Asia and Japan in particular. So now you are talking about this Buddhist quality and the exhibit was fascinating because of us talking about how this idealized and very orientalist idea of what the east was like and what Japan was like got translated into Danish modern, into what we now see and think of and valorize as Danish modern furniture. And that's about the same time that hygge becomes a valued part of Danish culture. This is the 1940s, 1950s, 1960s but after the Second World War. So it is interesting to start thinking about hygge as a concept that has points of origin coming from somewhere else. Rather than just being quintessentially Danish, which is how it is so often stereotyped.

Jeppe: Yeah, when you think about the early B&O designs, for example, you could almost think about Japanese sliding panels. I mean it's like … I can see the connection and the…

Jonathan: I remember so clearly my uncle and my grandparents both had a sort of slab Bang & Olufsen CD-changer that was like a whole-house music system, where you, like, I think, just waved your hand over it and this little sliding panel opened. It was kind of magical and you put the CD in there and it closed again. But yeah, there is definitely something … something there.

Jeppe: Yeah, there is.

Jonathan: So one of the other things we were talking about earlier, that would be interesting to discuss where we think research on hygge might go. What are your thoughts on that?

Jeppe: Okay, well, I think there are many angles … I mean you could start a whole program with several PhDs on various aspects of hygge and tie it all together in a beautiful way if you had the resource, I think, which would have been a clever thing to do a few years ago.

Jonathan: Before the hygge explosion!

Jeppe: Yes yes. I think, well, to start with one thing. Now, after the hygge explosion it would be interesting to take like a glocal perspective and see how hygge has been imagined in different ways all over the world. Because I think that people, you know, see many of their … they invest many of their own tensions, or dream of releasing many of the tensions of their society—of their particular society—in hygge. But then again there are also clearly similarities across those different appropriations of hygge. Which of course … there should be, because there is an actual phenomenon here, and so, of course, there should be some similarities in the way that it is understood.

Jonathan: A starting place would be to simply just take the inventory of all the hygge books and then finding, tracking down all of the translations. I was just in Vietnam and I was surprised to see a book about hygge in Vietnamese!

Jeppe: Well, that's true. You could do that, of course. You could also maybe go to the … you know, all the lifestyle articles and essays. I mean even those where the author is less knowledgeable about the actual phenomenon, but just writing to a domestic audience in whatever journal, yet still applying the concept of hygge and translating it. I guess … you know, the whole tradition of looking at cultural intermediaries, that would be an obvious concept to use in this regard, and global/local as well. And I mean: why has the UK in particular become so extremely obsessed with hygge? Well, I've had this conversation several times with journalists and I usually offer the idea of the hygge trend as a retreat from an insecure world, from anxieties around terrorism and whatnot. But also with Brexit. I think with Brexit, the Brits needed … well, they were sort of thrown back upon themselves as a nation suddenly, and some quite involuntarily, so since this was now happening, they were very attracted to the idea that you can draw on a, you know, a sort of national repository of cultural resources and achieve good things. I think hygge is maybe extra appealing to them because of that. It could be one underlying reason.

Jonathan: When those interviews get printed, do they contain that insight or that idea?

Jeppe: They do. Yes, I mean the journalists readily accept that interpretation, and yes … that's a whole story in itself, the experience of being interviewed again and again about this. But yes.

Jonathan: I ask because I've been interviewed a couple of times, not about the hygge phenomenon but just about hygge, and I have had to go out of my way to incorporate in those interviews what I see as the dark side of hygge. There are many problematic aspects and reasons as to why this concept is suddenly so appealing and that part never gets printed. The part where I say, "light some candles and call up some good friends and have a nice dinner" gets published. So that is also really interesting that there is this willingness to be critical I haven't seen, at least in the US. Why aren't we taking a step back and asking about "wait a minute, why is everyone writing about this?"

Jeppe: Well, I guess I have been fortunate sometimes to be contacted by some quite nuanced journalists or essayists, from *The Guardian* or *The New European*, who were able to devote a bit of time to what they were doing. So, some of these writers are not content with just writing a list of, you know, tips for how to hygge. I think when we talk about the materiality—I mean, clearly the material side of hygge has received a lot of attention, like the candles, for example, because it goes so well with a lifestyle approach. But I think there are some interesting issues around that, which have been overlooked. For example, it has been very much about domestic space, but not so much about public space. Not so much about, for example, how do the parts of a city, streets, squares, cafés and third spaces—how do they afford the urban experience of hygge. I think it has all become very much focused on the home and also feminized, turned into this sort of maternal phenomenon almost. I think a convention is emerging here, that should be challenged. I wrote this conference paper on something I called 'social sedimentation' and I kinda liked that concept and should probably publish it, but maybe I'm publishing it now. Which was simply about, you know, all these traces that people leave behind and other people perceive, even unconsciously. Like, a person who is now dead used to come and sit on that leather couch in this old restaurant or café. They left their marks, and today these add to the ambience of the place. Of course you know this very well from architecture, that it can't be designed and built a new. It has to … it takes decades to create it, that feeling that 'other people have been here'. That there has been life here for a long time. I think that in urban areas, we associate these social sediments with hygge. People leave marks behind and add their own layer to their surroundings; they contribute to that build-up of layers which is something that McCracken refers to as homeyness—the principle of encompassment. So this concept I am toying with, of social sedimentation, has less to do with feeling enclosed and more with recognizing how marks and layers of life are left behind, and how that contributes to a sense of urban atmosphere, like layers of torn posters covering a wall, for example…

Jonathan: I always think of it as a worn threshold or like, you know, something that has been worn down, like stone steps in a museum. It is this very immediate physical reminder that there have been many, many people there before you.

Jeppe: Yeah, I heard a talk by a Swedish archeologist Cornelius Holtorf. He used the concept of pastness. He said that, for example, the Disney cooperation is super good in places like Disneyworld at creating the experience of pastness. He used an example where they would create lines around … they would build a building, for example, somewhere that was supposed to look like, let's say like a Western-movie environment, and then they would create signs that look like marks of buildings that used to be there, but are now gone. You see these signs and at some level of consciousness you pick up the idea that there was another building here before the building that you are actually looking at. And that building is obviously brand new, while in itself made to look old, but in its surroundings you perceive signs that tell you that other buildings used to be. Even if obviously they never were. So it's not past but pastness, and I kinda like to think along with that idea and with this concept of social sedimentation; all these signs that there have been people here before us. They reassure us somehow, at least if it is in the right way, because there are many signs of other people's existence that we don't like. I mean, there are many remains or leftovers from other people that we find gross or, you know, that we don't want to deal with.

Jonathan: Yeah! Like what's the boundary between dirt and hygge?

Jeppe: Exactly, which is an interesting question because what will be hyggeligt for some people will be dirty or messy for other people, will be too intimate, too close, too chaotic…

Jonathan: There is this idea in cultural geography that the built environment is a sedimentation of culture, which I have always really liked. I think that goes back to Allan Pred. Something that could be investigated or mined a bit more is the relationship between hygge and the kinds of aesthetic styles that have been in fashion for the last ten years or so. We call it the hipster aesthetic in the article about Kinfolk. You know, it is reclaimed wood and handcrafted-looking things. This cultural yearning that hygge is filling, to what degree is that answered or accommodated in these reclaimed wood tabletops and industrial-style pendant lights and all of this kind of stuff?

Jeppe: Yes, yeah, I totally … I agree. To look at, for example, wood and to interpret it from an environmental psychology perspective. How does wood afford hygge? Why is it, that it is so good at that? What are the signs that we pick up on and why? I think that's an interesting perspective and reminds me also of a presentation I saw by Mikkel Bille once. He was talking about sterile environments and how they are not hyggelig. I mean, a sterile environment does not afford hygge, and it is interesting to think about the different antonyms to hygge, because it is clearly not 'uhygge' that captures the non-hygge. It is not the unheimlich, because that can be very hyggelig, at least if you are watching it on a screen, right? But 'sterile' is one significant antonym to hygge and 'stressful' is another, right?

Jonathan: I would suggest 'corporate'.

Jeppe: Corporate? Yes, corporate is definitely, but I guess … not for everyone, though, right? I mean, imagine that … hygge is essentially being familiar with the environment that you are in. And I suppose if the business world really *is* your world, where you know all the codes, then corporate could actually be home for you.

Jonathan: But I think in a way, this is at least how it has been constructed in the US. And it is funny that we are talking about wood now, because we are sitting around a wood table outside in wood chairs that are worn. That … I hope you don't mind me saying this, but they could use a coat of oil, right?

Jeppe: They could.

Jonathan: And I'm looking at the kolonihave and it's weathered wood that you can see and there is an area underneath the window where the water drips down probably in the winter and the paint is little bit worn off and it is going a little bit white and grey and it is interesting to look at because it is … it shows age and wear and gives you this sort of reminder of this sedimentation process that we are talking about. But I do wonder if part of the appeal you get in the US around hygge is that our built environment is nearly all made of low-maintenance, durable products. The result is that the surfaces of most of the buildings that Americans spend time in are all plastic. So interiors are covered with latex paint, flooring is laminated or vinyl, which is plastic even if it is putatively wood—it is wood covered with a thin layer of plastic. The exteriors of our buildings are often vinyl siding or what's called synthetic stucco, which is simply plastic. Windows are made out of vinyl too, so that they don't age and need maintenance. Those materials are not meant to show age, and when they do show age, they don't do so in an elegant way. They just sort of look worn out and thrashed, right? So I do wonder, again like, how much of this is wanting something that is missing and has been sort of systematically removed from the built environment.

Jeppe: So you mean, the yearning for hygge would be a yearning for the return of some of that…

Jonathan: Just that you are spending so much time in an environment where any kind of reminder of time passing is being either systematically erased or suppressed, right? So here comes along this concept that's all about, you know, reminding you of the cyclical nature of time and ritual and everything else, and you don't see that in your built environment, partially due to the materials that it is made out of, and maybe also because of some of the demographic changes. People are moving more often, you know, possessions are more liquid, all of these kinds of things that we know.

Jeppe: Yeah yeah, and also I mean in the US, before it came to Denmark, there grew this focus on hygiene, on, for example, always cleaning your hands with a disinfectant, with these little dispensers emerging everywhere. Which also relates to rules about avoiding bodily contact, immediately uttering excuses when brushing into other people on the street. I think compared to Danes, Americans would be more careful not to bump into each other. So there is something here about contact, and I think there are much tighter cultural rules in the US about who can touch whom, that apply to contact between grown-ups and children, between genders etc. A policing of the space between people.

Jonathan: The place that I see that so clearly is in the design of train seats. So in the US, you always have very clearly delineated seats with an individual seat for each person. 18 inches wide or thereabouts. Two or three across. The trains, for example, the S-Tog in Copenhagen, just has one continuous bench and there is, you know, you could put two people on it, or you could put six. It doesn't indicate how many people are supposed to sit there, so there are much different spatial codes. And in an older article about hygge, the one written by the Danish-American anthropologist Judith Friedman Hansen, she talked about how chairs around a table wouldn't have arms, so they'd fit better in a small space. But that also puts you closer in physical proximity.

Jeppe: Yeah, I think there is also something here, an aspect that has to do with space and its design, but not necessarily with smallness. I think Pennartz, you know, the Dutch writer. Is he a social scientist? I'm not sure.

Jonathan: Yes, I think so.

Jeppe: He is. Okay. In one of his articles, he mentioned how spaces allow … spaces that can be used in more than one way, they give us a sense of pleasure. He used the Dutch term *gezelligheid*, which is more or less similar to hygge in its meaning, for this sort of unreflected feeling we have of pleasure that, you know, you get from a bench that is just straight like this. You can sit on it in one way, you can sit in another way, you can sit a group of people turned to each other. Whereas you're much more told how to sit, and what to do, when the seats are designed in the way that you describe. And I think it's conducive to this sense of hygge pleasure when a space does not tell us very clearly how to behave or how to sit, how to go about it, and probably that is also one reason why we often end up in the kitchen at a party. Because it is this functional environment that does not really dictate clearly what should go on in there. Makes a lot of people relax, right? To smoke in the kitchen or something like that, you know, this is where people can be a bit more like, *woooh*, right? So I think there is something about the functional versus the symbolic, and the flexible versus the strict and rule bound, when it comes to which environments that people really like. For example, in Copenhagen at Vesterbro, where I live, on Sønder Boulevard, there has been some very successful ways of creating public squares, with just really simple concrete structures that are tall enough for people to sit on the ground and use them as a backrest, but you can also sit on it and you can also skateboard on it and it is not like, you know, it really is very very simple but sort of well-made and shows a good conception of the space in between one object and another. A down-to-earth quality, where the space does not communicate too much what it wants. This seems to be something that we humans like.

Jonathan: Yes! Flexibility and indeterminacy of use—that is so important as a general design principle! In part because it goes against so much of what designers try to do, which is to sort of match environments to people's behavior rather than provide the environments that afford flexible patterns of behavior. And that reminds me of something that I think you told me. I think you said this the very first time we met—a long time ago. I hope that I remember it correctly 'cause it always kinda cracks me up! You said that to other people in Scandinavia, Denmark was sort of the Jamaica of Scandinavia, where things were free and loose, and I got a big laugh out of that at the time because I was still at that point learning Danish and adjusting to life in this place that seemed so rigid. That was the summer that I came over here to study *Bo Bedre*, and there are aspects of Danish life that seem from an American perspective extremely rigid. People will … I remember that same summer I had bumped into someone I knew, and we were walking down the main walking street in Copenhagen, and a truck drove into the walking street to deliver something. This was during the time on the walking street that no cars or trucks were allowed, and a woman attached herself to the side of the truck and very loudly told the truck driver, in Danish that even I could understand, that this was not allowed and that, you know, he was really breaking the rules and he needed to stop right then and turn around and go the other direction. And I just thought, you know, even if I saw somebody violating rules in the US, I would never inform them so loudly and so clearly that this was not something that you should do. So that really sort of struck me as odd.

But when you are talking now about this flexibility of use, that is something that I see as quintessentially Danish. I'm thinking here of Jan Gehl's work, this tradition of letting places and spaces and people … letting the people that use those spaces determine them for themselves. Either through building flexibility into the design solution and making it simple, like the blocks you mentioned, or through, you know, truly participatory design, where you go and talk to everybody that use this space and then design it around them. That does strike me as an important cultural nuance, which may underpin some of the nice things about hygge. I'll put it that way.

Jeppe: Yes, yeah…

Jonathan: So what else is on your mind about hygge?

Jeppe: Well, there are still a few themes, somewhat interrelated, of course. I was just thinking about how, when people look at behavior in other societies, they *see* what culture is. Culture becomes noticeable, as a set of aspects that appear rigid to an outsider. For example, to Danes, certain kinds of behavior or certain designs in public space may seem alien, and these are often aspects that we feel detract from hygge, which may even lead us to the idea that these people don't "get it", get hygge. Now since Danes have a patent on hygge, allegedly, no one will be able to conclude, conversely, that Danes do not understand hygge. Because by definition they do, having successfully claimed the concept in a series of popular lifestyle books. But if hygge was a universal concept, something that we could all challenge each other about, then maybe non-Danes could also say "look at how rigid they are, the Danes. Look at this and that". That might challenge the idea of Danes as loose and informal, and counteract the, how to put it, the underlying national chauvinism of global hygge semantics.

A different issue around hygge has to do with what we are doing to our cities, how trade and pedestrian life interfere with each other. We are taking all the elements of actual trade and craftsmanship and industry out of the city—they can't afford to stay, and then it all becomes just one big consumption space, which is not very good for hygge in the long run. Because many of the signs that afford a sense of hygge, they rely on a city space created for industries of trade and production, not leisure and consumption. Many urban areas that gentrify, you know, where people create environments with cafés and creative industries that people often find hyggelig, they really owe that to industry. They have an informal quality to them that people like, and I think this informality has grown from spaces of trade and small businesses, from the everyday presence of shopkeepers and craftsmen. The way that these local people behave, the music they listen to and the food they eat, the zones for taking a rest that they create. Middle-class people with disembodied jobs really enjoy that, tourists love seeing it. They love going to some little port in Italy and looking at the blacksmith going bang bang bang or something like that. But if it all just becomes one big Starbucks, then that hygge goes away, right? That was sort of a bit tangential but maybe we will be able to make sense of it later.

Okay, what else, concerning angles on hygge? I would like to see some attention to the interrelation of the social and the material aspects of hygge. I would like someone to really analyze in-depth how what we do socially when we have hygge, how those social interactions relate to the materiality that gives us hygge. And also be a bit experimental in the research approach. What happens if the material aspects that support hygge are completely absent but the social ones are still there, or the other way around? What does that do to the experience of hygge? And as an aspect of this thought, what kinds of hygge are there? If we could start to classify hygge into some subkinds, that might get us beyond some of the conceptions that we are stuck with. Here I am thinking about hygge among different social groups, because a lot of the examples we actually have of hygge, and that we talk about, it's very much middle-class family life. Which strives for an ideal that contains the social as well as the material aspects of hygge, both in the way that people behave with each other, if it is a 'good' family, and also in the way we construct a proper home. Both of these aspects are present, and so become difficult to take apart and analyze separately. But how about, for example, the drug addicts at the center close to where I live in Copenhagen? They have a room there, where they are allowed to shoot heroine. And these people on the street, who are very much under the influence of something, they seem sometimes to have a kind of desperate intimacy with each other. And I mean, I think we all know the feeling of being intoxicated, being drunk, and just having a fantastic time with someone exactly because we are drunk, right? So to tie this string of thought together, about social groups and kinds of hygge, there are more kinds of hygge than the warm, wholesome, domestic kind. There are kinds of hygge that we can only achieve by intoxicating ourselves.

Jonathan: Yeah, that's been sanitized out of the US hygge discourse, I think.

Jeppe: We should bring that back. There is also hygge among people who are down and out and really fragile. Even if the material constituents of hygge are absent, there is the social hygge that we can give each other … we can also simply call it, I don't know, social life or whatever. Maybe we don't need to call it hygge, but anyway we mislead ourselves if we think that there is no hygge in a life that is unhappy and desperate and poor and unhealthy. There can still definitely be an intense feeling of social well-being, in fact a feeling of mutual forgiveness, among people who share hygge, for all the stupid choices that we have made. A feeling of being, you know, recognized and seen and safe with other people, one that is intensely rewarding because society is so much turned against you and you probably get so many looks on the street. This signaling from mainstream society that you are not worthy, I think it intensifies the feeling of well-being you get, when you end up with people who are equal to you, and you can identify with each other's life. So, I think one danger of the popular association between happiness and hygge is that we are led to believe that there cannot be hygge in an unhappy life—which there clearly can be. We can say that hygge is a component in life that may support an individual's happiness. Okay, I'm fine with that. But it does not go the other way. Happiness is not necessary for hygge. And hygge is not necessary for happiness either, though it may support it. It is important to see this intellectual inconsistency in the current happiness discourse around hygge. While still we might appreciate that angle because it sells books, it achieves volume, and thus might have an effect on how people live. I mean if it makes people slow down. If it makes it more legitimate to slow down, spend time, quality time with other people, be more attentive, turn off the mobile, then that's something.

Jonathan: Yeah, I think about it in a slightly different way. I have been thinking about it since you mentioned your neighborhood in Copenhagen. I think that somewhere on Istedgade there was a project that Søren Møller Christensen's former company, Hausenberg, was involved with. It was in a park [*Enghaveparken*] that was getting excavated to build the new metro station. This was a while ago. There were some problems because in this park there were some drug pushers and there were some alcoholics who sat around and drank all day, and then there were some people who were gentrifying the neighborhood, walking their dogs. And when the excavation for the subway started, it displaced all of these people from their usual spots and mixed them all together and there was a bunch of conflicts that resulted. Then this company, Hausenberg, came in and talked to people, and redesigned the park or redesigned the space to accommodate all of these different users. And one of the first things that they did was that they decided: "we are not going to call them alcoholics. We are going to call them beer-drinkers". I've taught this in a number of classes, and I think that this is one … this is like a really humane move, right? Because you're stepping back and saying "this person, maybe technically speaking this person is an alcoholic but for the purposes of this exercise we are going to humanize them and just describe them by what they are doing, which is sitting around all day and drinking beer". The form of that project was a long continuous and curving park bench. Very simple. Not that different from the ones you see all over Copenhagen or New York or any big city for that matter. But it looped around, so that there was a zone where the beer-drinkers could kinda hold court all day and drink their beer and they realized that the beer-drinkers would actually moderate the activity of the drug pushers because the beer-drinkers didn't want any trouble, and they realized that the pushers, especially the ones selling hard drugs, they were the ones that brought trouble. So they would actually get the really bad folks out of the park and then the yuppies could walk their dogs all they wanted and everyone was happy. But you look at that project both from a formal perspective, of the ways that it used enclosure, and the way that it sort of respected the kinds of social activity that people were having, and I do think that there is something there, right? Like thinking about hygge as something that is a sort of universal attainable state, right? And maybe leveraging some of its better qualities.

Jeppe: Yeah, sure. Well, I mean, people who sit on a bench and drink beer for most of the day could be referred to in Danish as people who "*hygger sig lidt for meget*" [are having a bit too much hygge], right? But the figure of the drunk, the public space drunk is also a humorous … it is a fun figure. They are harmless and a bit clown like. A bit childish perhaps in popular culture, in movies. I mean, you also have that in the US too—Laurel and Hardy, aren't they a bit…? No?

Jonathan: Sure, but that's old!

Jeppe: Of course.

Jonathan: In the absence of any kind of effective mental health system in the US, the primary response to anyone drunk on the street is fear, not humor. One is not inclined to engage.

Jeppe: Well, that's true. Someone calls the cops and they show up massively. I've seen it happen. One might actually write a very critical article about, on the one hand the American endearment with hygge, on the other the American policing of public space, the fear of people who step outside the norms in public space, and whether that at all leaves any possibility for urban hygge to arise.

Jonathan: Well, that's one thing that I think is interesting in the way that hygge has been socially constructed in the US. It is becoming something. It is about luxury consumption. You know I spent all that time looking through issues of *Bo Bedre* and it was so clear that there was this really … these three phases of hygge where it goes from being this expression of collective identity, to one that is an association with the imagined glorious past of Denmark, to one that I think is still in effect now of self-indulgence and getting something nice for yourself because you deserve it. And I think that is very compatible with the selfie culture that has emerged in the US. Maybe there is room for this concept to incorporate more dimensions. There is some action research potential here for ways to bring the concept back and widen its meaning.

Jeppe: Yeah, and I mean, there are many ways that you can be critical to the hygge wave and especially in this, as you say, selfie version where you deserve this extra silk pillow or whatever it is that you buy in order to have more hygge wellness in your life, posting images of your retreat experience with your girlfriend. Maybe it would be possible to actually exploit the concept and evaluate policy through it, so say: "Well, it's great that you all like hygge, but look at how we are designing our city and look at the role of the police, and look at the way that every single square meter of an American city is owned by someone who can dictate the rules for being there". I mean, there are very few places that you are allowed to be without consuming something, right? Which is the case in Copenhagen too. And I think from a philosophical-existential point of view, this ties into the parallel between meditation and hygge that I mentioned before.

Being allowed to be you, without producing, without consuming. That puts a modern person in a particular state of mind because it is quite rare. We usually have to do either of these: produce or consume, or both, to have a legitimate presence. Even when we are at home, we're producing for our family and we're producing because, you know, we have a scorecard with our partner about producing dinners, producing entertainment, entertaining conversation, whatever. There are actually very, very, very few spaces where we don't either consume or produce something for someone.

This theme of consumption and production gets me a bit philosophical, going back to the social sedimentation part, and how we like to be in a café that has maybe existed for a hundred years and we can see the signs of people who were there. These guests of the past, they were actually producing the space, its future atmosphere, as they consumed it—which I think is interesting, how we produce hygge simply by moving around and leaving small traces behind. Sort of adding an extra layer to the world or taking away an extra layer from the world or whatever we are doing, right? When we are talking third spaces we are there as consumers, and people were there as consumers 50 years ago as well, and they were producing the charm of the place as they were consuming it. And so are we. I guess there might be a, I don't know, a CCT (consumer culture theory) essay in there somewhere about producing as we consume. I don't know but, yeah … The concept of hygge can take you into many loops. I don't have so many other questions left right now. How about you? Do you have some angles that often appear to you, that we should be more attentive to?

Jonathan: This has been the curse of having an interest in architecture and in hygge, which is that everyone wants to talk to me about tiny houses and we're in … we're sitting outside of one right now. Well, actually from an American perspective, this is a way big tiny house, but the tiny house juggernaut and the hygge juggernaut, they pretty much exploded in parallel. I guess maybe the tiny house thing in the US happened a couple of years in advance of hygge, and I think that there is something interesting about, not so much the actual lived experience of hygge or even the lived experience of what it is like to be in a tiny house, but the process of imagining these … of imagining hygge and imagining life in a tiny house. Maybe it's just the political situation in the US that's made me have this perspective on it in the last couple of years but there is something about both of these phenomena that is like sticking your head in the sand. Like, there is this quality of hygge and I always … my visual indicator for it is lamps, like the one hung over your table, right? And Judith Friedman Hansen, she talks about how the light that is issued by a pendant like the one that you have hanging here, which has a metal shade that's sort of a funnel shape, it all gets directed down onto the table and it bounces off the table and illuminates the faces of the people at the table and because of that … because of the way that our eyes perceive that, we don't really see much beyond the other people who are at the table, right? So there is this idea of hygge and also of a tiny house … it's almost like a spaceship, or like when you were a kid and you would pull the covers up over your head and imagine that you were someplace else—someplace disconnected from the world around you. I think that it would be really interesting to mine and unpack and explore the quality of the desire for that kind of experience in a tiny house. When people are talking about knowing exactly how many changes of clothes that they are going to need, or how many cups and glasses that they'll need, or this experience of hygge which is a sort of idealized parallel reality where everything is perfect, if just for a little bit. I think that that's serving some sort of function, something that makes this kind of escape from reality very attractive and I do wonder also about the degree to which it is facilitated by information technology. The ways that people can surround themselves with images on Pinterest and Instagram and can live in that imagined parallel world. Some hashtag study of #hygge on Instagram would be amazing.

Jeppe: The tiny house thing, I think, connects to many hygge-related aspects of enclosure and also about fractality. I mean the whole Russian doll pattern that seems to be in so many ways connected to hygge. Spaces within spaces within spaces etc.

But now that you mentioned the hashtag, I had an IFTTT (if this then that) protocol running for maybe half a year, recording every instance of the hashtag hygge on Twitter. And of course, it produced a very very long spreadsheet and then it stopped at some point, and I was, like, okay, there is a lot of data there. I mean, if you want to get into big data and combine it with qualitative analysis, I know it would be possible to collect this kind of data and then, because we have already done so much thinking and interpreting around hygge, train an algorithm to report back on the patterns of what is being tagged as hygge, and what has been tagged that is still out there. Just survey and describe the online space of hygge for us, right? What kinds of color, how many people, what kind of people? Are they doing this? Are they doing that? It should be possible for a robot to find that out and then see how these findings resonate with some of the conclusions and ideas that we have made over the years concerning hygge. That would actually be interesting…

Jonathan: A network analysis on Instagram … there are all kinds of things. So I can see from your watch that we are coming to the end of our time, but I really must ask you about your watch!

Jeppe: Yes, you must, because the brand of it is 'Hygge'…

Jonathan: It says hygge at three o'clock. Ha!

Jeppe: It does. We can put a picture of that in the article.

Jonathan: So what's the story?

Jeppe: It is interesting. I was actually going to mention it when you mentioned the possible Japanese roots of Danish modernism. This is a Japanese watch brand and it has been in existence before the hygge wave. Maybe for a decade or so. And even a year after the hygge wave had begun, there was still no retailer of hygge watches in Denmark. Apparently the people behind this brand did not really pick up on what was happening in the world—they should have employed one of those Chief Cultural Officers that McCracken writes about. Anyway, I bought it through some online watch portal and had it shipped to Denmark. Now retailers have appeared, so now they are finally exploiting what is happening. But anyway, it is a Japanese brand and I think they employ some Swedish designers. Many of them are very colorful and some are rectangular. They have all these funny shapes.

Jonathan: It looks very Danish modern.

Jeppe: Yes, that's probably because I chose it. You know, it's the Dane in me. It is the modernist Dane in me, because this is one of the simplest watches that they produce. Many are much more, you know, all over the place in terms of colors and shapes.

Jonathan: It is just a large … maybe we can have a photograph of it, but it's a large round watch with a mesh band and a sort of patterned silver. Maybe a stainless-steel color.

Jeppe: Yeah yeah, I like mesh bands and I like the simplicity of it, that it has a few colors but like one of the dials.

Jonathan: But you've also put the box on a prominent place of display, so that when I look into your house I see a little sign in the window that says 'hygge'.

Jeppe: And that's what the watch came in. Yeah, that's true, yeah. Well, how could I not? I mean, maybe it's a bit overstating the point of this place, I don't know. But hygge has been so much in my life that it makes sense somehow.

Jonathan: It is a little funny, I should tell you a story that I remember. Maybe that will be the end but I had a ... before I went back to graduate school, I was maybe a little bit smitten with Danish culture, and I wanted to keep learning Danish. I only had two years as an undergraduate, so I wasn't particularly good. So I started a Danish meetup group in Portland, Oregon, where I had moved. And the first two people that we met were a Danish-American woman named Mette and her boyfriend. With my partner we all got together and spoke a little bit of Danish. This group grew and it became quite large quite fast and we ended up having *julefrokost* (the traditional Danish Christmas lunch that goes for hours and turns into dinner) at our house. I was a little bit house-proud, so I stashed paper towels around the house. In case anyone spilled red wine on my prize possession at the time, which was this very beautiful Danish light blue wool rug. Mette's mother had volunteered to come and help us have the lunch, so that it would be really a Danish lunch because she was really Danish. And as we were setting up, my paper towel rolls that I had stashed very conveniently around the house just in case anything happened kept disappearing. I kept putting them back and then they would disappear again. And then I realized that Mette's mother was taking the paper towel rolls and putting them away in the kitchen because she thought that they were really detracting from the correct atmosphere that it should have. And so I am pleasantly amused and a little bit reassured when I look at your house now and see a pendant lamp, a candlestick and a *køkkenrulle* [paper towel roll].

Jeppe: And a køkkenrulle, yes.

Jonathan: And a little sign of hygge, so...

Jeppe: Yeah yeah, so after all, you weren't completely off...

Jonathan: I wasn't. This is authentic!

Jeppe: Yes, indeed. Wow! Okay, so maybe we are at the end of our hygge talk here.

Jonathan: I think so. Hygge out. Hygge out.

Jeppe: Exactly, hygge out.

Works Mentioned in the Conversation

Bean, J., Khorramian, A., & O'Donnell, K. (2018). Kinfolk Magazine: Anchoring a Taste Regime. *Consumption Markets & Culture, 21*(1), 82–92.

Hansen, J. F. (1970). *Danish Social Interaction: Cultural Assumptions and Patterns of Behavior*. Berkeley: University of California Berkeley.

Hansen, J. F. (1976). The Proxemics of Danish Daily Life. *Studies in the Anthropology of Visual Communication, 3*(1), 52.

Hansen, J. F. (1980). *We Are a Little Land: Cultural Assumptions in Danish Everyday Life*. New York: Arno Press.

Hildebrand, G. (1999). *Origins of Architectural Pleasure*. University of California Press.

Holtorf, C. (2010). The Presence of Pastness: Themed Environments and Beyond. In J. Schlehe, M. Uike-Bormann, C. Oesterle, & W. Hochbruck (Eds.), *Staging the Past. Themed Environments in Transcultural Perspectives* (pp. 23–40). Bielefeld: Transcript Verlag.

Linnet, J. T. (2011). Money Can't Buy Me Hygge: Danish Middle-Class Consumption, Egalitarianism and the Sanctity of Inner Space. *Social Analysis, 55*(2), 21–44.

Linnet, Jeppe Trolle (2015). Cozy Interiority. The Interplay of Materiality and Sociality in the Constitution of Cozy 3rd Place Atmosphere. *Ambiances: Perception – In situ – Ecologie Sociale*. Retrieved from http://ambiances.revues.org/543.

McCracken, G. (1989). Homeyness: A Cultural Account of One Constellation of Consumer Goods and Meanings. In E. C. Hirschman (Ed.), *Interpretive Consumer Research* (pp. 168–183). Provo, Utah: Association for Consumer Research.

McCracken, G. (2011). *Chief Culture Officer: How to Create a Living, Breathing Corporation*. New York: Basic Books.

Om hygge [ti kroniker]. (1965). [København]: Politiken (Note: The Danish-language Politiken series from November and December of 1964 "Om

Hygge" [On Hygge] was collected and published as a book the following year. It has not been translated to English, but should be).
Pennartz, P. J. J. (1999). Home: The Experience of Atmosphere. In I. Cieraad (Ed.), *At Home. An Anthropology of Domestic Space* (pp. 95–106). Syracuse, New York: Syracuse University Press.

Part III

Epilogue

13

Nordic Consumer Culture Theory Research: Conversation in a Wine Bar

Benjamin J. Hartmann and Eric J. Arnould

It is a dark October day in Gothenburg, Sweden. Thick raindrops pouring onto the streets and windows punctuate intermittent fine misty rain—familiar seasonal weather. A wide palette of grey blurs the sight, shimmering in dim silver, only to then dissolve into black shadow. The night falls quickly as if the day were tired of the light. It seems there are two kinds of people who linger outside. There are those who negotiate with the wind in their umbrellas and throw back their hoods to hasten inside; and those who defy the weather with stoic indifference, slowly and steadily going on, hands in their pockets, and their heads lightly tilted downwards. On the inside, however, behind those rainy windows, we can spot a third species. It is reflection season and consumer culture theory (CCT) researchers gravitate toward warm and protected nests, like a wine bar submerged in a basement on Viktoriagatan near the School of

B. J. Hartmann (✉)
University of Gothenburg, Gothenburg, Sweden
e-mail: benjamin.hartmann@handels.gu.se

E. J. Arnould
Aalto University School of Business, Helsinki, Finland
e-mail: eric.arnould@aalto.fi

S. Askegaard, J. Östberg (eds.), *Nordic Consumer Culture*,
https://doi.org/10.1007/978-3-030-04933-1_13

Business, Economics and Law, taking their time to interrogate, discuss, and reflect.

Eric and Benjamin have found a cozy corner with low ceiling in Björn's Bar and ordered a bottle of red wine and a sharing platter of "mycket gott", a selection of freshly sliced hams and sausages, rillette, and pickles. The following are excerpts of this conversation, mildly edited for clarity and sobriety.

Paradox and Serious Irony

Benjamin: So, now we are in this beautiful wine bar. You made this nice reading list of Per Østergaard's research that we both read; and we know that Per has been here in this wine bar, sitting over there?

Eric: Yes.

Benjamin: Let's discuss or interrogate that collection of artworks—to see if we can find some common themes reflected in these works that are reflected also in the general nature of something like Nordic CCT research.

Eric: Right. Let's mention some of the works.

Benjamin: Yes. Okay, let's do it like this and go through some quotes. I have a first topic for starters.

Eric: Okay, great.

Benjamin: I will read some quotes from these articles, which we can then discuss. For the first topic, there will be three quotes from three articles.

> *One main characteristic (of the "Danish or Scandinavian culture") is the dichotomy of natural versus artificial. In a Danish context it is positive to be natural.* (Amy-Chinn et al. 2006, p. 398)

(While Benjamin browses his pile of articles to find the next quote, the waitress arrives with the wine bottle, opens it for Eric to taste, who then nods and approves of the wine by saying in Swedish with a Danish accent "*Det är fint*".)

Second quote, *Relationships can, and are, simultaneously real and imagined.* (Østergaard and Fitchett 2012, p. 246)

Third quote, *Individuals in consumer culture know that they are confronted with constructed enchantments when they shop, buy, dream and consume. Our analysis has highlighted the need to think beyond fixed categories of enchantment and disenchantment.* (Østergaard et al. 2013, p. 343)

These quotes highlight some kind of dichotomy, paradox, a word that appears frequently in his work, dilemma, dialectics that Per has seemingly been interested in. What do you think, how and in what ways does that reflect a more Nordic research tradition?

Eric: Well, when I think of this work or one of the things that we may notice about this work is that Per has often worked with other Nordic scholars. The scholars that he has worked with are not necessarily people in the near orbit of consumer culture theory work, but people who have an interest in fundamental social theory. I think of Christian Jantzen. I think of Frank Lindberg, and I think of Matthias Bode. All from the Nordic region. Although from different backgrounds, all interested in fundamental questions about ontology and epistemology being, as one of these articles says, being and meaning, or being and doing.

I am struck by a … link to a certain current of existentialism in Nordic scholarship. I don't want to necessarily evoke a dark outlook or something like that. I do think that you see indeed in this work a … Nordic questioning of being that is not present so much at all in the North American school of work, no matter how scholarly, which tends toward, as he has himself criticized … the more pragmatic orientation.

It seems always—again, I hesitate to use the word—dark. It's different than the French style of interrogation, I would say. Perhaps, we can see a certain constitution, the way this work is constituted by the things that it's different from.

Benjamin: I would agree, this reflexivity not only of the researcher but like it's highlighted in the reflexivity of society, of consumers, and this culture. I think that's a particularly Nordic thing. Here we have this—what one could call serious irony.

Eric: Yes, serious irony!

Benjamin: As a metaphor or analogy, if you look at the Wallander stories, there's always this nice and shiny, peace and quiet community. Then there's this serious drama going on at the same time. That dichotomy can be natural, and can be disturbing. That, I think, is something that characterizes Nordic consumer research as well. Here highlighted, for example, in Per Østergaard's underwear study: underwear is hidden but it's not meaningless.

Eric: Also, in fact, it is quite *eventful*.... I like what you've just said about those stories that you mentioned. Because it immediately made me think of Per's affection for the Danish filmmaker Lars von Trier and the whole school of film-making that was around; a very natural approach to film-making that was also ... often quite horrifying and violent.

The Manifesto, the work they've devoted in *The Manifesto*. There's natural lighting, real time. I make quotations signs, "Real time story telling." Not a lot of jump-cutting and things like that. Again it's a paradoxical level of superficial normality, but underneath something else is going on. I think it's characteristic of a certain type of—at least if you take Per's work—an example of Nordic scholarship. Particularly when you keep in mind his collaborators in some of these inspirations from other kind of endeavors like film-making, which was one of his marks [*sic*]. We can see that paradox of—

(The waiter brings the meat platter)

Benjamin: That reminded me of that quote or citation where it says—it's the first sentence in the introduction of the article "Relationship Marketing and the Order of Simulation"—

"Our approach here is to continue the well-established tradition of synthesizing marketing theory with social theory" (Østergaard and Fitchett 2012, p. 232). That is not particularly Nordic, to synthesize marketing and social theory. That's not Nordic.

Eric: Not particularly Nordic.

Benjamin: What can be Nordic, however, about that is, I think, the starting point of the paradox. There can be a theoretical paradox, but it can also be a methodological paradox. Let's say empirical paradox. By studying something intensely close like women's underwear and not letting go. Just holding on to that phenomenon, and scrutinizing it, deeply scrutinizing it. This supposedly ordinary, even the simple object becomes special just by studying it, right? Also by highlighting it. Because of that, you are able to show the specialty of the ordinary object. Similarly canoe trips, mountain climbing—these are extraordinary consumption experience I would say, but they're not treated as extraordinary.

It's like contrasting the special with the unspecial gift. He's using a categorical span, and thinking around the concept or the phenomenon under study in a wider form: in what kind of web it is embedded.

Eric: I want to go back to the thing about the original, the initial quote about the study of the underwear itself, because one of the points he makes in that article, one of the points that comes out in the study of these Danish women, is the way "I will definitely not say it's spectacular. I will say it's special. I'll just say the special." The way the special takes place through something mundane like underwear, but also takes place in a modest way because it's hidden.

If I think about at least my experience of Danish festivity, this usually takes place actually in an environment that's somewhat … that there's a way in which this is transformative and the special quality of the underwear. In particular, the underwear that's worn to produce special occasion or a special feeling was hidden. Takes place out of public view but in a private place. To me that is also very Nordic, in a way.

Benjamin: I think you're touching upon a very important issue here. That is the discussion of the intersection of the public and private domains. This idea that in order to construct an inside, you need the inside and an outside. You need the public and the private. We have state intervention, welfare in the welfare state. There's a strong public actor and that by itself creates the private. This pervasive dominance of the public creates a certain type of privacy or private domain.

Eric: Say a little more about that. How does that create a certain kind of privacy or a private domain?

Benjamin: If you look at consumption, for example, in Sweden, here, the state intervenes and says, "You're not allowed to consume alcohol as you like. You can consume it but we have to restrict your access to it, and we tax it extra hard." That's quite a strong intervention. In Denmark, you see a luxury-tax system as we can also see in Norway, where the state says "You want to enjoy the luxury of a car? We tax it extra hard." Of course, in Norway, there is in addition to the luxury tax a state monopoly on alcohol like in Sweden and Finland, but as far as I know, Denmark has only the severe luxury tax but no state monopoly on alcohol. So there are shades of intervention but there are interventions. The private domain is not neoliberalistic, free of any constraints, but it's severely governed by a mothering or nanny state if you like, to some degrees. That creates some tensions for the consumers who still believe in and are adhering to that consumer culture that we have.

On the surface, Nordic consumer culture is very much like most consumer cultures. It programs us to make supposedly individual choices and that we should be happy, perform hedonic consumption, which should be about experiential aspects. At the same time, we acknowledge that it's a little bit stricter and more governed than in, let's say, the Northern American context, where you don't see that.

Eric: Very much so. Again, back to the lingerie story and the way Per frames it there *in a Nordic framing*. You can see in the text from the informants that they engage in what we would think of as typical consumption choices, and engage in self-making and multiple self-making activities and so forth but in a very discreet way. In a very discreet way.

Benjamin: Delicates.

Symmetry

Eric: Very delicate. Very discreet. You also see the intervention in that study of something that … I associate with Nordic consumer culture is a concern for symmetry. That is, the women were quite unhappy with mismatched underwear. They were quite concerned with mismatches between the public and the private, the front stage and the back stage. Exposing a gap between the front stage and the back stage was something that they found monstrous that they wanted to avoid. That again seems to me like it's a Nordic thing.

Benjamin: That symmetry, that reminds me of something I read in a Swedish car magazine—that someone chose their car to fit the house they were living in. House and car in symmetry, like the Diderot effect (McCracken 1988), or consumption constellation. Is there a deeper level of symmetry?

Eric: If we think about consumer culture in the mid-East, it's based on a discrepancy with front stage and the back stage. That what you see—and you see that in architecture and in clothing—you don't see the person; you don't see the family. It's all hidden behind walls. The distinction is, but I think this dislike of a bad discrepancy showed up in that text.

I do think that's a Nordic thing, because in the US we would be quite ... so in the North American context we would be quite happy if the front stage was well managed. We could give a crap about the back stage as long as nobody sees it, because it's a facade. The facade is all important. You can see they're quite different in that discussion of—

Benjamin: artificial versus natural, which leads back to the first quote.

Eric: Natural.

Benjamin: We are engineers of our own identities and other life projects. We use technologies of self. We use consumption to engineer our lives, but the dominant discourse or rather ideology is that it should never happen in an artificial way. From this perspective, it should always appear to be natural, even if engineered. In other cultures, however, it's perfectly fine to be a cyborg, to follow a beauty ideal in which one engineers the body to the max. Here, on the other hand, it's more like makeup should be looking as if you don't wear makeup. You should never overemphasize anything because that would be unnatural. I think that's indeed a common theme in Nordic consumer cultures, the symmetry of modesty, the symmetry of humble and bragging—humble bragging.

Can't we see that in advertisements, too? Marketers are culturally not really allowed to communicate a message like "This is the best product ever. Buy it and you will be having a happy life." That's simply not acceptable on a cultural plane. It's unnatural. It's artificial. Culturally, you're allowed to advertise a product as such, but only in a certain modest and somewhat symmetrical way.

Eric: Yes! On that theme I was quite interested in the work on lingerie. The way in which the informants were pretty generally horrified by and put in a negative category anything that seemed again exaggerated. Hence, the lingerie that made them seem like, what they said was, made them seem like streetwalkers, which was a big contrast with the English women, who were quite happy to have fun with the Ann Summers trashy lingerie. Across the board, the Danish women found this unnatural. Said pretty much that. It's unnatural.

It's a really interesting study in that way, in that we don't have so many studies of this mundane consumption that is so deeply researched, and that reveals so much. It certainly goes on. It seems to me that, that's again quite Nordic.

Process

Benjamin: One other hunch that I have is that, although it's rarely explicit, there is a Nordic interest in process. Rather than studying the state of being, or state of action or something as given, I think it's very Nordic to have more process-oriented perspective.

Eric: Okay. Why would you say that?

Benjamin: If we embed Nordic consumer culture theory research into a larger tradition of Nordic marketing theories, like, for example, relationship-marketing theories, internationalization theories, the Uppsala model of how firms internationalize, if we look at these, there's…

Eric: Yes. The IMP (Industrial Marketing and Purchasing scholarship) work is fundamentally a relational one, which is another way of saying process.

Benjamin: Yes, exactly. I think we see traces of that tradition as a deeply rooted social constructionism. Again, one aspect might be this underwear study, which also reflects that, which rejects an existential ontology by foregrounding that nothing *is* a special object, but that something *is made* into a special object. It's rendered a special object.

We see that, for example, in Per's and colleagues' study on appropriation and singularization, where it specifically says two consumption processes, again touching upon that paradox.

Something, and I quote again just because I have it here in front of me:

> *But, the paradox of the society of mass production and consumption is that this enormous supply of goods, gadgets and things is used by the individual to shape the personal concept of what life is all about.* (Østergaard et al. 1999, p. 405)

Again, paradox and process.

In moving commodities from markets, from shops to public stores or displays to their homes goods become decommodified and individualized. In this process anonymous mass products are transformed into unique objects out of which the consumers' personal world of memory, fantasy and association is created. (Østergaard et al. 1999, p. 405)

[Eric: Looking at this article later, we see the authors talk about the paradox of mass production versus singularization, and how consumer appropriation (productive consumption) mediates this transformation. Their article builds meso-level process theory from Grant McCracken's macro- and Russell Belk's micro-level theories of meaning.]

I think the attention to process—that comes with a baggage of necessity to look also at the various different levels involved. We look at more institutional macro-structure levels and individual level or actions, behaviors, meanings, doings. What do you think about that?

Eric: Well, as you were talking I was thinking about the kind of conversations I often would have with Per about the constitution of subjectivity in the Nordic environment. Usually these conversations took the form of actually two things, actually three things. Jokes and stories about Jutland and Fyn, the conflicts between these two subcultures, regions who couldn't understand each other and so forth, at a larger level between Danes and Swedes, Danes and Norwegians. It was Per who was always telling me the kind of rude things that Danes would say about Norwegians (see the discussion of inclusion and exclusion in the Introduction for more on this theme).

That's one kind of process. One kind of process—this identity formation process is always about this sort of thing. The other thing I was thinking of is, often times we would be having a conversation about—this was a historical conversation—a historical conversation about the old nobility and the old peasantry, usually illustrated by discussing landmarks in the countryside. Which is, we're driving through a little village and here's a bunch of stones under a tree. Well, okay. Uh, this is the remnants of the Folketing. The village Folketing.

Benjamin: Folketing, yes.

Eric: Yes, reproduced at the national level in Copenhagen, where the parliament is called the Folketing. Very often, we had these conversations about identity as a special thing. Then, the third level is the idea of Denmark versus the world. This inside outside things, relationships of which Danes are almost always constantly aware for some reason, are reflected in the work of our colleagues in that department. The other people in the department, the other people who founded the department were really involved with small and medium enterprises that were at the same time born global.

Very small local enterprises that were born global and formed theoretical discourse at the other part of that department, the non-CCT part of the department. It's a process on three levels having to do with how identity forms that also reflects how markets form in the Danish context.

Benjamin: That's great.

Eric: Very central to what you were just talking about, I think, in terms of why the process is so important is the everyday experience: it seems to be something that's existentially present in the everyday experience, at least Per's everyday experiences as we talked about these in terms of processes.

Benjamin and Eric: Yes, processes.

Benjamin: I don't know why processes permeate this culture. Systems, process, institutions.

Eric: I've no idea. [laughs] That's a bit of a puzzle. We don't need an answer, but it's an interesting thing.

Benjamin: Maybe we don't need to know where it comes from, that process. But it would be interesting to know.

Eric: I notice in looking now at—in talking about—some of Per's work. There are two kinds of things: there are his empirical studies and then something else that is characteristic. The other part of Per's work is his constant attention to the philosophy of science. Unlike many scholars, there is a constant stream of work about philosophy of science, which is accessing … which again is a very processual oriented work and a reflexive work. Because rather than again, here we are and we can't just carry on, there's a reflection of where are we? Why are we—

Benjamin: How do we get somewhere else ontologically and epistemologically speaking?

Eric: Exactly. How can we get somewhere else? Precisely.

Benjamin: For example, this article "*A critique of the ontology of consumer enchantment*" is one of my favorites, I have to say. Written by Per Østergaard, James Fitchet, and Christian Jantzen.

Eric: This is a really good article.

Benjamin: Yes, and that is prototypical of that conceptual world. What kind of process do we have to understand when it comes to enchantment, because enchantment itself is a process theory.

Eric: Well, I think that their point is that the enchantment was not a process theory. That either—in Weber, it's a theory of the Fall [laughs]. It used to be great and now it sucks. Precisely Per and his colleagues are attempting to reassert that this is a processual phenomenon.

What's interesting about this article is it absolutely comes back around again in the lingerie story, because there are these moments of enchantment and disenchantment that women experience with their underwear choices. I don't know which came first in terms of inspiration. I think the lingerie study came first, but it's interesting that that process thing is very much—to me this paper is—I don't know if it's cited at all—is actually I think a rather major paper. Because taking on Weber's ideas about the disenchantment of society under capitalism. It's installing a processual view and a dialectical view.

Benjamin and Eric: Of course Baudrillard is in there as well!

Catalysts and the Modest Drama

Benjamin: A favorite! That's interesting because I think the way in which Baudrillard is used here and in other papers is as an analytical device to be able to crack open the paradox and even go beyond the paradox. Creating new paradox (as they say, "a certain irony," Østergaard et al. 2013, p. 344) and just messing with it, playing around with possible answers.

Eric: Say a little more about that.

Benjamin: I think if you use a, let's say, a purely Foucauldian approach, which we also see in many papers (Varman et al. 2012; Yngfalk 2016), that's a great thinking tool to reveal power structures, creation of subjects, creation of agency and so on and so forth. Baudrillard on the other hand is a radical component that's carefully introduced here and there as a catalyst to crack open an existing debate to diminish previous arguments made. It's this carefully introduced chemical agent, almost, that the authors carefully introduce at the last step. If you look at this article—

Eric: It is very catalytic.

Benjamin: Yes. We see there is Weber [Eric: the pessimist], we have Campbell, we have George Ritzer [Eric: the optimist] and then let's have a Baudrillardian discussion of all of that [Eric: the seducer dealing in second-order enchantment, or simulacra]. It's a process again and a carefully engineered and mixed process.

Eric: That's an interesting observation because if we look at this article we see it takes in a way what you might call quite traditional sociologists in a particular sociological tradition. Weber and then Campbell, who very clearly is trying to extend ... Weber without a critique of Weber. Then you add Ritzer, who again is pretty much a vetted sociologist in the same Weberian tradition. Perhaps the point is that the macro dimensions of epochal change in economic systems is an enduring theme in sociology. Per, along with his colleagues, is among the few "marketing" scholars to dare to participate. This seems not incidental to the Nordic university environment to this point less riven by neoliberal governmentality.

If you read those authors, you get a layer cake unfolding of social science in a modernist fashion, getting better in understanding what's going on. Then you toss, as you say, toss in Baudrillard, who's more of a bombshell. They use it judiciously; the judicious use of incendiary device strikes me as Nordic.

Benjamin: That's the drama.

Eric: Yes, it's drama. It's not the way the French would do. They would set this all up and then they would tear it all down, to say now we have to use the first principles again. That's not what Per does. They throw in a catalytic thing; that's something different.

Benjamin: This is the scenic scene, but now we need a little bit of drama, but the modest drama, please. There has to be drama at some point. I think this is just a great narrative device, which we also see used strategically in other articles like the classic article "*Relationship marketing* *and the order of simulation*," where it's there from the beginning. But it's a narrative device if you look at the critique of relationship marketing from a French philosophers' perspective.

Eric: Here of course, the Nordic approach is central; this is a paper that is directed at the heart of Nordic thinking in marketing, which is "*Relationship marketing and the order of simulation*," that is to say, the tradition as it was before. The aim is to understand the relational focus whether it is the IMP tradition or the service tradition associated with Evert Gummesson and Christian Grönroos, a host of other scholars, and the order of simulacrum that comes from, I guess this is a little, as you said, a little murder.

Because the order of simulacrum is a bit of a murder, Baudrillard is a bit of a murderer in terms of the classic—the relationship marketing literature, the IMP literature, you know the Grönroos and Gummesson literature in general focused on the material services in a very orderly, modest, an effort to codify, a certain way of doing business that "we," Nordics, can feel comfortable with.

It justifies the way in which we, Nordics, do business. It is a very sanctioning, legitimizing discourse. Not that it's wrong, it is just a thing. When we throw in Baudrillard, it introduces paradox and irony.

Benjamin: Yes, it is a very ironic article. I mean, it is serious irony and it works.

Eric: Is there a particular passage that you think is particularly amusing, telling, or insightful there? I don't see that you highlighted anything in particular.

Benjamin: In that article, yes. I mean, it is quite nice to have you here, because he is referencing your 1999 study of commercial friendships, right?

Eric: Yes.

Benjamin: Just to show that drama, so here is what you write in your 1999 article, page 50:

> *[I]n contrast to the bulk of the relationship marketing literature, we assert that qualitatively different marketing relationships exist. Both service providers and clients share a general sense of the content and behaviors characteristic of commercial friendships. Participants agree that commercial friendships, similar to*

> *other friendships, involve affection, intimacy, social support, loyalty, and reciprocal gift giving.* (Price and Arnould 1999, p. 50)

Now, Østergaard and friends enter the stage, blowing up both the transactional and relational paradigms:

> *The longing for meaningful commercial relationships between firms and consumers only conceals that such meaningful relations can never be "real" only real-assigns. It is the idea of the relationship that emerges as the sole entity, and not a relationship that can be "lived" (Baudrillard, 1996: 203) … a Baudrillardian inspired view would show this friendship form to be a result of the contemporary order of simulation, of object-signs. The idea (sign) of the hairdresser relationship is determined primarily by the code of the market, which operates by the concealment or disappearance of the fact that the encounter is an essentially economic/commodity exchange.* (Østergaard and Fitchett 2012, pp. 245–246)

Again, we see this authenticity, the genuine, real, artificial, as well as nature and that kind of drama that Baudrillard catalyzes.

Politicized Consumption

Eric: Yes, we wrote this article in the spirit of the RM tradition, which, as Østergaard et al. point out, was oppositional to the North American, transactional marketing management approach. Per's and James' critique here is that, because these relationships have been commodified and then signified, in other words, turned into signs, that they have become simulacra within the order of simulation. They are the signs of friendship, signs of intimacy and the signs of reciprocity, the signs of the gift—all of which are unnatural monsters.

Per and James are quite right because Per is, I think, he's asserting this Nordic concern for nature and naturalness which one could even argue is in a way preserved by, at a sociopolitical level, the regulatory authority of the welfare state, which continues to try to push back against commodification via political regulation, right? You already spoke about this.

Benjamin: Yes.

Eric: You can consume all the alcohol you want but only in a certain way, right? This is even more the case in Norway with the system of state monopoly in alcohol; highly tax it. Anyways, it is not the point that this restrains consumption in any way, not at all; but what it does do is that it inserts a political reality into that, like, "We Norwegians, we Swedes, we Danes". Via institutions the control of this order of simulacra is subordinated to a non-sign-based reality, the reality of the Nordic welfare state, which is not a sign, but just a system of exchange, in the nature of things. Whereas the poor could be described by Arnould (2007) in a paper in *Annals of Political and Social Science* as disempowered semiotically, they (we!) are completely unprotected from the order of simulacrum. There is no state regulation, which is madness.

Benjamin: From Baudrillard's perspective, individual identity politics are imagined and agreed on at the same time. We see a politicized consumption, but identity politics are inherent in ordinary consumption.

Eric: Yes, of course.

Benjamin: Like in other countries.

Eric: Every consumer culture.

Benjamin: The point here is that they are politicized in a different way by participating in consumer culture in a different way. In the Nordic, we see other actors participate that we do not see on the same playing field in other consumer cultures, and these actors are state actors. That, I think, is a unique, rather unique setting in the Nordics.

Eric: Totally unique.

Benjamin: The welfare state in Germany, in France or other social welfare systems are slightly different. It is supposed to be a kind of safe capitalism; you know social welfare and capitalism at the same time. Of course, we could say that the more welfare state you get the more intervention you get, right?

Eric: Yes.

Benjamin: In that case, on identity politics, identity consumption and the consumption projects in general, that is an interesting setting in the Nordics we have.

Eric: Absolutely. You're right of course to say we have social safety nets, well-developed social safety nets, in other countries such as Germany and

France and Spain and Portugal and so on, but I think that it is different somehow.

Benjamin: Yes, but what is that difference?

Eric: It is different in the sense that … well, again, here I cannot comment on the situation in Sweden because I am not in any way familiar. At least in terms of my experience in Denmark and Finland, until relatively recently, and for a quite a long period of time and with some exceptions, you have a relatively homogenous ethnic community—the Danes, the Finns. (See again comments in the Introduction that clarify the point that homogeneity versus heterogeneity misses the point. The more interesting dynamic is one of inclusion versus Exclusion.)

Benjamin: Okay.

Eric: In the same way that we Danes clearly exclude the long present Turkish community. This is not part of the … the Turks have lived there for a "hundred" years but are just not part of the equation. I think the state intervenes on behalf of the "We Finns" or in particular "We Danes." I think that is, in France you have much more heterogeneous community. You got all kinds of Maghrebins (North African) and (sub-Saharan) Africans [Eric writes later: in any case the law recognizes an equality of citizenship divorced from ethnicity]. You have places like France and England, aftermaths of an empire and an empire that also never existed in the German context. If it did, it was primarily among Germanic-speaking peoples. Austro-Hungarian Empire incorporated other peoples before they all—

Eric: Relatively powerful Germanic community. Anyway, I think that's something that I think underwrites the importance or relevance of regional identity.

Rites

Benjamin: Let's touch upon the issue of rituals. For me, that's very striking, at least in the Swedish context, that these rituals play an important role in this collective understanding of the Swedish self.

You have only one Christmas dish and everyone serves that for Christmas. There's no option around that. We have to have that; it's called the "Julbord," a dish which is itself a collection of dishes, right? It's for everyone.

No one should be excluded. You can eat fish, you can eat sausage, you can eat potatoes in Janssons Frestelse. It's for everyone—vegans, meat eaters, fish eaters—they're all happy. That *has* to be served.

It's culturally unacceptable to serve anything other than that. Midsummer traditions, of course, too, they are very old. But for Christmas we have commercialized Christmas traditions. For example, at three o'clock on Christmas Eve, you simply have to watch *Donald Duck*. So on and so on. Candy? Only on Saturdays. These rituals are deeply structuring ordinary weekly life.

Eric: This is true in Denmark and in Finland. [Eric writes later: I well remember my surprise in Denmark in 1996, that only bakeries and flower shops were open on Sundays, in order, I learned, to facilitate the Sunday tradition of visiting for coffee and cake.]

Benjamin: It's not so much tuned for the German context, I would say.

Eric: Copy. Certainly much less so in the English, the UK context. Yes, of course, there are certain things about the ritualization of everyday life and the ritualization of consumption choices. One of the things that I think, I mean this is not in Per's work, but of course, you see the high streets in Danish cities and the use of high streets in those cities.

There's a very weekly way in which—and it seems to me there's a bit of social policy—in terms of creating high streets and centralizing shopping districts. These, of course, are the places where people also see, are seen and be seen. We were talking earlier about the [fancy] baby carriages and so forth. Certain kinds of local social relationships are established there. It's very interesting to go to these shopping areas where I lived in Odense. It's [equally] very interesting to be there at five o'clock in the morning on Sunday.

Benjamin: Well, is no one there?

Eric: No, no, no.

Benjamin: What?

Eric: This is where you have the end of the drunken night.

Benjamin: All right. Okay. [laughs]

Eric: Consistently, you'll find a bunch of drunk people screaming at the top of their lungs and wandering the streets—[crosstalk]

Benjamin: [laughs]

Eric: and a police presence scooping them up. Nothing ever—[severe crosstalk as the bar fills up with people]

Benjamin: Escalates.

Eric: Nothing ever escalates. It's just how that would be. It's quite predictable. It's extremely predictable in initial—those sorts of things. Of course, in Denmark too we have—mid-summer is very important, Christmas is very important, the amount of—I can go on endlessly citing ritualized activities in the Danish context, then I'll then generalize. What should your windows look like? That is, people do not have curtains in their street-facing windows, but instead they are decorated with certain elements, typically potted plants, perhaps candlesticks, and such like (Garvey 2005).

Benjamin: Yeah, yeah, yeah. The point is, every culture has these rituals, right? It's a part of the definition of a culture. I think the interesting point here is that, we'll have rituals in anywhere and everywhere. They serve to construct the collective identity more than they serve to construct regional identity. I don't know if that's interesting but it's certainly ordinary for Swedes to engage in these ritual activities.

Eric: [laughs] No. I think it is interesting. I think it's interesting in terms of Nordic consumer culture.

Benjamin: Oh yes. Yes. Wouldn't know how though. Reflexive consumer freely recognizing the—

Eric: Something that I think is interesting to think about is, ask ourselves why was Baudrillard of such interest to Per, because after all, Baudrillard is a French thinker, not a Nordic thinker. So why do you think that Per thought that Baudrillard was one of the kinds of thinkers to bring to bear upon his work which, I think, always has the sort of foundation on his own experience of Nordic life.

Historicizing, Periodizing, Discussing Process Through Time

Benjamin: I think it is a good question. I don't know the answer but I can talk about it. And I think, beyond these, I think, catalytic abilities of that literature, I think Baudrillard himself resonates quite well with the thought that everyone is correct and everyone is wrong at the same time. So, Baudrillard often, to my mind, has this lateral solution.

To stick with these movie metaphors, you have that person locked into a room and the evil character is approaching: how should the hero escape? Then, all of a sudden the roof explodes like something you wouldn't expect, right? And that is the Baudrillard model, I think.

Because, for example, the order of simulacrum that it's the dialectical—the emphasis on dialectics, this and that at the same time. So *you* are right and *you* are right but you are both wrong at the same time. It is a very egalitarian way of theorizing while at the same time destroying your neat little world. So it is kind of making Baudrillard's research, or his thoughts, almost making everything else look a bit naive by introducing that new lateral solution.

And that has, I think, a certain kind of authority to lean on to when criticizing other people's works. And you can always use that as a voicing mechanism to raise your own critique. And in turn, this relates to the nature of conflict we see in Nordic culture. To raise a conflict by means of a system or to solve the conflict—create one and solve it—by a systemic perspective.

So that system becomes Baudrillard. Because it's not him saying, but his way of thinking, systemizing the system of the dialectics is used to kind of raise and create a conflict and at the same time working within it and resolving it. What do you think? Why Baudrillard would be of such interest?

Eric: It's interesting. Well, I have been trying to frame my arguments in terms of Nordic scholarship and here I run out of ideas about that. Instead, I think about Per and consistent with what we said about process framework, all sorts of processes and history, and I think Per was very,

very interested in history. Are Nordic scholars generally interested in history?

When I think about other Nordic anthropology that I love, I think about Orvar Löfgren from Lund, for example, who writes about the history of tourism, rail travel, emotional labor and other topics. And I think of some other work I have seen from Nordic anthropologists—*Trade and Traders in the Sudan*—a cultural historical analysis of the marketing system in Sudan, for God's sakes, quite a long way from here.

So Per was a … he was interested in the history of philosophy, he was interested in the history of history which is a kind of being, as you say, processional interest. So I think Baudrillard was very much interested in, as we have said before, process, but he also was interested in history.

It was the kind of language that he liked to adopt, was the language as if he was talking about historical periods, although I think in his mature work, he more or less used that as a rhetorical device while annihilating that truth claim. So I think that Per was interested in Baudrillard because of that.

Historicizing, periodizing, discussing process through time—I think that is why he likes that to intervene in his work. And why would he choose Baudrillard over some others. When you think about Latour, he is … criticized as being overly value neutral, overly descriptive in his approach (Mills 2018). And I don't know, I mean, it is hard to say.

Benjamin: Hard to say. But there is a good question there: Is Nordic research generally more, say, historicized, even when it doesn't necessarily have to be explicit? Even in popular culture, there is an amazing awareness of history. For example, when I researched guitar cultures and the Swedish guitar brand Hagström in particular, I was surprised to find that there is a book on the history of that brand Hagström.

You can buy that in the shops—you can go out and read up on that history of Hagström, on the history of that guitar from an accordion maker to a guitar played by Elvis Presley, Frank Zappa and others. So there is this general interest in history, and we see, for example, media research in Sweden that also had a historically descriptive overtone, like Karl-Erik Gustafsson, for example, who was researching the history of newspaper industries in Sweden.

It might be that there is this general interest, but I wouldn't say that every research is historical. There might be this general interest to history. My colleague Johan Hagberg is doing a study on advertisements—an archival study of several decades of advertising. There is an interest for that.

Eric: Well, as I said before, many of my conversations with Per revolve around historicizing discussions: About the history of Jutland, about the history of Fyn, about the history of Esbjerg. I have a lovely book which is "Odense: then and now" in then-and-now postcards.

And these books, as you say, sell [well] in the shops. It was like a return of nineteenth century. We have [an orientation of]—oh, let's look, and here is the before and after pictures. There is an interest in this.

Benjamin: Yes.

Eric: And, of course, we can contrast this very dramatically with North American scholarship in marketing and consumption, which in the mainstream denies temporality, fundamentally denies temporality. Markets are like this, consumption is like this, then we can discuss how it is, but there isn't any historical depth (with the exception of a few marketing historians and sociologists of consumption (Breen 2004; Cohen 2003; Löfgren 1999; Witkowski 2018), the standard approach to consumer behavior is cross-sectional and a-temporal).

Benjamin: Not a lot at least.

Eric: But very little.

Benjamin: Very little, you are right.

Eric: So this is not a characteristic of the mindset but the *zeitgeist* of marketing and consumption scholarship in the North American context or, I will say, in the French context with which I am familiar. I do not know about German scholarship, but some of the most famous German marketing scholars are all about 'how do you predict this from that' in a very contemporary framing. But this is not a characteristic of Per's work.

Benjamin: And I think it is interesting to highlight that modesty, even if you are historically informed, you don't necessarily write about that in the article. So it is not always that every Nordic researcher I think emphasizes that; it is not that Nordic research always has a history chapter in the article. I think it contributes ... this inquisitive Nordic mind includes history as a dimension of relevance into the research. How come this is like that? If this is like that today, how was it before, and where might it be at a different time? I think that's interesting to talk about—the history of hearing aid devices, for example.

Eric: Yes, our colleague, Anders, he wasn't Per's student but he found Per someone worthy to converse with, and yes, I think that's a very interesting thing to come out of that school at University of Southern Denmark.

Benjamin: Another study I think that relates to that in a broader sense is the study I would like to raise; it's called "*Just for Fun? The Emotional Regime of Experiential Consumption*," where we see that there seems to be a kind of that model of, maybe it's a Nordic model of writing and argument. Maybe it is an academic model that works well with publishers, I don't know. But it is like this cracking open that dialectic, cracking open that drama.

Eric: We should remember that, like so much of Per's work, this is a collaborative work.

Benjamin: Sure, yes.

Eric: And one where he takes—he's listed as a third author.

Benjamin: Yes, yes. But I think that it has a kind of—why I am raising this is because the arguments that are made here are all put into historical context.

Eric: Okay.

Benjamin: So when they argue about the emotions and experiential consumption, they always have that retrospective perspective and partly because these theories are quite old, but they always link back to that kind of original thought in an ontologically historicized way. Where does it come from? Why is it that we think of emotions in that way? What did, you know, Holbrook and Hirschman do back then, and how was it before? How can we understand it today? So it is a kind of a rather larger process, the study, but the arguments, they are in themselves a process.

Eric: Well, you know, I do not know why I just thought about it now because I could have raised this issue at any point in our—this particular part of the—discussion, but this concern to be extended as Per's concern clearly relates to Per's lifelong commitment to philosophy. And particularly to understand German philosophy; of particular interest to Per was Heidegger, but he was not disinterested in Hegel and not disinterested at all in all the genesis and development of German philosophy.

So I think that Per's interest—and I wouldn't want to claim this as a general Nordic interest—in historicizing comes from his interest in history of philosophy in particular. It was his philosophical position merged with other philosophical positions. And I think that Per often thought about our scholarly work as a question that one would naturally raise: "How does this work come out of some other work?"

Benjamin: Yes.

Eric: It's just a natural inclination in Per's scholarship. So that's a component of this piece on the regimes of experiences of consumption. It's inevitable that this would be referenced to the historical frame. Is there a particular passage that's interesting?

Benjamin: That one struck me as interesting. On page 151 they say:

> *Modern hedonism is anything but just fun. It may have severe consequences on personal identity by confronting the individual with their own deficiencies and inabilities.*

So again the contrast, right? Something looks nice but—

Eric: There is a drama somewhere.

Benjamin:

> *Most western citizens can make pleasure an independent goal in their life, but this does not imply that all kinds of pleasure are valued equally. This is precisely the meaning of an emotional regime: certain ways of 'doing emotions' are preferable to others.*

Eric: So this is the perspective for me to unpack all these different areas in full range of consumer culture that emotionally perfected from, some of, you were talking about before, the ritualized consumption events in

Nordic culture such as the Christmas lunch or the Christmas dinner or the mid-summer bonfire or the baptism, confirmation, etc. To things such as triathlons, or all these commercialized forms of exercise, pilates, and so forth, to the 12th party congress of the People's Republic of China at a very high-level scale or the World Cup or the Olympics, *Tokyo Olympics 2024* and so forth. *Paris 2020*, all of these legitimized spaces for congealed emotional expressions that are regimented and that are, as Wilk says, structures of common difference.

Benjamin: Yes, I like that concept a lot.

Eric: Brilliant concept.

Benjamin: Under-explored, or underused I should say.

Eric: It's underused, but Per and his colleagues, they're a bit—they are making a very similar context and point. It is actually a kind of a brilliant point, but how is that? How is it that these particular regimes of emotional expression are valorized and legitimized? This article makes a stab in that direction, that's quite significant—

Benjamin: I think the starting point—

Eric: Yes?

Specificity

Benjamin: … of that article that struck me as really interesting, I would say that page number 139,

> *A cultural account of emotions opens up the prospect of considering the idea that emotions are not only culturally variable but culturally constructed. Where, we might ask, is the evidence or rationale to assume that all cultures have the same experience of emotions? There are clearly many different ways to express an emotion such as grief for example, and in different cultures many different ways of expressing grief would be expected to be observed. But is it conceivable to imagine a culture in which individuals are unable to experience this emotion of grief, where the emotion of grief is completely alien and unknown?* (Jantzen et al. 2012, p. 139)

Eric: This is a deeply anthropological point, this—But it's also to my mind an assertion of Nordic specificity.

Benjamin: Okay, how do you mean that?

Eric: I think one of the things that we see in Per's work, and I think it's properly representative than Nordic CCT, is the specificity. This is something we would desire. That is the sort of found—to my mind the sort of foundational gesture in a Nordic CCT is to say "Yes, culture matters. Yes, consumption is present. Yes, we need to have a look at it through an interpretive lens."

If we put all those three things together, then lo and behold, we discover that we do it differently here in the Nordic countries than those North Americans have been claiming for the last 25, 30, 40 years. That's what I see is implicit in that. It's the plea for the emotions that we may experience in the Nordic countries around consumption activities—are again the same and different, the same and different.

People are committed to confirmation at the same time as they're committed to secularism and that this not getting, not participating in confirmation is not possible.

Benjamin: In Denmark.

Eric: In Finland.

Benjamin: Finland as well?

Eric: You cannot not participate. You can have a non-confirmation celebration, but this celebration must go forward. It's some form of a—that's an emotional effect that's associated with that— "Kids should go to confirmation camp," kids want to go to confirmation camp, they love going to confirmation camp even though we're secular.

There's no contradiction there because emotional expression, as they say, maintained here is particular to circumstance and yet we're ill prepared. I think they're opening—trying to open—the door to how do we socially construct legitimate emotions around particular culture at particular circumstances. I don't know about in Germany how people—how well people are committed to confirmation as an activity. Maybe there are those that people—

Benjamin: It's a pervasive factor, but it's not, as you described, like in Finland. It's more like—I think it's a very transactional perspective.

Eric: Hah! Not in Finland, not in Finland for sure. Kids love it. They want to go, even if they don't have any belief whatsoever.

Benjamin: No, it's not—

Eric: They'll learn their verses from the Bible in order to—

Benjamin: I couldn't say that's true for Germany.

Eric: I wouldn't think so, it's a different country. Anyway, this is a—the idea that we should think of emotions as regimes.

Benjamin: That's a nice touch.

Eric: I think it's not—I think one of the things that we see here in Per's work is that, again, is very Nordic in my way of thinking is the way in which incredibly paradigm-busting ideas are modestly expressed; not insisted upon.

Benjamin: Well informed and well argued, of course.

Eric: They're also hard to get on.

Concluding Remarks

Benjamin: And historicized. That would be my next question. So, if there is such a thing as Nordic consumer culture theoretics, is it just the "Other"? Is it the alternative? Is it this paradigm-shaking regiment that you just mentioned? Is that what characterizes Nordic consumer research?

Eric: I think those are two different things. Substantively, I think there is an insistence. There is a kind of a self-othering relative to a hegemon.

Benjamin: Using this Nordic consumer culture as we do right now.

Eric: Yes, exactly.

Benjamin: The Othering.

Eric: There's a self-othering, "No, we're not like that." Again that's consistent with this reflexive—reflexivity—

Benjamin: Self-othering is deeply Nordic.

Eric: Yes, I think that's it. The Finns: "We're not like—we're not like the Swedes, they're not—" That self-othering is, I think, a Nordic problem. But that's one thing. The other thing as I said is cracking open—that's a different thing.

I think that is—If we think of IMP, if we think of the service work in marketing in the Nordic countries, or the born global perspective or host of things that we can think of, there's all sorts of insistences, scholarly insistence's that are, as you said, historically founded and well researched, well integrated. But at the same time modest claims for a theoretical distinction—

Benjamin: Or infusion.

Eric: Or infusion is quite Nordic. If you look at the French, for example, what they want to do is join the conversation, "We're just as good," which is very different than the Nordic position. It seems to me that German marketing scholarship is—"We're not just as good, we're much better." Mainstreaming—

Benjamin: Don't go there [laughs]

Eric: "We're not emulating, we're setting…

Benjamin: …The bar

Eric: The bar, within this extremely normatized framework, and I admire that. "So-and-so came and taught us the latest techniques of hierarchical regression analysis, we're so fucking smart." Which is not something you would ever see coming out of a Nordic university. I can't even imagine that. There would always be a—"That's not what we do."

Benjamin: Modest excellence

Eric: We're modest, not even. This claim for being the best is something these horrible Germans and Americans do, but not us. We remain modest.

Benjamin: No, no, no, that's very wrong (laughs).

Eric: But each time, so many of the articles that I have read and reread, I was suddenly struck by the significance of the claims that are never highlighted. Nobody says, "We present a new theory of or a new approach to—"

Benjamin: That relates back to the advertising or marketing discussion we had. It's that reflexive awareness of "Yes, this is a nice solution, it might not be the best but it is one, a new one." It is interesting but perhaps not, that is the self-marketing, some might even say that these articles are underselling themselves.

Eric: Clearly.

Benjamin: Some might say these are modestly excellent.

Eric: They're modestly excellent. One of the things we haven't discussed about is the location of these articles.

Benjamin: Oh yes.

Eric: If we do an inventory of the locations of these articles, what do we discover? We discover that they're not located in the top-tier marketing publications which we have to say with a stentorian accent. Instead, they're quite—I mean, quite credible publications, and some even quite modest like the *Journal of Consumer Behavior*, a pretty modest publication.

Benjamin: Even the ACR—

Eric: *ACR Proceedings*.

Benjamin: These are great articles for an *ACR Proceedings*.

Eric: Brilliant.

Benjamin: These are conceptional works.

Eric: I would say that the practice, the scholarly practice that we see, is very reflective of the general strand of CCT—refusal to step forward.

Benjamin: In Per's case, that was a conscious decision.

Eric: Absolutely.

Benjamin: We have to just emphasize that. It's not trying to do the top journals first, and then meandering down below. But this was a conscious choice: where does a conversation happen? "If it's *marketing theory*, then this article is happening there, or perhaps the ACR [Proceedings]. To stir up a debate. That's where I want to be."

Eric: I think this strategy is varied. These are conscious choices that we should put forward. And indeed in Per's and James' critique of Arnould and Thompson—their critique of Arnould and Thompson, not Per and James Fitchett's; Per and Mathias Bode's. Their critique of Arnould and Thompson. Their critique of consumer culture theory.

You can see I think quite clearly the logic that informs a lot of the publication choices of Per's work, which is, "Let's be reflexive about what we're doing. We can either join the power pull for the power knowledge dialectic, or we can join the knowledge pull for the power knowledge dialectic." [In their critique, they argue that] Arnould and Thompson have rather unwittingly joined the pragmatic power pull for the power knowledge dialectic.

Then he chooses to endorse, and they say this quite explicitly in paper. We endorse what they call CCT1, which is knowledge production, the pull for the power of knowledge dialectic. I think that's reflective then, as

I say, in their choice of outlets for their work: conference proceedings. What role the international rankings, which of course, are an entirely neo-liberalized institutional apparatus refuse to play in those spaces.

Again, it speaks to the integrity of this position toward CCT1 or knowledge production rather than power consolidation. I think that's quite interesting. When we look at these papers that are published in journals of a "lower" level, it shouldn't be indicted.

Benjamin: I think the point you raised there is this self-othering happens to an extent, but not to the extent that this is not consumer culture theory. Right? If you scan these articles, the word Nordic is rarely mentioned. And of course, the context is mentioned in methods section.

But it's not made a point of departure. "Oh, this is Nordic." What I think is important to underline is that although we might frame this as being Nordic, it's not Nordic in the sense that is empirically Nordic. Nordic is more like a signifier of, not the regional or local but it's more like a different ethic way of theorizing, maybe understanding and analyzing.

But it's not a market of, "Oh, this is so different. We're on the moon, and you're on the earth, so we can't talk to each other." That's why this research naturalizes CCT but engages in a natural fashion to try and format the CCT discourse, and engages in the critique of Arnould and Thompson. And of course, why not? I think that's an important part to underline when you talk about Nordic consumer culture.

Yes, there's a different empirical context, but isn't by no way different enough to justify an old school of thought. Instead, I think it's this scholarly Nordic approach that is much more different than the empirical settings.

Eric: Yes, the distinctiveness of the Nordic is not the context per se, but is distinctive in their approach, that is, a certain way of proceeding, a certain way of proceeding. I was stumped as I was about to say in terms of ontology and epistemology, as well as—then I was stumped for a moment because not exactly the right distinction.

Benjamin: We're still looking for what that is, but I think maybe axiology is the—I mean it's not ontology. It's not an epistemology. Definitely not an epistemology.

Eric: No, in fact the empirical work is pretty straightforwardly interpretive without any fancy bells and whistles. In fact, you would even argue that the empirical work is rather classically positivist in the sense of—

Benjamin: Very streamlined.

Eric: early twentieth-century sociological positivist. What are people saying? What are they doing? Let's analyze their words and their actions which is a kind of humanist—

Benjamin: Existentialism, that you referred to at the beginning.

Eric: Yes, exactly.

Benjamin: That was an existential thing position.

Eric: It's not opposed. One thing we can say about this work is that it is resolutely not post-humanist.

Benjamin: No, this body of work. But the axiology, I think, there we find some point of departure and how do we value and how do we create value through scientific work?

Eric: Yes, of course. Absolutely [Adding later, the humanistic orientation]. Do you want to—

Benjamin: Should we have a break or move on?

Eric: Yes, I think we should move on. So we've made a tour of a number of articles and raised a number [of] points.

Benjamin: It's just a bunch of them. We have to write one chapter. This will be 50 pages already.

Eric: Yes, I wonder, do we have a concluding—

Benjamin: That will be nice, have some kind of concluding moment, and I mean—

Eric: I really like the idea of just sort of raising—I'd have to listen to the tape now, but I think we've raised lots of different interesting points. And in my view, a chapter would be one where we simply expose a certain number of these points.

Benjamin: Yes, definitely, and edit it for clarity because I mean—

Eric: Edit for clarity, but I'm not very interested in creating an overarching narrative.

Benjamin: No, it's a conversation, and that itself is Nordic, right?

Eric: Great, so let's not over—

Benjamin: I don't want to overly—

Eric: Over-storify, and take a modest conversation on—I think to make this accessible to a wider audience, I think the focus we had on exploring the Nordicness in this work, in other works, is finding this generalized dimension. I think that makes it accessible, and to use these articles as a platform to explore these arguments.

Benjamin: Yes. I think that was really nice, but it would be nice to have some kind of concluding…

Eric: But I do think that we should … we are not concluding a life, but we might say…

Ben: No, no we are not concluding a life.

Eric: We are concluding a discussion about a body of work. We should think about how we want to conclude in a non-concluding way and so we should think about how we want to conclude a discussion about a body of work in an unconclusive [*sic*] way I would think.

Ben: Yes, I think … concluding a body of work is too tall an order for me. Maybe you knew Per better, but for me, I wouldn't be able to conclude his body of work. But what might be nice as a conclusion is kind of to highlight something about the last points we made. About "what is this Nordic research?" We have the Nordic interest, but then researchers differ, there is self-othering and … But what this is about, in some ways, is generalizing in an inconclusive way: concluding what Nordic consumer research is about, and we came to that conclusion by using Per's work in shaping Nordic consumer research.

Eric: Absolutely, a key point to make is this modest cracking open that is to say, unpacking.

Ben: this modest cracking open—

Eric: is quite central to this work.

Ben: And this little drama inside the ordinary, the beautiful, calm, romantic setting: "Everything works. All your theories work nicely. You must be so happy; all these theories you have worked out and worked with." But then there is a crime scene, and the criminal investigation. Very thorough, robust, methodological …

Eric: Yes, how do we call this, uh, forensic?

Ben: The forensic.

Eric: There is a very forensic quality. (Ah, I like this.)

Ben: And not necessarily a solution.

Eric: You know that television series, Broen/Bron? It's perfect. It's the perfect metaphor and indeed the bridge is a perfect metaphor for Per's work. It bridges time, space, cultural tradition, and it deals with a situation in which everything is fine and all middle class and then there are two [very disruptive] things that don't quite get together; that are joined by a bridge [NB: Rather like Per's work, a bridge joins rather than ends or brings closure].

References

Amy-Chinn, D., Jantzen, C., & Østergaard, P. (2006). Doing and Meaning: Towards an Integrated Approach to the Study of Women's Relationship to Underwear. *Journal of Consumer Culture, 6*(3), 379–401.

Arnould, E. (2007). Should Consumer Citizens Escape the Market? *Annals of Political and Social Science, 611*(May), 96–111.

Breen, T. H. (2004). *The Marketplace of Revolution: How Consumer Politics Shaped American Independence*. Oxford and New York: Oxford University Press.

Cohen, L. (2003). *A Consumer's Republic: The Politics of Mass Consumption in Postwar America*. New York: Knopf.

Garvey, P. (2005). Domestic Boundaries: Privacy, Visibility and the Norwegian Window. *Journal of Material Culture, 10*(July), 157–176.

Jantzen, C., Fitchett, J., Østergaard, P., & Vetner, M. (2012). Just for Fun? The Emotional Regime of Experiential Consumption. *Marketing Theory, 12*(2), 137–154.

Löfgren, Ö. (1999). *On Holiday: A History of Vacationing*. Berkeley and Los Angeles: University of California.

McCracken, G. (1988). Diderot Unities and the Diderot Effect. In G. Grant McCracken (Ed.), *Culture and Consumption: New Approaches to the Symbolic Character of Consumer Goods and Activities* (pp. 118–129). Bloomington, IN: Indiana University Press.

Mills, T. (2018). What Has Become of Critique? Reassembling Sociology After Latour. *The British Journal of Sociology, 69*(June), 286–305.

Østergaard, P., & Fitchett, F. (2012). Relationship Marketing and the Order of Simulation. *Marketing Theory, 12*(3), 233–249.

Østergaard, P., Fitchett, J., & Jantzen, C. (1999). On Appropriation and Singuralisation: Two Consumption Processes. *Advances in Consumer Research, 26*, 405–409.

Østergaard, P., Fitchett, J., & Jantzen, C. (2013). A Critique of the Ontology of Consumer Enchantment. *Journal of Consumer Behaviour, 12*, 337–344.

Price, L. L., & Arnould, E. J. (1999). Commercial Friendships: Service Provider-Client Relationships in Social Context. *Journal of Marketing, 63*(October), 38–56.

Varman, R., Skålén, P., & Belk, R. W. (2012). Conflicts at the Bottom of the Pyramid: Profitability, Poverty Alleviation, and Neoliberal Governmentality. *Journal of Public Policy & Marketing, 31*(Spring), 19–35.

Witkowski, T. H. (2018). *A History of American Consumption: Threads of Meaning, Gender and Resistance*. New York and London: Routledge.

Yngfalk, C. (2016). Bio-Politicizing Consumption: Neo-Liberal Consumerism and Disembodiment in the Food Marketplace. *Consumption Markets & Culture, 19*(3), 275–295.

Index[1]

[1] Note: Page numbers followed by 'n' refer to notes.

S. Askegaard, J. Östberg (eds.), *Nordic Consumer Culture*,
https://doi.org/10.1007/978-3-030-04933-1